A Companion to Lucca

Compiled and introduced
by
ANDREAS PRINDL

Illustrated by Sergio Tisselli

maria pacini fazzi editore

© 2000 ɱƥ maria pacini fazzi editore, lucca

ristampa 2002 maria pacini fazzi, editore
via dell'Angelo Custode, 33 - 55100 Lucca
tel. 0583 440188 - fax 0583 464656
www.pacinifazzi.it - mpf@pacinifazzi.it

Proprietà letteraria riservata
Printed in Italy

For illustrations:
© copyright: Veronica Prindl

ISBN 88-7246-429-3

For Veronica

TABLE OF CONTENTS

LUCCA AFTER UNIFICATION WITH TUSCANY

12

ILLUSTRATIONS

ACKNOWLEDGEMENTS

Acknowledgement is made to the following for their kind permissions to reprint extracts appearing in this Companion:

MAGDALENA AND BALTHASAR by Steven Ozment. Copyright © 1986 by The Steven Ozment Family Trust. Excerpted by permission of Simon & Schuster.

Andre Deutsch Ltd. for passages from two books by Olive Hamilton: PARADISE OF EXILES, copyright © 1974 Olive Hamilton; and THE DIVINE COUNTRY © 1982 Olive Hamilton.

"Marriage II" from DAY BY DAY by Robert Lowell. Copyright © 1977 by Robert Lowell. Reprinted by permission of Farrar, Straus and Giroux, LLC.

Excerpts from THE INFERNO OF DANTE: A NEW VERSE TRANSLATION by Robert Pinsky. Translation copyright © 1994 by Robert Pinsky. Reprinted by permission of Farrar, Straus and Giroux, LLC.

ITALY: A CULTURAL GUIDE by Ernest Hauser. Copyright © 1981 Ernest Hauser. Reprinted with the permission of Scribner, a Division of Simon & Schuster.

Roger Morgan for permission to reprint portions of SPARKENBROKE (Macmillan, 1936) and THE WRITER AND HIS WORLD (Macmillan, 1960) by his father Charles Morgan.

Penguin UK for passages from LIVES OF THE ARTISTS by Giorgio Vasari, translated by George Bull (Penguin Classics, 1965) copyright © George Bull, 1965 and from MICHELANGELO: A BIOGRAPHY by George Bull (Penguin Books, 1995) copyright © George Bull, 1995.

University of California Press for permission to reprint a letter from the Ricciardi firm appearing in RENAISSANCE FLORENCE by Gene Brucker. Copyright © 1983 The Regents of the University of California.

University of North Carolina Press for passages from RUODLIEB, THE EARLIEST COURTLY NOVEL (CA. 1050) translated by Edwin H. Zeydel. Copyright © 1959 by the University of North Carolina Press. Published for the University of North Carolina Studies in the Germanic Languages and Literatures. Used by permission of the publisher.

Francis Warner for part of his poem LUCCA QUARTET.

Excerpts from LUIGI BOCCHERINI: HIS LIFE AND WORK by Germaine de Rothschild, trans. by Andreas Mayor. © 1965 Germaine de Rothschild. By permission of Oxford University Press.

Excerpts from SHRINES AND CITIES OF FRANCE AND ITALY by Evelyn Underhill, Longmans Green, 1904, by permission of Pearson Education Ltd.

Excerpts from THE JOURNALS OF ARNOLD BENNETT, ed. Frank Swinnerton (Penguin, 1954) by permission of A.P. Watt on behalf of Mme V M Eldin.

Harper Collins Publishers Ltd for excerpts from ITALY – *The Places between* by Kate Simon.

PREFACE

This is a book about the most special small city in Italy. There are grander cities, some more important historically or more filled with sublime art and architecture. Yet Lucca is *sui generis*. No other Italian, hardly any European, city has kept its original form and its spirit as Lucca has. This is due to the magnificent, glowing walls which protect it and shape its outlook. Had the walls which were started under the Romans, expanded in medieval times and grandly rebuilt in the Renaissance, been torn down, then Lucca would look like other ancient Tuscan city-states, with a few beautiful buildings in the midst of a noisy, modern town.

Being inside the walls has meant both little physical change and a conservative mentality. Lucca remains a jewel: a city of marble churches, a city of beautiful palaces and piazzas, a city for pedestrians and bicycles. It has a human scale – you can walk across it in fifteen minutes or stroll around the walls in one hour. Nothing towers over you, except a few stunning towers themselves: Torre Guinigi with its living oak trees on top and the Torre delle Ore in via Fillungo, and the slender bell towers.

Many of the "hundred churches" which characterised Lucca historically are still there and used daily, for Lucca is a pious and observant place. Festivals are held in and around the churches, which date from the twelfth and thirteenth centuries, and at times animated processions sweep through the town's narrow streets as they have since medieval days.

Lucca was a republic for 400 years, proud of its independence and producing a remarkable coinage with the face of Christ on one side and *Libertas* on the other, unique in numismatics. That face represented both Lucca's deep Catholic traditions and the revered statue of the Volto Santo in the cathedral. The sheltering walls, the physical constancy, the quiet religious affirmation and belief in freedom have produced a city and an atmosphere of the greatest charm.

Lucca is also a city of music, with many vibrant concerts in its churches, courtyards and palaces. The Teatro del Giglio has a winter opera season, complemented by the summer opera festival in nearby Torre del Lago, where Puccini composed several of his operas. Puccini, Boccherini and Catalani are Lucca's most famous musical sons; the Boccherini Conservatory educates fine professional musicians to this day.

The town has always been a magnet for visitors: Julius Caesar, the Longobards who made it their capital in Tuscia, pilgrims, crusaders, Holy Roman Emperors, and northern Europeans on the Grand Tour. They were my focus; this volume is not a detailed guide to Lucca nor a history, neither of which I am qualified or inclined to write. Rather it is a companion for modern visitors who want to know what Lucca represents. My aim was to portray interesting people who came to Lucca, and important things which happened here, over the last 2000 years. I selected what such visitors saw, what they wrote about it and point out what is the same today as they described. Tales of Lucchese personages and Lucca's own history complement their comments. My object was, where possible, to let anecdotes, stories, songs and poems speak for themselves. These are presented as I found them, with archaic or idiosyncratic spelling unchanged. Of course, such a selection is personal and prejudiced. There is very little here of the internecine wars between Lucca and its neighbouring city-states, hardly any politics and not much of religious history or the many battles between Popes and Emperors. Even some of the most beautiful churches are omitted (but readers can seek them out for themselves). The book won't help you find a good restaurant or hotel, nor how to spend the time between 12.30 and 4 p.m. when museums and churches are closed (going up on the walls with a picnic is a good choice). But perhaps it will give a deeper appreciation of the development of the beauty and history of this place.

Many friends helped me to finish this book. Daniele Vanni, a Lucca writer now living in Rome, wrote the longer entries on major aspects of Lucca, such as the introduction, the walls, the churches, the tower houses, to expand the litany of shorter individual anecdotes. Helen Askham read my drafts several times and translated large swathes of Italian; without her advice this *Companion* would have been disorganised and inconsistent. Claudia Sander, an architect, helped mightily in translation and layout. Laura Giambastiani of the Archivio di Stato di Lucca helped me to find some important new material in the City archives. She is the main energy behind the effort to preserve the English historical presence in Bagni di Lucca. Jenny Wraight, Admiralty Librarian in London, showed me how to dig into the rich resources of the British Library by Internet (during which I was forced to use a computer for the first time) and worked very hard with me on the final text. Barbara Newlands typed a cumbersome manuscript with her customary efficiency, patience and good humour. Other friends suggested new sources, made constructive suggestions, threw out irrelevant items (even if they were at first my favourite ones) or just encouraged me when the spirit was flagging: Dick and Laura Neagle; Dr Ro McConnell; Liz Clifford; Michela and Mario Marchi; Professor Antonio Romiti of the Istituto Storico di Lucca; Susan Jarman of the local English magazine *Grapevine*; Charles Nicholl; Ben and Jenny Schutz; Ilse and Paul Guglielmetti, and Enrico and Paola Chiesa. Our daughter Kari made some real improvements to the text. To all of them, I am greatly indebted; any remaining errors or infelicities are mine alone.

I found the sources for this book in many libraries: the Biblioteca Statale in Lucca, I Tatti in Florence, the Reform Club library in London, where the librarian Simon Blundell was particularly helpful, the London Library and the British Library, from all of which I received a great deal of friendly assistance.

My wife Veronica, who is *inlucchesita*, kept me going through her constant support, and was responsible for devising and commissioning the striking illustrations by Sergio Tisselli. This book is dedicated to her, and everybody else who loves Lucca, or will.

Andreas Prindl

INTRODUCTION
by Daniele Vanni

Nomen omen, said the Romans, in the name you will find the omens. We cannot foretell Lucca's destiny from its name, however, because ours is a city with no etymology and the meaning of the word Lucca and why it has that name is unknown or, at least, doubtful. Recent research by the great linguist Professor Ambrosini links Lucca once again with *luce*, light, and puts forward the hypothesis that it is derived from the Indo-European word *leuk*, meaning a luminous place.

The Romans liked to make an anagram of a name in order to read the omens and if we do this with Luca (the name when Lucca was a Roman colony), we get *lacu*, ablative of *lacus*, meaning "from water". This would support the body of rather romantic research which derives the name from *luk*, a Celtico-Ligurian water-place-name denoting a marshy place or bog.

Lucca wasn't founded on a hill or in some other naturally fortified place. Instead, it was built between the branches of the River Serchio which originally flowed into the Arno, making a marshland of the whole plain as it did so. When the river found a new route to the sea, some of the land dried out. This is where Lucca was built, in constant danger from the river, until San Frediano came from far-away Ireland to live as a hermit on the mountains near Pisa; it was he who changed the course of the river with his miraculous rake and saved the city. No doubt every miracle has some foundation in fact but, in this case, it also took another thousand years' work and many, many kilometres of embankment before Lucca could co-exist peacefully with the Serchio.

The earliest references to Lucca concern the crushing defeat that Hannibal and his elephants inflicted on the Romans in the Po valley, on the banks of yet another river, the Trebbia, in 218 BC. After the terror and humiliation that these great animals caused, the Consul Titus Sempronius beat a very hasty retreat back over the Apennines to Lucca and took refuge there for the first few months of 217 BC. This wasn't, in fact, the Romans' first experience of elephants – sixty years earlier they had encountered them in the south of Italy in a savage battle against Pyrrhus and had given them the name *Bos Luca* after the site of the battle. But this is a whimsical coincidence.

Archaeologists in the last fifteen years have taken giant strides towards helping us to understand Lucca's remote origins better. Thanks largely to the outstanding work of Professor Michelangelo Zecchini, we can now be certain that Villanovan communities lived and died here and that they preceded the Etruscan settlers with whom they eventually merged, though by how long is not clear. The evidence provided by the most recent excavations means that we also know that the Versilia mountains and the Garfagnana were occupied by the Ligurians from at least 300 BC, and that for about a century and a half they made incursions south over the plain as far as Pisa. Scholars now suggest that Lucca is Etruscan in origin and the finding of a unique *tesoretto* supports their hypothesis. There are remains of farms and perhaps also of a necropolis, but no other signs of a city.

In short, without there ever having been an Etruscan city like Volterra, Tarquinia, Arezzo, Pisa or Fiesole here, the plain on which Lucca stands was colonised by Etruscan peoples who merged with the earlier Villanovan settlers, as so often happened in this region. The settlements were frequently destroyed by floods (there was a particularly destructive one in the fifth century BC); and, in the last phase before the stabilising influence of the *Pax Romana*, by the invading Ligurians (300-200 BC) who turned this area into a border zone.

But, in truth, do the origins of Lucca really matter much? Better to be content with the present – with the silence of this noble little city and its calm self-possession which gives it the atmosphere of a northern town. It is loved by the many tourists who come here and find themselves staying on, beguiled by something which is more than the climate and more than its natural beauty.

Its uniquely splendid isolation made Lucca an enclave like no other in Italy, for hundreds of years. Its Catholicism was shot through with a lay spirit so that only the minds of the people belonged to the Church and the Inquisition never really took hold. Its government was oligarchic but Lucca was proud of its liberty and anyone intent on empire-building was given short shrift. Out of their love of independence and sense of pride, the Lucchesi bled themselves almost white to build walls better suited to a greater power. For the same reason, and also to persuade the people that they were indeed truly free, their rulers wrote the word *Libertas* obsessively in stone and marble on all their major buildings. Later, this became the motto of the Christian Democrats, the white whale of Italian politics and, at one time, the largest party in the country. Just to reconfirm the city's uniqueness, it attracted such support here that Lucca was the only white spot on the otherwise red map of Tuscany.

There are many sides to Lucca but everything is understated, nothing forced or showy. In nearby Etruscan Pisa you can see the strong tones and colours of the temples of Tarquinia, Volterra and Vejo, but not here. Nor will you find the bravado of Livorno or the grandeur of Florence, only a nordic subtlety. Lucca isn't for people looking for mandolins and tomato red, because it is the white marble recycled from the Roman forum, the green of Matraia stone and the red bricks that predominate – bricks for the sake of the building industry, you understand, not as a matter of taste.

We live in an age losing touch with much or even all of the past as we arrogantly rush along with the progress of the present. This book is the result of someone needing to reconnect with the past and with the past of Lucca in particular.

And so we come to the author. Lucca has a long history of tourists who became Lucchese, in part or in whole. It began with San Frediano and a king called Richard and now we have Professor Andreas Prindl, economist and musician. One day, he found an unpublished diary written by an Ipswich traveller in Lucca in the seventeenth century and that inspired him to start collecting what people have written about Lucca, his second homeland. His collection is the book that you hold in your hands.

Sempronius retreats to Lucca after a battle with Hannibal

ROMAN LUCCA

216 BC

Sempronius, a Roman Consul, retreats to Lucca after a battle with Hannibal

from Thisdore Ayrault Dodge: *Hannibal*

The Carthaginian commander Hannibal (c. 247 BC-183 BC) was one of the great military leaders and strategists in history. Hannibal's invasion of Italy in 218 BC with his elephants was a shock for the Roman State. Hannibal was supported by the resources of the Carthaginian empire in Spain and out to revenge Carthage's losses in the first Punic War. Coming across the Alps, where most of his elephants died of cold, Hannibal had a series of brilliant victories between 218 and 216 BC, especially at Cannae. Sempronius' retreat to Lucca, not yet a colony, was perhaps the first time Lucca appears in recorded history.

Sempronius' defeat at the Trebbia had not served to discourage or teach this officer caution. He had now returned from Rome. With his fiery impetuosity, for which to a certain degree he deserves credit, he determined, before retiring from Hannibal's front, again to cross swords with the Carthaginian. The opportunity was soon afforded him. Hannibal, after his mountain adventure, had returned to within ten miles of Placentia. One day, apparently while intent on making a reconnaissance in force, with twelve thousand foot and five thousand horse, Sempronius sallied forth to meet him, and to accept Livy's relation, the consul's attack on Hannibal's line was so sharp that he forced him back to camp, and even went so far as to attack the camp intrenchments. Then, satisfied with the seeming advantage, he began to withdraw. This was Hannibal's opportunity. He debouched from camp with the bulk of his force, the foot from the front-gate, and the cavalry from the side-gates with instructions to fall on the Roman flanks. A hotly contested combat was the result, which only night arrested. Sempronius withdrew from the field with a loss of six hundred foot and three hundred horse, including five Roman war-tribunes, three allied praefects and many other officers. Hannibal's loss was about equal. Livy calls this a drawn battle, but the advantage had remained with Hannibal.

The Roman generals had determined to retire from Placentia before going into winter-quarters. They had become convinced that they could not longer hold the line of the Padus to advantage. Leaving garrisons in Placentia and Cremona, Scipio retired on Ariminum; Sempronius retired on Luca, across the Apennines into Etruria. By this division of forces, the two consular armies protected the two lines of operation from Cisalpine Gaul to Rome, the one east, the other west of the main range of the Appennines.

Hannibal broke up in early spring, probably March, 217 B.C. He had wintered in the vicinity of modern Alexandria. The first part of the march towards Etruria was not over-burdened with difficulties. The range from the Ligurian country to Genoa is rugged; but his troops had campaigned in Spain, and the Gauls knew the land tolerably well. From Genoa to modern Spezia, he kept along the cliff-roads. Near the Luca country, he also neared the Arnus marshes. Just what the extent of this submerged section was, we only know from the ancient authors. It does not now exist. It is called a marsh. It probably was alluvial land covered by the usual spring overflow, this year excessive. At first blush, especially to judge from the fact that Luca was a Roman colony, one would suppose that there must have been a practicable road around the north of the flat land of the Arnus. But that there was none must not only be assumed from the authorities, but is evident from the structure of these foothills. Roads in plenty there may have been, up into the valleys of this southern slope of the Apennines, and some across the range; but to attempt to march along the length of the slopes would have been to encounter a never-ending succession of precipices and torrents, as well as a zig-zag path as long in miles as the entire peninsula. Hannibal was obliged to essay the passage of the marsh. Through this there was a road, fairly good during the dry weather, but at this time considered impassable.

But the Carthaginian knew not the meaning of the word. There was no road he could not utilize. He set out confidently on his perilous march. In the van he sent the Spanish and African troops, with the most necessary and valuable of the baggage, so that these, his best troops, should not suffer, and that the treasure and essentials should be got across the marsh before the road was too much trodden down by the column. It is not probable that a large quantity of baggage was taken. Hannibal was well aware that if he lost the game, he would need none; if he won, he would have food and treasure in superabundance. He probably kept his treasure in small bulk. Next came the Gallic allies – the least reliable of his army – followed by Mago with the horse, whose duty it was to persuade these troops to diligence, if possible, but, if necessary, to push them on by the use of force.

The van with the baggage got through without all too great loss. They were old and hardened troops, and found the road, such as it was, still unbroken by recent travel. But the Gallic column, unused to and impatient under such exposure, lost heavily from fatigue and deprivation. The whole army was four days and three nights marching through water, where only the dead horses, dead beasts of burden or abandoned packs afforded any chance to rest. Many horses and mules cast their hoofs. Hannibal personally made the march on the last remaining elephant – the rest having all perished at the Trebbia or in the Apennines – and during this season of exposure lost an eye from an inflammation which he was unable to attend to, and which was seriously aggravated by overwork. Cornelius Nepos states that he had to be carried in a litter from this time until after the battle of Trasimene.

180 BC

Lucca becomes a Roman colony

from Livy: *History of Rome*

The Romans had taken Lucca from the Ligurians after a long siege in about 250 BC. Lucca was included in Gallia Cispadana when the Empire was broken into provinces. Its range was large, extending to nearly Parma in the North and Volterra in the South. Here the Roman historian Livy is reporting the main events of the year 180 BC.

Several prodigies were reported this year: that at Crustuminum a bird, which they call the ospray, cut a sacred stone with its beak; that a cow spoke in Campania; that at Syracuse a brazen statue of a cow was mounted by a farmer's bull, which had strayed from the herd. A supplication of one day was performed in Crustuminum, on the spot; the cow at Campania was ordered to be maintained at the public expense, and the prodigy at Syracuse was expiated, the deities to whom supplications should be offered, being declared by the auspices. This year died, in the office of pontiff, Marcus Claudius Marcellus, who had been consul and censor; and his son, Marcus Marcellus, was chosen into the vacant place. The same year a colony of two thousand Roman citizens was settled at Luca. The triumvirs, Publius Aelius, Lucius Egilius, and Cneius Sicinius, planted it. Fifty-one acres and a half of land were given to each. This land had been taken from the Ligurians, and had been the property of the Etrurians, before it fell into their possession. Caius Claudius, the consul, arrived at the city, and after laying before the senate a detail of his successful services in Istria and Liguria, a triumph was decreed to him on demanding it. He triumphed, in office, over the two nations at once. In this procession he carried three hundred and seven thousand denariuses, and eighty-five thousand seven hundred and two quinariuses. To each soldier fifteen denariuses were given, double that sum to a centurion, triple it to a horseman. The allied soldiers received less, by half, than the native troops, for which reason they followed his chariot in silence to show their disgust.

Why Rome built such colonies

from Indro Montanelli: *Rome: the first thousand years*

Roman colonies started in Italy itself, long before the more famous overseas colonies and the eventual Roman empire. Colonies provided agricultural and other goods, as well as soldiers. The historian Strabo said of Luca that "some of the people of this part of Italy dwell in villages, nevertheless it is well populated, and furnishes the greater part of the military force, and of equites, of whom the Senate is partly composed".

After her experience with the Latin League, Rome had realised that one could not put one's trust in protectorates and forced allies. Partly for this reason, and partly owing to over-population in the City, the Romans really began to Romanise Italy by the system of "colonies", a process they had already inaugurated after the first Samnite war. Enemy territory was confiscated and distributed to landless Roman citizens, especially to those with military merits. In fact, it was to the ex-soldiers that most of it was assigned, men who could be relied upon to rally promptly to their own defence – and Rome's. The natives naturally received them coldly as robbers and oppressors, and from the name of one of them, a certain Caphus, a corporal in Cæsar's army, the word "cafone" was later coined, a term of contempt meaning a coarse and vulgar person. This hostility also gave rise at this time to the mocking, derisive sound with which the defeated peoples greeted the Romans when they entered their cities and which, it would seem, was at first mistaken by them for a manifestation of welcome.

Of course one cannot hope to enlarge one's territory from five hundred to twenty-five thousand square kilometres, as the Romans did during this period, without treading on somebody's corns. On the other hand, all central and southern Italy began to speak the same language and to think in terms of nation and state instead of village and tribe.

How it looked

The colony of Luca was laid out in traditional grid fashion within a ring of walls, approximately 500 metres square. Two main streets criss-crossed the town: the Decumanus Maximus, *roughly via San Paolino and via Santa Croce today, and the* Kardo Maximus, *roughly the path of via Fillungo and via Cenami. They met just above the Forum, now Piazza San Michele, where until recently Lucca farmers sold their wares in the square and gossiped as did their predecessors two millennia ago. Four gates were placed in the sides of the fortifications.*

The amphitheatre near the end of via Fillungo – then outside the walls – has kept its shape, and one senses its atmosphere inside the great ellipse, but only a few of the arches and walls can be seen along the outside perimeter, the rest having been plundered for building materials (as was the Coliseum in Rome) or integrated into the more modern buildings around it. The public theatre inside the walls has been subsumed in the area around Sant' Agostino.

The seat of government would have been where the Palazzo Ducale is (today's seat of Government). A few portions of the Roman wall are visible, especially in the church of Santa Maria della Rosa and near the Botanic Gardens. Roman columns abound in the city churches. Remains of Roman baths are beneath the church of SS Giovanni and Reparata.

56 BC

Caesar plots with Pompey and Crassus

from Laurence Echard: *The Roman History* (1699)

Luca had become a municipium *in 89 BC. Later it became known for the Congress of Lucca in 56 BC, when Julius Caesar and the generals Pompey and Crassus met to plot their takeover of government in Rome. Pompey was married to Caesar's daughter*

Julia and Crassus was famous for having put down the slave revolt led by Spartacus. They agreed in Luca that Pompey and Crassus would be the next year's Consuls, and thereafter have the Governorships of Spain and Syria respectively. Crassus was to lead an army to the conquest of Parthia. Caesar would remain pro-consul of Gaul, which he had defeated and annexed to the Empire. The arrangement didn't last long. Crassus died in Parthia, while Pompey was killed in 48 BC during the Civil War, where he and Caesar represented opposite sides. Julius Caesar then became the supreme ruler of the Roman Empire, until the Ides of March in 44 BC.

As Caefar's Conquefts eftablifh'd his Reputation in Rome, fo his Humanity, and other excellent Qualities, abfolutely gain'd him the Hearts and Affections of his Soldiers. He had now got great ftore of Wealth, by which he not only difcharg'd his Debts, but likewife made many great Friends by his Magnificent Prefents, efpecially to the Ladies, corrupting alfo the *Ediles, Praetors* and *Confuls* themfelves. In this Winter he pafs'd into *Italy* to *Luca*, where he took up his Head-Quarters, where there was fo great a Concourfe of People to pay him their Refpects, that 200 Senators were prefent together, and fo many *Praetors* and *Pro-confuls*, that 120 Bundles of Rods were feen there at a time. Here the *Triumvirate* took new Meafures, and *Caefar* fearing he might be recall'd from *Gaul*, procur'd *Pompey* and *Craffiss* to endeavour at the Confulfhip the following Year, and fo continue him in his Imployment for five Years longer. This Defign was fo difpleafing to the Senate and the Diffentions fo violent concerning it, that they went into Mourning as in publick Calamities; faying, *That the Proceedings of the Triumvirate were dangerous to the Quiet and Liberty of* Rome. *Cato* with great Eagernefs fet up *Domitius* to ftand againft 'em; but *Pompey* refolving to remove all Obftacles, fent fome Armed Men againft *Domitius* as he was going to the Election, who kill'd the Slave that carry'd the Light before 'em, and difpers'd all their Company, *Cato* himfelf receiving a Wound on the Arm, and *Domitius* hardly efcaping: And thus by Force and Violence both *Pompey* and *Craffiss* obtain'd the Confulfhip.

and a Lucca priest is still proud of Caesar's visit 1774 years later

from V. Marchiò: *Il Forestiere informato delle cose di Lucca*

Marchiò was a priest in Lucca and wrote the first comprehensive guidebook about the city.

Thus, all the world finds Lucca memorable for its most famous guest, when it received Julius Caesar in the Roman year 698, or 53 years before the delivery of the great Virgin Mother; because of the Triumvirate in Lucca Rome's liberty was taken away and the great structure of the Roman Republic torn down.

Caesar's stay was not short, but of longer duration, and it encouraged a great group of eminent people to come to Lucca, such as Pompey, Crassus, many praetors, women and matrons of Rome. Also all the magistrates of Rome, and all the most noble citizens, and in a short time 200 senators, 120 senior officials and other dignitaries met before the gates, demonstrating that the City of Lucca could receive at the same time the three principal leaders of Rome and a great number of personages of every level, confirming that 1774 years ago Lucca was a commodious, celebrated City capable of hosting and lodging such a great quantity of noble guests, and Lords of greater and lesser parts of the world, just as it was 163 years before that, when it was capable of receiving the Consul Titus Sempronius, a supreme leader of the Roman Republic, and his entourage.

How Diecimo got its name

from Hilaire Belloc: *The Path to Rome*

Diecimo is a very small village just north of Ponte a Moriano in the Serchio Valley. Hilaire Belloc (1870-1953) wrote a number of charming travel books, including The Path to Rome, *an account of his pilgrimage on foot from France to Rome in 1901. Belloc slept in the woods and walked the whole way like a medieval pilgrim, usually more than thirty miles a day. The eleventh century church he mentions is sparse and beautiful, made entirely of a subtle grey stone.*

I will give up this much, to tell you that at Decimo the mystery of cypress trees first came into my adventure and pilgrimage: of cypress trees which henceforward were to mark my Tuscan road. And I will tell you that there also I came across a thing peculiar (I suppose) to the region of Lucca, for I saw it there as at Decimo, and also some miles beyond. I mean fine mournful towers built thus: in the first storey one arch, in the second two, in the third three, and so on: a very noble way of building.

And I will tell you something more. I will tell you something no one has yet heard. To wit, why this place is called Decimo, and why just below it is another little spot called Sexta.

LECTOR ...

AUCTOR. I know what you are going to say! Do not say it. You are going to say: "It is because they were at the sixth and tenth mile-stones from Lucca on the Roman road." Heaven help these scientists! Did you suppose that I thought it was called Decimo because the people had ten toes? Tell me, why is not every place ten miles out of a Roman town called by such a name? Eh? You are dumb. You cannot answer. Like most moderns you have entirely missed the point. We all know that there was a Roman town at Lucca, because it was called Luca, and if there had been no Roman town the modern town would not be spelt with two c's. All Roman towns had milestones beyond them. But why did *this* tenth milestone from *this* Roman town keep its name?

LECTOR. I am indifferent.

AUCTOR. I will tell you. Up in the tangle of the Carrara mountains, overhanging the Garfagnana, was a wild tribe, whose name I forget (unless it were the Bruttii), but which troubled the Romans not a little, defeating them horribly, and keeping the legionaries in some anxiety for years. So when the soldiers marched out north from Luca about six miles, they could halt and smile at each other, and say, "At *Sextam* ... that's all right. All safe so far!" and therefore only a little village grew up at this little rest and emotion. But as they got nearer the gates of the hills they began to be visibly perturbed, and they would say, "The eighth mile! Cheer up!" Then "The ninth mile! Sanctissima Madonna! Have you seen anything moving on the heights?"

But when they got to the tenth milestone, which stands before the very jaws of the defile, then indeed they said with terrible emphasis, "*Ad Decimam*!" And there was no restraining them: they would camp and entrench, or die in the venture: for they were Romans and stern fellows, and loved a good square camp and a ditch, and sentries and a clear moon, and plenty of sharp stakes, and all the panoply of war. That is the origin of Decimo.

```
LIBERATORI ORBIS
ROMANI RESTITVTORI LI
BERTATIS. ET REIPV. CON
SERVATORI MILITVM
ET PROVINCIALIVM
DN II CLAVDIO IV
LIANO INVICTO P P
//MPER AVGVSTO
```

```
LVCENS. CIV. SVB PROBO
IMP. AVG. MAR. AVR. LAV
PROCON INTER. GALLIAS
ENS. FABR. RETENTVRAE
IVSQ. COH. PR. LEGEND
MENS. RES. A DVO LAT.
```

Roman inscriptions found in the Renaissance in Lucca,
dating from the time of Augustus

The Volto Santo responds to a wandering minstrel

MEDIEVAL LUCCA

The White Oxen bring the Volto Santo to Lucca

from Janet Ross and Nelly Erichsen: *The Story of Lucca*

The Volto Santo is a large figure of Christ, surrounded by a little temple by Matteo Civitali in San Martino Cathedral. A stunning fresco of the story of its arrival in Lucca by Aspertini can be seen in the Gentili Chapel in the church of San Frediano. The Volto Santo is said to have been carved by Nicodemus, who had removed Christ from the cross and placed him in the tomb. He carved all but the head which he felt incapable of doing. One night when he was sleeping, angels came down and finished the countenance.

Then, it is said that after the death of Nicodemus the Holy Cross was in that cave for many, many years; none knew about it, all the descendants of Nicodemus being dead. An angel appeared to the good and devout Bishop Subalpino and said, "Bishop Subalpino, arise, and go to Mount Cedron, there shalt thou find a spacious and fine cave. Search therein and thou wilt see a precious image fashioned by divine wisdom. It was made by the saint Nicodemus. For it thou must build a rich tabernacle in the form of a ship, and when well secured launch her into the sea. God wills that it shall no longer be hid, but be reverenced and honoured, and He will lead it where it pleases Him." The bishop at the head of much people went into the valley and with prayer and hymns they searched for the cave, found it, and entering saw the True Cross. The bishop's joy was unspeakable when he beheld so sweet and rare an image. He carried it to the shore, built a ship adorned with many lamps and other ornaments, placed the Cross within her, and with his own hands made it secure on all sides. And there arose a wind so soft and so laden with sweet odours, that it seemed as though all the spices of the earth had been strewn around, and the ship gently left the shore and entered into the high seas.

Then it is said that when the ship had left the land she met

Genoese trading vessels, whose crews, greatly wondering at such a marvel, resolved to capture the ship. Up and down, from one side to another, they followed her. Those sailors who knew how to swim threw themselves into the sea with hooks and ropes, and used every artifice, but the ship always eluded them. At length they came near to the city of Luni, and the Bishop, seeing the vain endeavours of the Genoese to capture the tabernacle-ship, called his people and promised absolution to any man who took that ship. Galleys and vessels of all sorts were launched, and the bishop stood on the shore with his people to witness so wonderful a sight. The ship ever eluded them and they could never get near her. There was then in Lucca a bishop named Giovanni, so holy, and through whom God worked such miracles, that he was called Giovanni the Glorious. To him came an angel and said, "Bishop Giovanni, arise. Call together thy people and go with great devotion to the sea-shore at Luni to receive the gift sent to thee by God. Thou art to take the ship sailing on the sea and the Holy Cross which is therein, and mind to be courteous to the bishop of Luni with that which thou shalt find inside the Cross." Next morning Giovanni of Lucca summoned his clergy and his people and told his dream, and they set forth. They saw the vessels trying to take the ship, and Giovanni of Lucca said to the bishop of Luni and his people, "Noble gentlemen, I pray of you to be satisfied with what Our Lord has said," and he told his dream. The bishop of Luni then begged for one day, during which his people would try to capture the ship. All day and all night the Genoese and the people of Luni tried to take her, but without going far from the port of Luni she ever escaped them, hither and thither, now here, now there. At break of day next morning bishop Giovanni went down to the shore and found the sailors worn out. They said to him, "By God, begin your prayers so that we can see this great wonder and what is in it, for we have had enough of it and are tired." The bishop caused his people to kneel and he prayed devoutly with many tears. When his prayer was finished a gentle breeze arose, bringing so sweet an odour that all marvelled, and borne by the soft breeze the ship came over the sea. Giovanni of Lucca stretched out his arms with great devotion towards the ship, and with his hand drew her to earth as though she had been a feather. Then he unfastened the boards and in the tabernacle he beheld the Holy Cross and the glorious Face. He caused candles and torches to be brought and examined the Holy Cross. Inside it he found a writing describing how it had been fashioned by Nicodemus, and another describing how Bishop Subalpino had found it in a cave. Then he found a portion of the crown of thorns, part of the vestment of Our Lord, one of the nails with which He had been crucified, a small phial containing His blood, and the sheet in which His Body had been wrapped when laid in the sepulchre, besides other precious relics. Thereupon Giovanni gave to the bishop of Luni the phial containing the precious blood, which he received with great joy. But many of the people were dissatisfied, and debated whether it would not be possible to keep the Holy Cross at Luni.

Then it is said that hearing this the bishop of Lucca proposed that a handsome four-wheeled waggon should be made, the Holy Cross be placed in it, and that two unbroken steers should be harnessed to the waggon while all prayed that God should guide it to the place chosen by Himself. The people cried with one voice, "We are content." The young steers bent their heads to the yoke like old, well-trained oxen, and without human guidance, save that Bishop Giovanni and his clergy walked in front, took the road to Lucca. When the people of Lucca saw the precious gift of God approaching they rang the bells and went forth to meet the Bishop with trumpets, fifes, cymbals, and other instruments, singing and praising God. The steers stopped in front of San Martino, which is the principal church of Lucca, and Bishop Giovanni most reverently with his own hands bore the Holy Cross into the church. Then he built a chapel and an altar whereon he set the Holy Cross with many fine ornaments. And this happened in the year seven hundred and forty-two, in the time of Pepin and Charles, illustrious kings.

The Volto Santo, Lucca's King

Lucca has never had a king. She was ruled by Roman emperors, of course, but that was when the Lucca we know and enjoy today was still in its cradle. There were barbarian and Byzantine kings, but even they had to bow to the obstinacy that made Lucca difficult to take by siege and to the diplomatic skills that it used to avoid being conquered – the very qualities that allowed it to evolve slowly and remain almost intact right up to the economic boom of the post-war period.

Internal lordships never lasted very long as the fluctuating fortunes of merchant, banking and ecclesiastical families rose and fell. Castruccio degli Antelminelli ruled for only a few years and although Paolo Guinigi held power for thirty, he left no heir. Napoleon made his sister Princess of Lucca and later it was ruled by Italian kings, though Lucca always felt detached from the rest of Italy. By that time, its subtle, quasi-nordic character was already fixed and no-one will ever change Lucca now.

In one sense, however, Lucca has always had a king and one king only. He is celebrated every year on 13 September in a procession which is both triumphal and triumphant; as the summer sun begins to fade, the evening streets light up with a thousand candles and torches in honour of the city's true ruler.

In the pagan world, there were important festivals in September to mark the end of summer and the approach of autumn. Every religion absorbs and superimposes itself on the rhythms of earlier beliefs, producing a blend of elements which reflects human life better than many philosophies do. Many Christian observances were superimposed on ancient pagan rites, sometimes duplicating their forms and emphases. In the Middle Ages, there were September festivals and fairs, when people from the country had a last chance to buy and barter before the winter set in. September takes its name from the Roman calendar in which the year started with the beginning of spring (as it is still celebrated in Florence) and was therefore the seventh month of the year. This is when the sun, with his radiant crown symbolising regal divinity and kingship, crosses the constellation which is called the Plough in English and *il Carro*, the cart, in Italian. And it just so happens that there is a legend in Lucca which tells of a king brought to the city in a cart one September long ago.

The origins, tradition and continuity of the September fairs and the Luminara (festival of lights) of Santa Croce are closely linked to the cult of the Volto Santo. This crucifix has symbolised the city's religious and political cohesion for more than a thousand years, and is venerated in the Cathedral of San Martino. The spirit of the Lucchesi may never have tolerated a permanent Signoria, as happened in Florence and Ferrara, and there may never have been a dominant figure in this little republic like the Doge in Venice. Nonetheless, Lucca had its own king-figure – the Volto Santo.

The legend of the Volto Santo is said to have been written by a certain Leobino and the question is how much truth there is in it. Why does it say that the Volto Santo, with the power to work a thousand miracles, was carved by Nicodemus, head of the Sanhedrin and close enough to Christ to be converted by Him? Why does it say that this Cross sailed all alone from one end of the Mediterranean Sea to the other, in order to choose Lucca with great portents?

There is one historic fact. In 742, the year of the legend, the Bishop of Lucca was not Giovanni, as the legend says, but Walprand, son of Walper, duke of Lucca, which was then the capital of the Lombard duchy and therefore with jurisdiction over the port of Luni as well. Under Giovanni, who became bishop soon afterwards and held office between 780 and 808, there was a period of great religious enthusiasm; it was probably at this time that a crucifix (or, at any rate, Lucca's most important religious symbol) was transferred from the Church of San Frediano to the new cathedral – the very route that the ritual procession has since followed faithfully for perhaps 1200 years.

According to the legend, the Volto Santo had made another ritual journey, namely, the journey from Luni, ancient capital of the Cento-Ligurians, where it had arrived from the Holy Land, to Lucca, carried on a cart drawn by a pair of white oxen like a Roman or Etruscan procession.

These elements give us the first inkling of the origins of the festival and why it grew up in the days around the summer solstice. Historians and art historians give a further clue. According to some, the present Volto Santo (no-one excludes the possibility that there was at least one earlier version) dates from the end of the twelfth century or the beginning of the thirteenth. By that time, Lucca had risen to the status of city-state and, thanks to its silk industry and commercial success, was enjoying its greatest splendour. She was extending her boundaries and thinking of building new walls, and the picture of her "king" began to be reproduced everywhere

– on coins, seals and coats-of-arms. Every Codex dating from that time had "To the glory of the Volto Santo ..." as its preamble. A Lucchese in danger or a merchant in difficulties abroad invoked the cross with the cry, "Oh Volto Santo, help me now!" When an alliance was drawn up, it began, "In the name of the Volto Santo".

This was so common that Dante accused the Lucchesi, in no uncertain terms, of using their Christ as little more than a catch-phrase, which was probably true, but he was also acknowledging that the city's unity and its very identity depended on the Volto Santo. Perhaps what the author of the *Divine Comedy* might have said was, "The typical Lucchese, with a servant girl for his holiest saint, is very religious, but when it comes to masters, he prefers to have one only and that one in the other world rather than in this."

In the light of these "facts", the whole history seems to have its centre of gravity at the end of the eleventh century and to be connected with the First Crusade (1096-1099). The Lucchesi did business in all parts of the known world and were *au fait* with contemporary ideas, but here they lost a great historical opportunity. Put simply, they couldn't believe that such a seemingly desperate enterprise would succeed, and they therefore had nothing to do with something which, in the event, changed the course of history. Their hated neighbours in Pisa took part, however, had enormous military and political success, and came home laden with wealth (which they used to build the famous tower and the piazza rightly called "of the Miracles") and important relics – including, most significantly, the body of St Nicodemus which lies in Pisa Cathedral.

It is difficult to say to what extent the eternal rivalry between the two cities prompted the emergence or revival of the cult and its legend, but it cannot be a coincidence that both the Volto San-to and its saint-creator crossed the sea from Palestine a thousand years after the event and landed in Italy less than twenty kilometres from each other. Nor can it be mere chance that the legend reports that the Pisan fleet was on coastal patrol as the Volto Santo sailed by. They followed it closely, having the sea power that Lucca would never have, and it seemed as though they were intent on seizing the holy unmanned ship – and that was why the Cross was forced to land at Luni, the first port further north which was not in Pisa's control!

The traditional procession of the Volto Santo (or Santa Croce) was originally celebrated on a September night to conquer the darkness of the coming winter (at its darkest, according to popular belief, three months later on Santa Lucia's Day on 13 December) but it must almost immediately have acquired the religious symbolism and political aspects which both identified the community and drew it together. Then as now, in a night at summer's end, the entire city and its territorial possessions gathered round this symbol of a religious faith which was expressed by reference to a remarkable image, famous throughout Europe in the Middle Ages and visited by foreign kings and rulers.

In order to perform both its religious and political functions, the procession had a special, fixed order. At the head was their king; the city authorities followed, reaffirming their power by this act of obeisance to the king, and then came the people of the community itself, in order of their lay, religious or voluntary affiliations.

Naturally, all citizens of Lucca and all the subject territories were obliged to perform this act of double reverence. Old statutes made it clear that everyone, apart from a very few exceptions, had to take part in the procession on 13 September. A law passed in 1308 listed all 300 communities under the rule of Lucca and which were therefore required to be present. The highest office-holders of the magistrature, the Captain of the People and the Governor also had to take part and had to be preceded in the procession by two large candelabras with lighted candles. A law passed in 1398 decreed that the obligation applied to all males of the outlying villages between the ages of 14 and 69 and set out the tributes to be made to the Volto Santo with pedantic precision. It was even so absurd as to list territories which had been lost, on the grounds that "should they ever return within the jurisdiction of and obedience to the law of Lucca, they will be required to attend at the Luminara". Another statute, this time of 1539, stated that only the Officer of the Guard, innkeepers, bread sellers and butchers were exempt – the enormous influx of people into the city made these exceptions necessary.

You may find it hard to believe how important it was to take part in the Luminara, but consider the story of Iscariccio, a lawyer in Castiglione in the Garfagnana. The Garfagnana had obtained

Frederick Barbarossa's permission to be governed locally by the Cattani family, who were the feudal lords of the area, while the people of the Garfagnana were granted the right to obtain Lucca citizenship and, if they chose, to go and live within the ambit of the Volto Santo. Iscariccio, citizen of Lucca, did his duty and took part in the Luminara in 1243, carrying the candle appropriate to his status. (By that time, even the numbers and types of candles and lights were meticulously prescribed by law according to the *census candeli*, which said, in effect, that the richer you were, the bigger your financial contribution and the candle you carried in the procession had to be.) It seems, however, that the lawyer was involved in some kind of intrigue with the Cattani family against the vassalage of Lucca, because the authorities regarded his taking part in the September procession as an act of treason and his right hand, found guilty of having carried a candle, was cut off.

Nowadays this socio-political, religious, ritualistic event is faithfully re-enacted by the city and provincial authorities, bands, representatives of public institutions and local town halls and all the emigrants and members of the "Lucchesi nel Mondo" societies who come back for the occasion. The festival has been greatly expanded and now occupies the whole of the month of September with cultural events, a funfair which has taken the place of jousting, sports meetings and markets, but the high point is still the evening of the 13th.

You need to use a little historical imagination to understand the attraction that this festival had for the people who lived outside Lucca and to picture the annual pilgrimage of people on foot, in sedan chairs, on the backs of mules or donkeys, with the better off on horseback or in carriages. Most people walked with a bundle of things to eat or to sell and, with luck, make enough money to pay for a bed in the city – though it can't have been easy to find somewhere to stay in Lucca during the days of Santa Croce if you didn't have friends or acquaintances or protectors there.

For the people who lived farthest away, coming to the city and seeing "the world" must have been something to talk about through the winter months. People looked forward to this holiday all year, to immersing themselves in life and religious faith in the crowded streets lit by candles whose wax polished the flagstones and whose flames lit up the festival of the king who entered the walls of the city in a cart.

Even now, once a year on this special evening, just as it was centuries ago, in the dense crowds, when the night is banished by the lights, you lose your sense of time and you feel, not as if you are reliving a precise moment in the life of the city, but as if you have always belonged to these houses and these piazzas and this community. (Daniele Vanni)

A French traveller hears a different version

from Maximilian Misson: Nouvelle Voyage d'Italie

Maximilian Misson (1650-1722) was a very early venturer on the Grand Tour. He was a Protestant judge in the "chamber of the edict" in the parliament of Paris. Upon its revocation in 1685, he found refuge in England and was tutor to the young Earl of Arran. They made a tour of Europe in 1687-8, and his detailed Nouvelle Voyage d'Italie *became a sort of handbook for other travellers for the next fifty years.*

The Volto Santo was first brought to the Church of St. Fredian, but it remov'd from thence to the Cathedral, and remained in the Air in the same place where they first saw it, till they had built an altar under it, on which it rested, and about which they afterwards built a magnificent chapel. This Image does not work so many miracles as several others; but every thing that it does, is wonderful in the highest degree. 'Tis the principal Object of the Devotion of their people, and they stamp it on the Coins with the Arms of the Republick.

You may easily imagine that this Crucifix met with a very high reception at the Cathedral; yet 'tis hard to divine the reason why it preferred St. Martin to St. Fredian, since 'tis certain that this City was much more obliged to the latter than the former.

The Volto Santo responds to a wandering minstrel

From a 14th century French storyteller.

Jenois, a poor young minstrel on his way to Rome, who had sworn not to break his fast until by singing to his lute he had gained his meal, sang one Sunday to seven hundred men who gave him never a farthing. So he wandered into the chapel and saw the newly arrived crucifix. He noticed that the hands and the feet were pierced with nails, and it seemed to him that blood flowed from the side. Addressing a man, he asked, "Who is this I see so sore afflicted? In what war was he so sore afflicted? In what war has he been thus maltreated; is he dead or is he alive?" The man answered, "Friend, you are making fun of me. That was never made of flesh and blood. It is a *Vou* (crucifix) fashioned beyond the seas to show that God was thus maltreated to save the world." When told how Our Lord had suffered, pity seized him, and taking his lute he began to sing before the Holy Face. When the Holy Ghost saw the pity that was in the minstrel heart, He descended and caused the Holy Image to move and to speak. Lifting one foot free of the nail the Figure extended it and kicked its gold and silver shoe studded with precious stones to Jenois. With joy he received it and exclaimed, "Now I will go and sup." But the bystanders ran and fetched the bishop, who imperiously ordered Jenois to give the shoe back. He obeyed, and placed it on the foot of the Holy Figure, which angrily kicked it off, commanding him to keep it until he had been well paid for it. The bishop then filled the shoe with gold pieces, and as Jenois again approached the Cross the foot of the Holy Figure was raised to receive the shoe, and then once more nailed to the Cross. Whereupon, like a dying man, the Figure bowed its head and became paler than anything born of woman, and the Holy Ghost withdrew from the crucifix as the light fades from the setting sun and the waves melt away under the sea. With the money bestowed upon him by God, Jenois gave a dinner to the poor of the city, and when all had eaten and drunk well he distributed what was left in alms and said farewell. Many accompanied him far out of the city, and when they lost sight of him they kissed the earth whereon he had trod. Thinking of God, he arrived at a palace inhabited in infidels, who, after making him sing all day, led him at vesper time into a cellar and asked him whether he believed in One who had allowed himself to be crucified. "Yes," answered Jenois, "all my thoughts are with Him." So the ruffians tied him to a pillar, beat his white body with thorns, and then struck off his head. If you doubt this, go to Rome, where his body lies encased in shining silver and pure gold.

The Via Francigena

Lucca's importance in the Longobard period and later in medieval days came from its position on the trade and pilgrim route called the Via Francigena, which led from Northern Europe to Rome. The standard journey would start (for English pilgrims) at the Boulogne coast, go through northeastern France to Rheims, across the Jura to Besançon, skirt the corner of Lake Geneva to the San Bernardo Pass, through Aosta down through Lombardy, over the Apennines by the Cisa Pass into Lucca. This journey, which can be done in two days driving, took over a month. Chaucer during his visit to Tuscany in 1372-3 took 39 days from London to Genoa; William Way on his pilgrimage to Jerusalem in 1462 took the same time to go from Gravesend to Venice. The time of year was critical, as winter would close all the Alpine passes and even those in the Apennines. Lucca was a major, and welcome, resting point for travellers and their animals. It provided hospices, food, provisions and a chance to see relics of saints known throughout Northern Europe, as well as the Volto Santo. You can walk along the old Via Francigena today, with the right guide book.

St Willibald goes through Lucca, where his father dies

from *The Hodoeporicon of St Willibald*

*The eighth century churchman Willibald was the son of Richard,
"King" of an unknown part of southern England. They made a
pilgrimage to Rome in 721, walking from Southampton. Willibald,
later Bishop of Eichstatt in Germany, was perhaps the first English
pilgrim to Rome and the Holy Land. He was also the nephew of St.
Boniface, the Apostle of Germany. His trip is minutely described in
the* Hodoeporicon *(guide-book), written by one of the nuns of the
Abbey of Heidenheim, a monastery founded by St. Boniface. The
author, an English lady probably called Roswida and a relation of
the Bishop, had listened to Willibald's own accounts of the trip.*

Afterwards that youth ... opened the secrets of his heart to his
father according to the flesh, and begged him with earnest prayers,
to give his advice and consent to the desire of his will, and he
asked him not only to give him permission to go – but also to go
with him himself ... And he so allured him by the sweet promises
of the oracles of God to accompany his sons, and to visit the
renowned threshold of Peter, prince of the Apostles. Now his
father, at first, when he asked him, declined the journey, excusing
himself on account of his wife, and the youth and frailty of his
growing children, and answered that it would be dishonourable
and cruel to deprive them of his protection, and leave them to
strangers. Then that warlike soldier of Christ repeated his solemn
exhortations, and the persistence of his prayers ... so that at last,
by the aid of Almighty God, the will of the petitioner and exhorter
prevailed, and that father of his and his brother Wunebald
promised that they would start on the course he had desired and
exhorted them to run.

... And going on, they came to the city which is called Lucca.
Hitherto, Willibald and Wunebald had conducted their father with
them in their company on the journey. But he was all at once
attacked with a sudden failure of bodily strength, such that, after
a short time, the day of his end was at hand. And the disease
increasing upon him, his worn out and cold bodily limbs wasted

away, and thus he breathed out his life's last breath. Those two brothers, his sons, then took the lifeless body of their father and with the affection of filial devotion, wrapped it in beautiful clothes, and buried it at St. Frigidian, in the city of Lucca. There rests their father's body.

Richard "King of England"

Willibald's father Richard was indeed buried in San Frediano. He was the first important English traveller to die in Italy and to be canonised. He now apparently lies in the small sarcophagus in the Trenta Chapel near the main altar. In 1094, the Archbishop Gillam, on his way home from Rome, also died in Lucca, where his sister Ermingard was a nun. His remains, buried in the convent of Santa Giustina, gave rise to miracles which permitted his canonisation. The fifteenth century statue which adorned his tomb in the convent chapel is now in the National Museum in Villa Guinigi. John Evelyn recorded King Richard's epitaph in 1645 as:

> Hic rex Richardus requiescit, sceptifer, almus:
> Rex fuit Anglorum, regnum tenet iste Polorum.
> Regnum demisit pro Christo cuncta reliquit.
> Ergo Richardum nobis dedit Anglia sanctum.
> Hic genitor Sanctae Walburgae Virginis almae
> Est Vrillebaldi Sancti simul et Vinebaldi,
> Suffragium quorum nobis det regna Polorum.

> Here King Richard lies, gentle and regal.
> An English king, he is now in the kingdom of heaven.
> He left his kingdom, he abandoned all for Christ.
> So from England he comes to us as Saint Richard.
> He was the father of St. Walburga the virgin
> And father of the saints Willibald and Winnebald:
> May their prayers earn for us the kingdom of heaven.

Misson is sceptical about this king

from Maximilian Misson: *Nouvelle Voyage d'Italie*

In the same church we took notice of a Tomb-stone with these words enscribed upon it, Hic jacet corpus Sancti Riccardi Regis Angliae: here lies the body of St. Richard King of England. I cannot imagine who this Royal Saint should be. Richard I if my Memory does not deceive me, dy'd in France of a Wound, after his return from his Voyage beyond Sea, and was interred in the Abbey of Fontevrant. Richard II was dethron'd by the Parliament and the Duke of Lancaster, and afterward stabb'd at Pomfret, from where his Body was carried first to St. Paul's, then to Langley, and at last to Westminster, where his Tomb still remains. And Richard III who was no more a Saint than his Predecessors of the same Name, but rather a very wicked man, was slain at Bosworth in Leicestershire and buried in the City of Leicester.

Besides I do not remember that ever there was a King Richard in England before the re-union of the Heptarchy. So that the Epitaph puzzl'd us all.

(1896)

A pilgrim hymn to the Volto Santo

INNO
dei Pellegrini al Volto Santo di Lucca

Evviva la Croce	Long live the Cross
La Croce evviva;	To the cross long life;
Evviva la Croce	Long live the Cross
E chi l'esaltò.	And all who exalted you.

Ti cingi la fronte D'un serto di fiori, T'adorna d'allori, O esarea città	You encircle your forehead With a wreath of flowers, Adorn with laurel your City of the River Serchio.
Un canto al Signore Innalza giuliva; Del Serchio la riva Risponder s'udrà.	A song to the Lord Sing joyously! The Serchio's bank You will hear respond.
A te dall'oriente Sull'onde portata, Da un angel guidata L'Immago volò.	To you from the Orient Brought on the waves, Guided by an angel Your sacred image flew.
O Lucca, fra cento Te scelse il Signore, Quel Volto d'amore Te sola beò.	Oh Lucca, one in a hundred The Lord chose you, That Image of love Blessed only you.
Ridesta degli avi La fede gloriosa; Ti prostra pietosa Innanzi al tuo Re.	Glorious faith of The ancestors revived; Makes you humbly kneel Before your king.
Quel Volto ritorna La pace e l'amore; O Lucca, il Signore Trionfa con Te.	The Image brings back Peace and Love; Oh Lucca, the Lord Triumphs with you.

San Frediano diverts the Serchio with his rake

50

A Hundred Churches and a Thousand Saints

The Longobards who poured down through Italy in 568, almost immediately taking Lucca, very soon realised that, in order to govern their diverse Italian possessions, they would have to embrace the religion which Constantine had already made the state religion, and become Christians. These people were the first barbarians to integrate with the established Roman population and they chose Lucca to be the capital of their Marquisate of Tuscia.

Matilda Countess of Canossa was a direct descendant of those men of the north, and, in particular, a member of the Longobard-Lucchese family, the Attoni. She was also so passionately attached to the Church that she became a champion in its struggles against the Holy Roman Empire, whose centre of gravity was in the German lands so closely related to her in race, laws, habits and culture. When she was young, her total commitment to the Papal faction cost her a period in a German prison but it also guaranteed her a place in history. One episode is especially remembered. In 1076, she arrogantly took up her position with Pope Gregory VII at the castle of Canossa in Emilia, in order to humiliate Emperor Henry IV, who waited for three days in the snow at the foot of the castle – wearing, they say, a penitent's shirt – before he was forgiven and his excommunication lifted. The countess must also have had greatness of soul if – as I believe – she is the same Matilda that Dante made a symbol of the journey of mortification towards asceticism.

There's always been a tendency amongst the people of Lucca to make icons of certain women, whether bad (Lucida Mansi) or good (Santa Zita). Popular belief in Lucca invested this great woman, who had everything and could do anything, with a mysterious aura of dissatisfaction and the impossible dream of becoming a nun and saying Mass. This theological idea is so modern that it might have been created on purpose to anticipate the schism in the Anglican church. Naturally, Christian doctrine barred Pope Gregory from granting her wish, but not wanting to discourage her in view of her great merits and thinking, in any case, of how it might be of advantage to the church, he – so the legend goes – asked her to build a hundred churches. That done, she would be allowed to celebrate Mass and administer the sacraments. Matilda set herself to the task with Teutonic spirit and covered the area straddling Tuscany and Emilia with lovely churches – sadly, she drew her last pious breath when she was in the middle of building the ninety-ninth. Maybe one day you'll ask an old man standing at a crossroads near Lucca, "Who built that charming church?" Chances are he'll say, "Countess Matilda!"

Legends are founded in truth. This particular legend has its basis in the extraordinary interpenetration of the Church in Lucca with the city's history. It is no coincidence at all that Lucca, erstwhile capital of Tuscia and seat of Matilda of the Attoni, is called the city of a hundred churches. Were there really a hundred? Well, yes, almost as many as the legend says if you count the churches which adorn the city, and certainly many more if you include the chapels of religious and charitable institutions and those inside cloisters and convents. Every penthouse and attic inside the walls has views of campaniles where crows roost and pigeons nest; every now and again they fly off in flocks to the innumerable little stone and marble squares in front of the churches.

A hundred churches within a perimeter of slightly more than four kilometres. And a thousand saints. Every area of Lucca and its surrounding parishes is named after a saint and it's not easy finding your way around this display of religious fervour. Even natives of Lucca have difficulty remembering which is Baluardo San Colombano and which is Santa Maria or San Pietro ... Porta San Gervasio e Protasio, Porta San Jacopo ... You remember the San Concordio, San Filippo, San Donato and SS. Annunziata areas because they're bigger, and the streets that you use – San Girolamo, Santa Giustina, Santa Croce, San Giorgio.

They say that Lucca was the first city north of Rome to be converted, by a disciple of Peter who landed at the mouth of the Arno. It is logical, therefore, that this cradle of the faith should have produced countless bishops and more than fifty cardinals. According to the Reverend Signore Vincenzio Marchiò in his 1721 guidebook *Il Forestiere informato delle cose di Lucca*, seventy saints went to their blessed and well-earned rest in Lucca and were buried within the walls. The limited power of the city, however, meant that it produced only one Pope, or possibly two, and that both of these were elected when Lucca was at the apex and the world centre of the silk trade. Pope Lucius III, who was born in Lunata of the Allucignoli family and died in 1185, was certainly Lucchese while Lucius II was either Lucchese or lived here for a long time. (Daniele Vanni)

～～

San Frediano diverts the Serchio with his rake

from St Gregory: *Dialogues*

San Frediano – the Irish priest Frigidian or Finnian – was called to become the Bishop of Lucca in 560. Eight years later, the Longobard invasion started; it laid waste to Lucca and its diocese, which extended to Livorno, Florence, Pisa and Volterra. Bishop Frediano lost his church of SS. Giovanni e Reparata (the later building which now bears the name has been deconsecrated and is used as a beautiful concert hall) but started a new church on the site of San Martino to take its place. He repaired Lucca's walls and tried to convert the Longobards, who made Lucca the capital of their new province of Tuscia; he died in 588. The present church of San Frediano was built in the twelfth century. It contains his tomb, as well as that of "Richard King of England", a magnificent twelfth century baptismal font, and the shrine of Santa Zita. Among its many frescos is one showing the miracle of San Frediano diverting the Serchio away from Lucca. Fra Filippo Lippi also painted this miracle. Frediano is the patron saint of harvests and good seasons, as well as protector against floods.

Nor shall I be silent on this also which has been related to me by the Venerable Venantius, Bishop of Luni. I heard two days ago, for he told me, that at Lucca, a city not far distant from his own, there had lived a bishop of marvellous power, by name Frediano, of whom the inhabitants relate this great miracle, that the river Auxer (Serchio) running close under the walls of the city, and often bursting from its bed with great force, did the greatest damage to its inhabitants, so that they, moved by necessity, strove with all diligence to divert its course into another channel, but failed in the attempt. Then a man of God, Frediano, made them give him a little rake, and advancing to where the stream flowed, he knelt in prayer. He afterwards raised himself to his feet, and commanded the river that it should follow him, and dragging the rake after him, the waters, leaving their accustomed course, ran after it, making a new bed wherever the saint marked the way. Whence this ever following on, it ceased to cause damage in the fields and among the fruits raised by the countryside.

1087
The son of William the Conqueror comes to woo Countess Matilda

from Janet Ross and Nelly Erichsen: *The Story of Lucca*

Matilda of Canossa (1046-1115), Countess of Tuscany, was known as the "great countess". When her father Boniface was murdered in 1052 and a brother and sister died three years later, Matilda was at nine the sole heiress to the richest estate in Italy. She was a friend and supporter of several Popes, particularly Gregory VII. It was her castle outside which the Holy Roman Emperor Henry IV stood barefoot three days in the snow in 1076. Matilda was a great patron of churches in Lucca and the contada; she built many new churches and the dramatic Devil's Bridge near Borgo a Mozzano.

After the death of Gregory VII, Mathilda defended the cause of Victor III against the anti-pope Guiberto, protected by the Emperor, and used her influence to ensure the election of Urban II in 1088. In the interests of the Church he persuaded the Countess, a woman of forty-three, to marry a lad of nineteen, Guelph d'Este, son of the Duke of Bavaria, an arch-enemy of the Emperor, from whom, however, she soon separated. She would have done better to listen to handsome, gallant Robert of

Normandy, the rebel son of William the Conqueror, who went to Lucca in the spring of 1087 to woo the Great Countess. She entertained him royally, but not being backed by papal influence, he failed in his suit.

A monk from Iceland writes a diary

from F.P. Magoun: *The Pilgrim Diary of Nikulas of Munkathvera*

Nikulas di Munkathvera had one of the most complicated pilgrimages to Rome – by ship to Bergen and on to Aalborg – then on foot. He kept a detailed diary of his trip between 1151 and 1154, recording roads taken, churches visited, the locals and their religious tales. He was abbot of the monastery of Thingir.

Then one must cross the mountain-range that is called *Munbard* (i.e., the Ligurian Apennines). Lombardy is the name of the region south from the Apennines and north to the Alps; one end of the Alps runs to the sea westward in the region of Stura, the other eastward to the lagoons in the region of Venice. Up in the Apennines is *Fracka skáli* and *Crucis markaor*.

Then comes Pontremoli. Then it is a day's journey to the Guild of St. Mary. Then comes Luni, where the Lunigiana region is near the town; there one can walk ten miles over these same fine "sands of Luna", and there are towns in all directions and from there there is an extensive view. Between the Guild of St. Mary and Luni is Borgo S. Stefano and Mary's castle. Some men say that the snake-pen that Gunnar was put in was in the Lunigiana. Then south from there is *Kjófor(m)unt*. At Luni the routes from Spain and from Santiago de Compostela join.

It is a day's journey from Luni to Lucca; there the bishop's throne is in the church of St. Mary, where that crucifix is that Nicodemus made in the image of God Himself: it has spoken twice;

once it gave its shoe to a poor man; another time it bore witness in favor of a calumniated man. South of Lucca is that town that is called Pisa; thither merchants with large trading vessels from Greece and Sicily, men from Egypt, Syrians, and Berbers repair.

There is to the south a village that is called *Arn blakr*. Then comes Matilda's Hospice; by this she redeemed her pledge to Monte Cassino to have a hospice built; and it must put every man up for the night. Then comes *Sanctinus borg*. Then comes *Martinus borg*. Then comes *Semunt*. Then comes Siena, a good town where the bishop's throne there is in the church of St. Mary; the women there are very good looking. It is a three days' journey from there to San Quirico, another day's to Acquapendente. Then one goes over the mountain that is called *Clemunt*; there is a castle on its summit that is called "Mala Mulier," "Bad Woman" as we say, where the people are very bad. Acquapendente is south of *Clemunt*. From there north to the Ligurian Apeninnes it is called Tuscany. Then it is twelve miles to Bolsena, where the saint Christina rests and her footprint is there in a stone. Then it is eight miles to Borgo S. Flaviano. Then it is a day's journey to Viterbo; Thithrek's Bath is there. Then it is ten miles to Sutri; this is near Monte Mario, which is near Rome on the north.

died 1278

The legend of Santa Zita

Santa Zita is one of Lucca's main saints. She is the patron saint of serving girls and her intervention offers special curative powers. The local medical clinic is called Casa di Cura di Santa Zita and lies next to the prison. Both can be seen from the walls near San Frediano church. The Zita fountain, located in nearby Via Fontana was thought to have particularly healthy water (until it was closed 20 years ago because of serious pollution). Santa Zita, born in Monsagrati north of Lucca, was a servant to a wealthy Lucca family; she took food from their larder to feed the poor. One day she was creeping out

56

with her apron full of bread for the poor, when her patron stopped her and asked what she was carrying in her apron. She replied "only flowers"; when forced to open the apron, flowers fell out. Santa Zita can still be seen in her glass tomb in San Frediano, tiny and delicate and emotive after 700 years. One writer on Lucca was shown that she is missing a little toe, which relic had been sent to a small chapel in Lincolnshire.

Puccini rented a villa in Monsagrati for a while, about which he was of two minds. In 1898 he wrote from there, "Hot! Hot! Hot! One sleeps by day and works by night. And the night here is really black. I am in a hideous, hateful place, amidst woods and pine trees which shut off all view, closed in by mountains and lighted by a boiling sun with not a breath of air. But the evenings are delicious and the nights enchanting." He soon moved to a villa in Torre del Lago.

Dressing sacred buildings in horizontal stripes

from Mary McCarthy: *Stones of Florence*

The style of dressing sacred buildings in horizontal stripes of alternating black and white came from Pisa, the mariner-city on the coast, whose sailors had fought the Saracens in Spain, defeated the Emir of Egypt, and gone on crusades; wherever the Pisan influence reached in Tuscany, the black-and-white stripes appear and, with them, a suggestion of the Orient, like the markings of an exotic beast. You find the gleaming stripes in rosy Siena, on the ferocious, tense Cathedral that sits in the Piazza exactly like a tiger poised to spring; you find them in Lucca, the silk town, where the Pisan style was enriched with decorative reliefs, polychrome marble inserts, stone lions on supporting columns, writhing stone serpents. The Pisan style, sometimes fusing with the Luccan, and rich itself in sculptures and tiers on tiers of graceful loggias, made its way into the remote parishes of rural Tuscany, like the spices from the

East – to steep Volterra and Carrara, far south to the ancient mining town of Massa Marittima, inland to Arezzo and the wool town of Prato, across the water to the islands of Corsica and Sardinia. This tigerish architecture stopped short of Florence, where the classic tradition was proof against the exotic.

The façade of San Michele

from John Ruskin: *Letters to his Parents (1845)*

Ruskin spent many afternoons in Piazza San Michele, drawing the rich façade of the church, still breathtaking although having been restored in the mid-nineteenth century.

The cornices of San Michele of Lucca, seen above and below the arch ... show the effect of heavy leafage and thick stems arranged on a surface whose curve is a simple quadrant, the light dying from off them as it turns. It would be difficult, as I think, to invent any thing more noble: and I insist on the broad character of their arrangement the more earnestly, because, afterwards modified by greater skill in its management, it became characteristic of the richest pieces of Gothic design.
... [The façade] is white marble, inlaid with figures cut an inch deep into green porphyry, and framed with carved, rich, hollow marble tracery. Such marvellous variety and invention in the ornaments and strange characters. Hunting is the principal subject – little Nimrods with short legs and long lances – blowing tremendous trumpets – and with dogs which appear running up and down the round arches like flies, heads uppermost – and game of all descriptions – boars chiefly, but stags, tapirs, griffins and dragons, and all indescribably innumerable. The frost where the details are fine has got under the inlaid pieces, and has in many places rent them off, tearing the intermediate marble with them, so as to uncoat the building an inch deep. Fragments of the carved

porphyry are lying about. I have brought away three or four and restored all I could to their places.

It has four stories of arches, two of fourteen and two of six, and owing to this attitude of proportion, it produces the most sublime impression of any church I know in this style.

The holy mint and the marketplace

The Holy Mint and the Coins of God

Lucca is a city of priests, nuns and a hundred churches. Perhaps no other place in the world has a little city centre like Lucca's with so many monasteries and convents, some of them closed orders. It is also a city of a thousand merchants with the same reputation for being "careful" as the Scots and the Genoese – perhaps there's a link to be found between the Celts and the Ligurians. I can't think of another moderate place with such a blatant contradiction between the deep religiosity that pervades its streets and stones and this charge of tight-fistedness. But the facts speak for themselves – almost certainly no other historic city centre has such a formidable concentration of banks. Lucca has held the savings record several times since the end of the last war, with no fewer than one per cent of the population having at least L. 1,000,000,000 in the bank.

This apparent contradiction has a kind of synthesis in the extraordinary history of the Lucca mint which was once one of the most important in the world. First of all, think of the American dollar. It reads "In God we trust" but maybe, as a joker in Lucca suggested recently, it should read "In Gold we trust". Lucca took this idea a bit further. The Romans may have put an emperor on their *sesterce* but the Lucchesi stamped their *denarius* with the Volto Santo. As far as I know, it is the only coinage in the world to be stamped with an image of Christ.

By one of the strange, magical coincidences and the historical continuity to be found in Lucca, the earliest mint was situated on the "highest" part of Lucca beside the Corte Regia, now Piazza San Giusto, where Lucca's strongbox, the Cassa di Risparmio bank, has its head office. It was from this little elevation sloping down to Piazza Grande that the much prized coinage made its way into the world, from the sixth century and the Lombard domination right up to the middle of the nineteenth century.

And with what spectacular success! Throughout the Middle Ages, the coins minted in Lucca were sought after in all the markets and fairs. It was used all over Europe and the Levant, not only because the words *Flavia Luca* meant that the money came from a prosperous city, but also because it guaranteed an established, stable exchange rate. Its reputation was so high that there were plenty of counterfeiters, working in particular on behalf of the hostile Pisans. Only a few families were in a position to compete for the honour and hugely profitable advantage of minting – generally the privilege was awarded only to consuls of the free state – but Frederick Barbarossa famously granted it to the Mansi family, perhaps because of their Germanic origin.

You can still find old loan and security documents using the Lucchese coinage as their standard. These coins were beaten out by hand with heavy hammers, in gold, silver, copper and alloy, up to the introduction of the press towards the end of the fifteenth century. For thirteen centuries, the pounding of the Lucca mint echoed within the walls producing 272 different types. Forty of these were gold, including the florin *d'oro lucchese*, which became a way of saying that something was 100% pure. There's also an old proverb which says: *È d'oro di Bologna, che a passar da Lucca si vergogna* (It's Bologna gold, which you'd be ashamed to spend in Lucca), which means that someone is making unguaranteed claims about an object. Nearly 170 different silver coins were minted, including the *danaro grosso* which originally bore the image of the Holy Cross, but the Teutonic emperors, who reformed the old Italian Mints, ordered the coins to be stamped with their name. More than fifty different copper and alloy coins left the Lucca mint to travel the world and many of those bore sacred images up to the time of Napoleon's sister, Elisa. She was alive to contemporary anticlerical and secular ideas, however, and these symbols of the "holy" Mint of Lucca were removed from the coins.

When the devils in the *Inferno* were prodding a famous swindler from Lucca ("where everyone's involved in corruption") into the boiling pitch, Dante made them shout, "There's no place for the Volto Santo here!" In one sense, of course, this means that the forces for good have no power in Hell, but it also implies that money can't buy anything there, not even money stamped with the Volto Santo. (Daniele Vanni)

Lucca and the Crusades

Lucca was a major stopping-off point for participants on their way to and from the Crusades. In the first Crusade, Robert Curthose, son of William the Conqueror, went through Lucca in 1096, where his army was met and blessed by the pope. Barbarossa was in Lucca in 1162. Edward I came back through Tuscany after fighting in Palestine, greeted by crowds crying, "Long live the Emperor Edward". Such grandees had a large retinue of soldiers and retainers, which would have greatly strained Lucca's resources. Lucca furnished a great deal of the coinage used to pay common soldiers in the Holy Land, where its small denaro was daily currency. Examples of this thirteenth century coin with a cross on one side can still be bought in antique shops or in the monthly antique market near San Martino, held every third weekend of the month.

The Lucca merchants abroad

from Gene Brucker: *Renaissance Florence*

Tuscan merchants, especially from Lucca, Florence and Prato, were active all over Europe from the early twelfth century. The first multinationals, they maintained networks of offices and agents abroad, as well as a database on inventories, customers and markets which resembled that of a modern trading house. They knew foreign languages and had a thorough knowledge of coinage, tariff systems, weights and measures and market conditions throughout the Continent. The Lucchesi were the first Tuscans to be involved in trade with England on a large scale. This is a letter from the Lucca firm Ricciardi, which helped finance Edward I's Crusades, to its London office in 1297.

We tell you that, as you know, our men in Champagne have loaned to the Bonsignori of Siena a great deal of money and they have told them to pay it back to our men over there [in England] or Ireland. Therefore, until now we have not known, nor have we been able to find out if they have been paid back, either all or in part, nor how much you have gotten back. Therefore, we ask you to let us know how much you have received and when, both you and the men in Ireland.

Bankers to the Kings of England

from Louis Green: *Lucca under Many Masters*

Such Italian merchants quickly became bankers through a natural extension of their trade credit and their growing wealth. Lucca merchants became important sources of credit for two Plantagenet kings.

The size of the advances made to Edward III by members of the Lucchese mercantile community in London between 1337 and 1342 is testimony to its wealth. It is interesting that, whereas at this time the great Florentine banking companies of the Bardi, Peruzzi and Acciaiuoli, having over-extended their resources in attempting to meet the financial needs of the English monarchy, were on the brink of bankruptcy, the more modest Lucchese trading enterprises appear to have been able to recoup enough from the royal revenues to remain solvent despite the claims made upon them. What seems to have enabled them to survive was first the relatively small scale of their operations that acted as a constraint on excessive lending; and secondly access, through silk-cloth sales in France and elsewhere to steady, though not spectacular gains that could offset losses occasioned by delays in the repayment of money borrowed by their clients. It is also worth noting that, as Edward III became more desperate for funds, he was prepared to make concessions to those still able to provide him with them, which could bring significant benefits to merchants to whom he was indebted, through the grant to them of favourable trading conditions. That some of the Lucchesi resident in London took advantage of these, particularly by transporting English exports to Flanders, is evident from the sources from about 1339 onwards. Thus, in the September of that year, Azzolino Simonetti received permission to load two bales of rabbit skins and two of serge to an unspecified friendly port, while in the next month Banduccio Mascarelli and Bonaccorso Balbani were allowed to carry four bales of blankets, serge, hare and rabbit skins to Antwerp. In November, Mascarelli was empowered to despatch 322 sacks of wool to the same destination and to deduct the duty on them from what the king owed him. In February 1342, he and his associate Parente Roberti were authorised to load another 67 sacks and transport them to Flanders, paying a reduced tax on them. In the following May, Lando di Poggio was to be granted the same concession in exporting fifteen sacks of pure wool and thirteen of lamb's wool from Bristol; and, in September of the same year, "Nicholas Barthelemeu" had the duty on 100 sacks of wool from Dorset he was to ship from London waived completely to reduce Edward III's indebtedness to him.

Lucca and the international trade fairs

An important way to develop exports and find new customers was by going to international trade fairs, especially in Northern Europe. Lucchese firms with traditional products such as shoes, paper, machinery or agricultural wares continue this tradition today. From the twelfth century the fairs of Champagne were the most prominent European marketplace. Six fairs were held each year, and they provided an almost continuous site of market activity. Merchants from Milan were attending the fairs by the 1170s, soon followed by traders from Piacenza and Lucca. By the second half of the thirteenth century the interchange between northern Italy and the fairs of Champagne produced a financial industry. The Tuscan merchants who had originally visited the fairs to buy cloth and sell alum and leather now travelled north purely to settle debts and offer exchange to the commodity merchants. In this way the fairs became a financial clearing-house as well as an international trade market. For example, in 1257 a merchant from Lucca was able to buy Chinese silk at Genoa, promising that a colleague based in Piacenza would make the payment at the Champagne fairs.

Life at the Troyes Fair

from Joseph and Frances Gies: *Life in a Medieval City*

The Hot Fair (of Troyes) is the climax of weeks of preparation. Apprentices have been up early and late, sewing, cleaning, sorting, finishing, storing, and repairing. The big halls and little stalls of the fair area have been put in order for their guests, as have the hostels and houses used for lodgings. In the taverns the dice are freshly cleaned, a precaution that may prevent a few knife fights. The cadre of regular prostitutes has been reinforced by serving wenches, trades-women, and farmers' daughters. Cooks, bakers, and butchers have added extra help and lengthened their families' working hours.

An army of officials ensures that all goes smoothly. At their head are two Keepers of the Fair, chosen from the ranks of both nobles and burghers. They are appointed by the count at the excellent stipend of 200 pounds (livres) a year, expense allowances of 30 pounds, and exemption from all tolls and taxes for life. Their chief assistants, the keepers of the Seal, receive 100 pounds apiece. A lieutenant of the Fair commands the sergeants, a hundred strong, who guard the roads and patrol the fair. There are tax collectors, clerks, porters, roustabouts, and couriers. Notaries attest all written transactions. Inspectors check the quality of merchandise. Finally, heralds scour the countryside to advertise the fair to the rustics.

The hubbub of the fair is as sweet a sound to the count as to the citizens of Troyes. Notaries, weighers, and other fee collectors divide their earnings with him. Thieves and bandits come under his high justice, their booty confiscated in his name. Sales taxes, the "issue" fee levied on departing merchandise, and other charges go to the count. So do rents on many stalls, booths, halls, stables, and houses. The bishop profits, too, drawing a sizeable income from rents, as do burghers and knights of Troyes. The Knights Templar draw revenues from their monopoly of wool weighing.

In return for all the fees and charges, the visiting merchants get freedom and protection. Fair clients are guaranteed security for themselves and their merchandise from the day of arrival to the day of departure, sunrise to sunset. At the height of the fair the streets are even lighted at night, making them almost safe.

Merchants are not only protected from bandits and robber barons, but from each other, and in fact today this is the more important protection of the two. Crimes committed at the fair are answerable to special courts, under the supervision of the Keepers of the Fair, but both town and provost try cases too, and law enforcement becomes a lively three-way competition. The special courts were actually created because the foreign merchants demanded protection against the other two agencies. Merchants can choose which court they will be tried in, and the most important cases fall to the courts of the fair. Energetic measures are taken to ensure collection of debts. A debtor or a swindler will be pursued far beyond the walls of Troyes and stands little chance of escaping arrest if he shows his face at another fair. This is not all. He is liable to arrest in any city of Flanders or northern France, and if he is Italian he will be least safe of all in his home town, for the keepers of the Fair will threaten reprisal against his fellow townsmen if they do not assist in bringing him to justice. The extent to which these guarantees are actually enforced was graphically demonstrated eight years ago when a caravan of merchants was set upon by robbers on the highway between Lodi and Pavia. It was ascertained that the bandits were from Piacenza. The aggrieved merchants reported the offense to the keepers of the Champagne

Fairs, who promptly and effectively threatened to exclude the merchants of Piacenza unless restitution was made.

The fair, though primarily a wholesale and money market for big business, is also a gala for common folk. Peasants and their wives, knights and their ladies, arrive on foot, on horses, on donkeys, to find a bargain, sell a hen or a cow, or see the sights. Dancers, jugglers, acrobats, bears, and monkeys perform on the street corners, jongleurs sing on the church steps. Taverns are noisily thronged. The whores, amateur and professional, cajole and bargain.

For a farmer or backwoods knight, the fair is an opportunity to gape at such exotic foreigners as Englishmen, Scots, Scandinavians, Icelanders, and Portuguese, not to mention Provençaux, Frenchmen, Brabanters, Germans, Swiss, Burgundians, Spaniards and Sicilians. Most numerous are the Flemings and the "Lombards", a term which includes not only men from Lombardy, but Florentines, Genoese, Venetians and other north Italians. The rustic visitor hears many languages spoken, but these men of many nations communicate with little difficulty. Some of the more learned know Latin, and there are always plenty of clerks to translate. But the *lingua franca* of the fairs is French; though there is little sense of French nationality, and though French is not universally spoken throughout the narrow realm of the king of France, nearly every merchant and factor at the fair can acquit himself in this tongue. French is already acquiring exotic words which the Italians have picked up from their Arab business contacts. Eventually *douane, gabelle, gondran, jupe, quintal, recif,* and many more will find their way into French. English will acquire *bazaar, jar, magazine, taffeta, tariff, artichoke, tarragon, orange, muslin, gauze, sugar, alum, saffron.*

Lucca merchants arrested in London

from George Parks: *New Roads to Italy*

Brawling and murder were commonplace in the Italian community in London, although the Lucca merchants in this story were arrested in retaliation for arrests of Englishmen in Pisa. Some Lucca citizens in England, however, reached very high office. The Lucchese Pancio da Controne, for example, was physician to Edward II.

In June 1345, a royal mandate in England required the arrest of all Pisa and Lucca merchants in England in retaliation for the arrest in Pisa of three Englishmen, later identified as Jerusalem pilgrims: Robert, son of Thomas de Bradeston, knight; John de Sancto Philberto, elsewhere called knight; and William Dachet. It appeared that a ship of Pisa had been captured by some Englishmen; the English government refused responsibility, calling the pirates banished men; the English pilgrims had been arrested in Pisa as hostages; and now the far more numerous Pisans in England were in their turn arrested as counter-hostages. Much commotion followed in England. In August letters of protest were written to the Italian cities and to neighboring nobles, including the lord of Milan; Sir Robert Bradeston demanded action before the Council; it was ordered in November that six of the arrested merchants of Lucca give bond for the ransom of the three Englishmen. In June, 1347, the case was still pending, the Luccans in England being still constrained to raise ransom money before October unless before that time the prisoners were conducted from Pisa to freedom in Florence or Pistoia or San Miniato or Santo Stefano. We do not have the rest of the story. Undoubtedly the government of Pisa was as much moved by the stolen ship as the English government by the arrest of its nationals. In the end the latter were released, and we suppose it was the Italian merchants in England who bore the brunt of the cost of the ransom. We find the travellers again in England, Bradeston in November of 1348, St Philibert in December of 1349, a long time after their release. The case had evidently taken two or three years to settle.

1434

Arnolfini goes to the Netherlands to trade, where he is painted by
van Eyck

from Johan Huizinga: *The Waning of the Middle Ages*

*The enigmatic portrait of a rich merchant and his young wife, now
hanging in London's National Gallery, was commissioned by the
Lucca merchant Giovanni Arnolfini from van Eyck when he was
living in Antwerp. Maurice Hewlett says of Arnolfini, "This
composed, smooth-faced, wise man was of Lucca and shall be chosen
emblem of his nation's virtues. John Arnolfini is like his town, which,
seated prosperously, hidden in a bower of green wealth, has a peculiar
grace, and sets great store by it." The Arnolfini Palace still stands in
Lucca near Piazza Napoleone.*

Time the destroyer has made it easy for us to separate pure
art from all these gewgaws and bizarre trappings, which have
completely disappeared. This separation which our aesthetic sense
insists upon, did not exist for the men of that time. Their artistic
life was still enclosed within the forms of social life. Art was
subservient to life. Its social function was to enhance the
importance of a chapel, a donor, a patron, or a festival, but never
that of the artist. Fully to realise its position and scope in this
respect is now hardly possible. Too little of the material
surroundings in which art was placed, and too few of the works of
art themselves, have come down to us. Hence the priceless value
of the few works by which private life, outside courts and outside
the Church, is revealed to us. In this respect no painting can
compare with the portrait of Jean Arnolfini and of his wife, by Jan
van Eyck, in the National Gallery. The master, who, for once, need
not portray the majesty of divine beings nor minister to aristocratic
pride, here freely followed his own inspiration: it was his friends
whom he was painting on the occasion of their marriage. Is it really
the merchant of Lucca, Jean Arnoulphin, as he was called in

70

Flanders, who is represented? Jan van Eyck painted this face twice (the other portrait is at Berlin); we can hardly imagine a less Italian-looking physiognomy, but the description of the picture in the inventory of Margaret of Austria, "Hernoul le fin with his wife in a chamber," leaves little room for doubt. However this may be, the persons represented were friends of van Eyck; he himself witnesses to it by the ingenious and delicate way in which he signs his work, by an inscription over the mirror: *Johannes de Eyck frit hic, 1434.*

Lowell writes a poem about the portrait

Robert Lowell (1917-1977), American poet, travelled extensively in Italy as a Fulbright scholar in Florence. He formed part of a group of artists and writers who gathered together in Lucca.

Marriage II

I turn to the *Arnolfini Marriage*
and see
Van Eyck's young Italian merchant
was neither soldier nor priest.
In an age of Faith,
he is not abashed to stand weaponless,
long-faced and dwindling
in his bridal bedroom.
Half-Jewish, perhaps,
he is freshly married,
and exiled for his profits to Bruges.
His wife's with child;
he lifts a hand
thin and white as his face
held up like a candle to bless her ...
smiling, swelling, blossoming ...

Giovanni and Giovanna –
even in an age of costumes,
they seem to flash their fineness ...
better dressed than kings.
The picture is too much like their life –
a crisscross, too many petty facts, this bedroom
with one candle still burning in the candelabrum blushing in
    the windowsill,
Giovanni's high-heeled raw wooden slippers
thrown on the floor by her smaller ones ...
dyed *sang de boeuf*
to match the restless marital canopy.

They are rivals in homeliness and love;
her hand lies like china in his,
her other hand
is in touch with the head of her unborn child.
They wait and pray,
as if the airs of heaven
that blew on them when they were married
were now a common visitation,
not a miracle of lighting
for the photographer's sacramental instant.

Giovanni and Giovanna,
who will outlive him by 20 years ...

There is no state that winds the peny more nimbly

from James Howell: *Instructions for Forreine Travell*

James Howell (1594-1666), historiographer to Charles II, resided in Florence for several years, and wrote a series of engaging letters home. In this one, he remarks on the business sense of the Lucca people, a theme mentioned throughout the centuries. A well-known proverb is, "It takes twelve Jews to make a Genovese, twelve Genovesi to make a Biellese, and twelve Biellesi to make one Lucchese."

There is a notable active little Republic towards the midst of Tuscany called Lucca, which, in regard she is under the Emperour's protection, he dares not meddle with, though she lie as a Partridg under a Faulcon's wings, in relation to the grand Duke; besides there is another reason of the State why he meddles not with her, because she is more beneficial unto him now that she is free, and more industrious to support his freedom, than if she were become his vassal; for then it is probable she would grow more careless and idle, and so would not vend his comodities so soon, which she buys for ready mony, wherein most of her wealth consists. There is no State that winds the peny more nimbly and makes a quicker return.

A silk weaver

The Plain of Silk

I need hardly mention the incomparable quality of Lucchese silk – gorgeous brocade and samite, the simpler dimity and trimity, and especially the *diaspore* and *lampasso* created by the extraordinary criss-crossing and interlacing of thread woven like the plot of a fantastic play. Such silks went to every court in the world, to every cathedral and to the See of St Peter, and every potentate had a robe or a bolt of Lucca silk in his treasure house. A miracle of nature was turned into treasure in Lucca, enriched with gold and silver thread and patterned with angels, harpies, winged dragons, parrots and the whole medieval bestiary. Thanks to an astonishing combination of nature, capital and culture, the land of the silkworms and the trade routes, the beauty of Lucchese silk displayed the city's oriental connections: Byzantine, Arabian, Persian and Chinese.

Fifty years before Christ, the Romans passed a law to stop people (not just wealthy patrician women) from spending too much money on silk. The silk came to Rome on the longest trade route to be named after cloth. In Book 8, 33 of his *Epigrams* Martial wrote about silkworms and their delicate work which he must have seen on the Roman plain. Legends and medieval accounts tell of pilgrim monks who hid the precious cocoons in their hollowed-out staffs in order to smuggle them into the West. They also stole the secrets of the art which the Chinese had developed over thousands of years.

For almost five hundred years the plain of Lucca could have been called the Silk Plain because of its extraordinary output. Lucca established a silk industry in the city and in the surrounding countryside, which eventually made it one of the world centres of accumulated wealth. By a twist of fate, quiet, sleepy Lucca found itself in the forefront of history. If it hadn't been for the civil wars between the Guelphs and the Ghibellines, and the refugees who, not unnaturally, carried the jealously guarded industrial secrets into the outside world, in particular to Florence, Bologna and the Po Valley, Lucca might have been as powerful as the wool trade made Florence during the Renaissance. As regards the silk industry, however, the period from the eleventh and twelfth centuries to the middle of the sixteenth century, must be regarded as Lucca's.

Silk was first produced in the Arab west of Sicily in the tenth century. It then spread to Normandy in the eleventh century and in all probability, it was from there that canny Lucchesi merchants introduced the production process to their home town. There are surnames in Normandy to this day which are derived from Lucca surnames. While silk production in Sicily was limited and supplied to the one court, in Lucca it became a modern industry. At first, the merchants got their raw material from abroad, but very soon it began to be produced on the plain, and they became industrialists employing silk workers who carried out the work at home, rather like home workers in present times. The merchants lent money, arranged labour exchange and even bought and sold the tools of the trade. Payment, however, was always on the basis of piecework.

Despite the fact that the work was done on a fragmentary basis, each process was kept secret. Certain operations had to be carried out by particular skilled workers and others by specialists. Anyone disclosing information was severely punished and even put to death. Nonetheless, confidential information began to leak out from the middle of the thirteenth century onwards, chiefly due to some of the people who fled from the different factions involved in the struggle for power in Lucca. Because of this early example of industrial espionage, silk production was established in Florence and the north of Italy, in particular, and had an important influence on capital accumulation, and therefore on the birth of modern industry in many parts of the Po valley, where the mulberry trees thrived.

At first only the black mulberry was grown, but in the second half of the thirteenth century, as Marco Polo was leaving for Cathay, the white mulberry began to be established on the Lucca plain. This silk tree continued to spread even after the beginning of the slow but irreversible decline of the silk industry in Lucca. The first signs of decline were noticeable from the middle of the sixteenth century although the death throes were prolonged into the nineteenth. Apart from the ruthless competition, it is difficult to understand why, but just when the market was growing to enormous proportions and customers were increasing in all parts of the world, Lucca, the first in the west for quality and efficient production, let its lead slip away, in all probability because it could not keep up with the world politics that a modern industry required.

Florence, the north of Italy, and especially Lyons in France, came into our city's inheritance. The mulberry trees spread to the north, to Como, into France, over the Florence plain and in particular to the Valdinievole. There, in Pescia, the history of Lucca silk continues with the famous *Filanda* of the Scoti family. (Daniele Vanni)

Tending the worms

from Tobias Smollett: *Travels through France and Italy*

The English writer Tobias Smollett (1721-1771) is one of several travellers who give an account of the smelly process of breeding and feeding silkworms in North Italy.

In the beginning of April, when the mulberry-leaves begin to put forth, the eggs or grains that produce the silk-worm, are hatched. The grains are washed in wine, and those that swim on the top, are thrown away as good for nothing. The rest being deposited in small bags of linen, are worn by women in their bosoms, until the worms begin to appear: then they are placed in shallow wooden boxes, covered with a piece of white paper, cut into little holes, through which the worms ascend as they are hatched, to feed on the young mulberry-leaves, of which there is a layer above the paper. These boxes are kept for warmth between two mattrasses, and visited every day. Fresh leaves are laid in, and the worms that feed are removed successively to the other place prepared for their reception. This is an habitation, consisting of two or three stories, about twenty inches from each other, raised upon four wooden posts. The floors are made of canes, and strewed with fresh mulberry-leaves: the corner posts, and other occasional props, for sustaining the different floors, are covered with a coat of loose heath, which is twisted round the wood. The worms when hatched are laid upon the floors; and here you may see them in all the different stages of moulting or casting the slough, a change which they undergo three times successively before they begin to work. The silk-worm is an animal of such acute and delicate sensations, that too much care cannot be taken to keep its habitation clean, and to refresh it from time to time with pure air. I have seen them languish and die in scores, in consequence of an accidental bad smell. The soiled leaves, and the filth which they necessarily produce, should be carefully shifted every day; and it would not be amiss to purify the air sometimes with fumes of vinegar, rose, or orange-flower water. These niceties, however, are but little observed. They commonly lie in heaps as thick as shrimps in a plate, some feeding on the leaves, some new hatched, some intranced in the agonies of casting their skin, some languishing, and some actually dead, with a litter of half eaten faded leaves about them, in a close room, crouded with women and children, not at all remarkable for their cleanliness. I am assured by some persons of credit, that if they are touched, or even approached, by a woman in her catamenia, they infallibly expire. This, however, must be understood of those females whose skins have naturally a very rank flavour, which is generally heightened at such periods. The mulberry-leaves used in this country are of the tree which bears a small white fruit not larger than a damascene. They are planted on purpose, and the leaves are sold at so much a pound. By the middle of June all the mulberry-leaves are stripped; but new leaves succeed, and in a few weeks, they are cloathed again with fresh verdure. In about ten days after the last moulting, the silk-worm climbs upon the props of his house, and choosing a situation among the heath, begins to spin in a most curious manner, until he is quite inclosed, and the cocon or pod of silk, about the size of a pigeon's egg, which he has produced, remains suspended by several filaments. It is not unusual to see double cocons, spun by two worms included under a common cover. There must be an infinite number of worms to yield any considerable quantity of silk. One ounce of eggs or grains produces four rup, or one hundred Nice pounds of cocons; and one rup, or twenty-five pounds of cocons, if they are rich, gives three pounds of raw silk; that is, twelve pounds of silk are got from one ounce of grains, which ounce of grains is produced by as many worms as are inclosed in one pound, or twelve ounces of cocons.

Ruodlieb buys a pair of silk gaiters

from Edwin Zeydel: *Ruodlieb: the earliest courtly novel*
(after 1050)

The very first documented mention of Lucca silk is in a poem in
Latin written around 1050 in the monastery of Tegernsee, Bavaria.
The hero Ruodlieb leaves home to seek his fortune in Africa and
has many adventures, including capturing a dwarf. The author's
knowledge of French, Spanish-Arabic and Byzantine culture must
have been acquired at the German imperial court, and in earlier life
he was likely a nobleman and courtier who spent time at Emperor
Henry III's court. On his way home, Ruodlieb stops off in "Lukka"
and buys silk gaiters. In the second passage Ruodlieb sends the silk
garters of a woman he is wooing, lost while she was in bed with a
monk, back to her. The dots indicate parts of the original text which
are now illegible.

He bound his shins with bands bought in Lucca.
... might flow toward him
and over his gaiters low silken shoes
... of silk.
His kinsman wore red socks under shoes of cordovan leather,
... he wore, with skilled handiwork.
He bound both legs with double bands.
... are all in the border,
and from which many bells hang on every side.
After this he soon put on a striped fur,
with an incision in front and in back and with a red border all
  around,
... by placing a pelt reaching to the floor,
edged with a very broad and black beaver fur.
He took the ring which the young lady had given him,
barely fitting his smallest finger.

... the undergarment badly washed (washed threadbare?)
The marten coat dark with age and sweat.
Thus they were dressed, and soon they repaired to the ladies,
whom they found at the latticed windows looking out.

Standing at the window, she opens that box,
while in it, she saw, was a delicate kerchief
so well fastened with twice two seals
of his ring that she wondered much what it was.
She breaks the seals of the kerchief and unties the knots,
until she sees a beautiful scarlet cloth tied together.
Opening it, she finds the headdress and the knee garters
which had fallen off of her while the cleric was in her embrace.
When she saw these and remembered where she had lost them,
she trembled all over, paled, and felt a chill
and she does not doubt that he is truthful who was feigning,
except that she sees that he is acting quite innocent.

1392

The Mercers of London wear Lucca silk

from an unpublished history of the Company

The Mercers (the name means traders of consumer goods) are the most eminent of the livery companies in London, and were founded before 1350. Then and now they were known for their elegance. I checked the Mercers' membership records back to 1348 (when they start), but no Lucca or Italian name appears.

First the livery companies contributed to a magnificent reception for the King and Queen on 21 August 1392. The monarchs were then met by the crafts of the city on horseback, each craft in a parti-coloured livery chosen by themselves for this special occasion, a glorious spectacle of red, violet, white, blue, green and tawny. The Mercers chose to wear splendid gowns of the expensive Lucchese patterned silk called *baldekin* – they had clearly been instructed to spare no expense to please the pageant-loving King. The King and Queen were accompanied by this brightly coloured escort through the city, along Cheapside to St Paul's, the route hung with cloths of gold and silk and the conduits running with wine. Pageants and minstrels entertained at the vantage points and suitable gifts were presented: horses accoutred in red and white, the colours of the city, gold crowns and precious images of the Crucifixion.

13th century

Lucca silk at the Champagne Fairs

from Joseph and Frances Gies: *Life in a Medieval City*

The first week of the fair is occupied with the merchants' entry – registration, unpacking, setting up displays. Then the fair opens with a ten-day Cloth Market. The Italian merchants pass from one to another of the halls of the famous cloth cities, examining the bolts, which have already been subjected to a rigid inspection at home, for every cloth town guards its reputation like Caesar's wife. It is an offense to sell defective cloth abroad; below-grade or irregular material must be marketed locally.

The tables in the cloth halls are a kaleidoscope of colored bolts, ranging from ecru, uncolored and little finished, through gray, brown, vermillion, rose and scarlet. The reds, highly prized and expensive, are a speciality of the famous *Arte di Calimala* of Florence, whose agents at the fair buy undyed cloth and sell dyed. Here and there is cloth heavy with gold and silver thread. Though wool predominates, there are also silks, mostly from Lucca; cotton from Italy, France and Flanders; flax in the form of linen for sheets, sacks, purses, and clothing, and of hemp for nets, ropes, bowstrings, and measuring lines.

The Saxon spy describes the town elders

from G.C. Martini: *Viaggio in Italia (1725-1745)*

Georg Christoph Martini (1685-1745) was a painter from Saxony, who took up residence in Lucca after his first trip to Italy in 1722. Some thought he was a spy, seeing him around town drawing and writing in his notebook. His minute journals in German, with many pictures of Lucca personages, such as those described here, and fortifications, were found in his belongings at his death and indeed looked like secret information. These are now in the Archivio di Stato di Lucca, which has fostered publication of an edition in Italian.

The costume of the Gonfaloniere varies, depending on the season of the year and in the quality of the materials, but is unchanged since ancient time. In the summer it is made of red damask, in winter of red velvet, and on Good Friday, when it is the custom for him to visit the Church of the Capuchins, of purple velvet. Regarding its fashion, the costume has the form of a long and wide toga, with ample sleeves sewn up to the armpit. A red stole hangs down from the left shoulder, the width of a hand and the length of an arm, moving across the chest and the back. The Gonfaloniere carries in front of him a little flat, thick hat of red colour, with gold lace around it. Around the neck he has a short ruffled collar, as priests in some parts of Germany wear, and on his head a great wig, or when this isn't customary, a red beret like those worn by Cardinals. Below the toga is a short vest decorated with gold; his shoes and stockings are red. In the Palace he wears this red French outfit and over it the ordinary black toga of the governing nobles.

The robes of the town elders are similar to that of the Gonfaloniere: only the colours are different. In the summer they wear black damask, in winter black velvet. Their stole is made of black satin, their hat is black and decorated with black lace. The nobles which sit on the Governing Council are dressed in black; in the summer they wear clothes in Italian fashion, rather similar to those in Spain, except the pantaloons which are made with an apron. Their doublet is left open; under it they wear a white shirt which goes under a waistcoat and over the pantaloons. This whole outfit is ornamented with black ribbon and lace in Spanish style. Over all this they wear a black taffeta toga, or when they are in mourning, one of pleated wool. The toga is long enough to touch the ground, and without sleeves, open at both hips; in front it has two bands which fall to the ground. Those who are not in the Governing Council can wear whatever style and colour of clothes they wish, according to the fashion of the moment.

1696

An Ipswich merchant fears competition

from an unpublished manuscript journal

I found this in a Brighton bookshop; it is an extract from an English cloth merchant's account of his trip from Ipswich to Rome at the end of the seventeenth century.

Lucca June 1696

Sixteen English miles from hence & 24 from Livorne stands Luca Which is the chiefest & only place of note in this small Republick – is pretty Large, handsomely built and Extraordinary well peopled. also very pleasantly situated in a Large fruitfull vally abounding in vines and Olive Trees producing ye best oyle counted in ye World & the Country houses scattered here and there afford a Lovely prospect from the Walls of the Citty, wch are well furnished with Brass Cannon & Strongly Fortified according [to] ye Modern Art. In Compass about 3 Little miles and regularly planted with 4 handsome rows of Trees atop, which invites the people to divert themselves Every Evening here, some in Coatches & others afoot according to their Quality. In this Citty you observe more freedom & good nature Especially to Strangers than in any other place In Italy, which good Temper is Certainly Influenced by the happy Liberty they Enjoy, & of this they are so Extreamly Jealous that the Chief Magistrate remains in his office but 10 months & cannot be Chose again under 6 years, his Guards are paid by the Publick & his revenu is only a Pissole per Diem for his table, the Dukes of Florence, as well as others of their Ambitious Neighbors, Envious of their Prosperity have often endeavoured to Subvert this Citty, but without Success they being always in readiness to repel such Ravanous Beasts & for an offensive or Defensive warr are able to raise some 15,000 men, & for greater Security have putt their Common wealth under the Emperours protection. So that at present they contribute, tho not immediatly Engaged in this warr. Several faire Churches present themselves to a Travellers view in this Citty. The Choisest & most beautiful is dedicated to St. Martin. In one of the others lies interred the body of St. Richard, who by the Inscription was King of England, but Certainly they impose upon us a king wch we never had. For the Chronicle mentions expressly that those three of that name since the Conquest were buried in England, & twould be hard to find another before. In this place of late the weaving of Silke Stockings is become a Considerable Manifacture – wch by how much they worke cheaper, by so much that more will prejudice our trade, but the strength of ours so much Exceeds that many Still wear them finding it the best husbandry in ye End.

Tower Houses

After the year 1000 had passed, and with it the fear that the world was coming to an end, the powerful families of Lucca left their castles in the countryside and came back to live within the walls of the city, where business was enjoying something of a boom. Life carried on, however, in an atmosphere of bitter rivalry and bloody power struggles as the disputes of the countryside were transferred to the city. The important families therefore built tower houses for themselves, their families and their merchandise. These houses could be austere, or spacious and luxurious with galleries where business was done, but they were all dominated by a high tower built of stone or brick. Taking into account only the biggest of these, it is estimated that there were no fewer than 250 of them when the city-state period was at its height. In the fourteenth century, Fazio degli Uberti wrote in his *Dittamondo* that, "*Andando, vedemmo in piccol cerchio, torreggiar Lucca a guisa di boschetta*", (As we walked, we saw Lucca towering like a little forest in a small circle).

In the frequent struggles for supremacy in the city, members of each family, along with their fighting men, allies and friends, could take refuge in the tower house, barricade themselves in and defend themselves for weeks and months at a time. On occasions when two families made a peace treaty, almost always sealed by a marriage, neighbouring towers could be linked by bold wooden bridges. When an enemy family, or a family which was an enemy on account of some alliance, was defeated, all of its towers were dismantled by law.

Little by little in the Italian cities the strongest families prevailed, establishing themselves as rulers and taking control by settling the conflicts between the local inhabitants. As a result, fortified towers became redundant. For a very short period, Lucca was ruled by the Guinigi family who were silk merchants, bankers and financiers to the French and English kings. The dynasty was short-lived, but it lasted long enough for them to build imposing houses of the old conservative type whose Romanesque-Gothic style was reminiscent of the tower houses and old castles.

Perhaps it was to soften the bellicose appearance of their houses that the Guinigi planted holm-oaks on the top of their

The towers

towers. Perhaps they were also remembering that they had built their house where once there had been oak forests, and that the area had in fact been called *in Lischia* because of the abundance of acorns, which were part of the staple diet of people as well as animals. Perhaps these trees growing more than forty-four metres above the ground had a special significance because the tree was a potent medieval symbol of rebirth. Whatever the reason, the fact is that these oaks in their roof-top garden have almost become the symbol of Lucca.

Of the towers that stood at each corner of the Guinigi palace, only one is still standing. A visit is essential because you cannot know Lucca properly without seeing it from the Torre Guinigi. It is the most distinctive surviving example of this type of dwelling.

You should also look out for the Torre delle Ore, the tower house converted into a clock tower, the towers near the corner of Via Fillungo and Via Buia, and the Torre del Veglio in Piazza della Misericordia. If you look carefully, however, you will see that almost every important *palazzo* has a corner or a part where a tower once stood. The sight of these towers soaring in their hundreds amongst the campaniles must have been breathtaking. Some idea of what it was like can be seen in the drawings of Sercambi who was a lawyer, Paolo Guinigi's secretary and, thanks to his writing and sketches, one of the first journalists of modern times. (Daniele Vanni)

died 1405

The tomb of Ilaria del Carretto

from Charles Morgan: *The Writer and his World*

Ilaria del Carretto was the wife of Lucca's leader Paolo Guinigi. She died in childbirth in 1405; her grieving husband erected a marble tomb for her which can be seen in San Martino. Ruskin wrote to his father about her in 1845, "It is impossible to tell you the perfect sweetness of the lips and the closed eyes, nor the solemnity of the seal of death which is set on the whole figure. The sculpture, as art, is in every way perfect – truth itself, but truth selected with inconceivable refinement of feeling. The cast of the drapery, for severe natural simplicity and perfect grace, I never saw equalled, nor the fall of the hands – you expect every instant, or rather you seem to see every instant, the last sinking into death."

As the word serenity appears and reappears in my thought like the face of an angel looking in through a window that I can seldom open, I am visited by the remembrance of two works of art of which I have often written in my novels, and now, as I write this, I seem to understand them anew, or, rather, I would say, to receive them anew. They are The Agony in the Garden by Giovanni Bellini in the National Gallery in London, and the tomb of Ilaria del Carretto by Jacopo della Quercia in the cathedral at Lucca ... The Bellini will wait, like an absolution, until I am able to receive it again.

Ilaria meanwhile waits in Lucca. She is calm and, at the same time, an embodiment of the distinction between calmness and serenity. What is that distinction? However we attempt to define it, the idea of light enters into our definition. From Ilaria there shines an interior radiance such as exists, within my knowledge, nowhere else in sculpture, the same radiance as glows, about the head of the kneeling Jesus, in Bellini's Italian sky – a sky so profoundly serene that Bellini, who has given a halo to each of the sleeping disciples, has given none to their Master; the sky itself being, of His holiness, a sufficient emblem.

Now, it is remarkable that of these two masterpieces, so triumphantly serene, one is the figure of a young woman dead – "L'homme seroit encore plus noble que ce qui le tue, parce qu'il meurt"; and the other, a picture of the garden of Gethsemane, marks a supreme point in the Christian tragedy, beyond which, in the Christian way, lies neither despair nor chaos nor any destructive finality, but that "solution" of the human tragedy which, in the Christian context, is called redemption and is precisely analogous to the Greek tragedians' idea of expiatory release.

Jacopo della Quercia

from Giorgio Vasari: *Lives of the Artists*

Jacopo was the son of Master Piero di Filippo of la Quercia, a place in the territory of Siena, and he was the first sculptor after Andrea Pisano, Orcagna, and the others named above, who, by applying himself with greater study and diligence to sculpture, began to show that it was possible to approach Nature, and was also the first to inspire others with courage and the belief that it would be possible to equal her in some sort... Through the efforts of some friends he was invited to Lucca, and there made a tomb for the wife of Paolo Guinigi, the lord of the city, who had recently died, in the church of S. Martino. On the pedestal of this he made some infants in marble bearing a festoon, so beautifully finished that they are like living flesh and blood. On the sarcophagus which is upon this pedestal he did the effigy of Paolo's wife, who was buried there, with admirable finish, and at her feet, and on the same stone, he made a dog in full relief, emblematical of her fidelity to her husband. After the departure, or rather the expulsion, of Paolo from Lucca in the year 1429, when the city won its freedom, this sarcophagus was removed from its place and all but entirely destroyed because of the hatred which the Lucchesi bore to the memory of Guinigi. Yet the reverence which they felt for the beauty and the ornamentation restrained them, and led them soon after to set up the sarcophagus and the effigy at the entrance door of the sacristy, with great care, where they now are, the chapel of Guinigi becoming the property of the community.

The Florentine Guelphs are driven out, and wind up in Lucca

from Giovanni Villani: *Croniche Fiorentine*

The internecine battles between Guelphs and Ghibellines in Italy mirrored the long conflicts between Holy Roman Emperors and Popes from the twelfth to the end of the fifteenth century. The names come from the contest for the imperial throne in 1138 between Conrad of Hohenstaufen, Lord of Wiblingen (hence Ghibelline) and Henry, nephew of Welf (Guelph) Duke of Bavaria. Conrad won, but the Pope and many Italian cities took sides with the Guelph faction. Manfred (1232-1266) was King of Sicily and a natural son of Frederick II. He was appointed by Frederick to be the representative in Italy of his half-brother Conrad IV. The "grievous discomfiture" was the Battle of Monteaperto on 4 September 1260, when the Ghibelline forces defeated the Guelphs decisively. Other Florentines fled to Lucca later; the painter Donatello's father was involved in the Ciompi Revolt in 1378, and as a ringleader had to cool his heels in Lucca for some time.

The news of the grievous discomfiture being come to Florence, and the miserable fugitives, returning therefrom, there arose so great a lamentation both of men and of women in Florence that it reached into the heavens, forasmuch as there was not a house in Florence, small or great, whereof there was not one slain or taken; and from Lucca, and from the territory there were a great number, and from Orvieto. For the which thing the heads of the Guelphs, both nobles and populari, which had returned from the defeat, and those which were in Florence, were dismayed and fearful, and feared lest the exiles should come from Siena with the German troops, perceiving that the rebel Ghibellines and those under bounds which were absent from the city were beginning to return thereto. Wherefore the Guelphs, without being banished or driven out, went forth with their families, weeping, from Florence, and betook themselves to Lucca on Thursday, the 13th day of September, in the year of Christ 1260.

The Guelphs of Florence took their stand in Lucca in the quarter around San Friano [Frediano]; and the loggia in front of

San Friano was made by the Florentines. And when the Florentines found themselves in this place, Messer Aldobrandi, seeing Spedito, who had insulted him in the council, and bade him look to his breeches, drew himself up and took from his pouch 500 florins of gold that he had, and showed them to Spedito (who had fled from Florence in great poverty) and said to him reproachfully, "Just look at the state of my breeches! This is what you have brought yourself and me and the rest to, by your rash and overbearing lordship." And Spedito answered, "Then why did you trust us?" We have made mention of these paltry and base altercations as a warning, that no citizen, especially if he is a popolano and of small account, when he chances to be in office, should be too bold or presumptuous.

1314

Dante and Lucca

from Dante: *Inferno*
trans. Robert Pinsky

Lucca, where Dante Alighieri was also a Florentine exile in 1314, is mentioned several times in the Divine Comedy, *with little affection. In Canto XVIII, the Alessio Interminei mentioned was from a prominent Lucca family. In Canto XXI the* Malebranche *(Evil Claws) is the overseer of devils in this part of Hell. Barratry is financial malpractice carried out by public officials; here a demon is bringing in another barrator from Lucca (referred to as one of Santa Zita's elders).*

Dante came to Lucca after years of wandering when it was held by his friend Ugoccione. He composed the last cantos of the Purgatory *here and dedicated them to Ugoccione. Dante left Lucca in 1315 after Ugoccione had lost both it and Pisa. These first three extracts are from the* Inferno.

CANTO XVIII

The bottom is so far down
That we could nowhere see it until we scaled

The ridge's high point at the arch's crown.
    When we had reached it, I saw deep down in the fosse
    People immersed in filth that seemed to drain

From human privies. Searching it with my eyes
    I saw one there whose head was so befouled
    With shit, you couldn't tell which one he was –

Layman or cleric. Looking at me, he howled,
    "And why are you so greedy to look at me
    When all of these are just as filthy?" I called:

"Because, if memory serves me properly,
    I saw you once when your hair was dry, before –
    I know you are Alessio Interminei

Of Lucca, which is why I eye you more
    Than all the rest." And he then, beating his head:
    "Down here is where my flatteries, that store

With which my tongue seemed never to be cloyed,
    have sunk me."

CANTO XXI

Hurrying from behind us up the rock
    Was a black demon. Ah, in his looks a brute,
    How fierce he seemed in action – running the track

With his wings held outspread, and light of foot:
    Over one high sharp shoulder he had thrown
    A sinner, carrying both haunches' weight

On the one side, with one hand holding on
    To both ankles. Reaching our bridge, he spoke:
    "O Malebranche, here is another one

Of Santa Zita's elders! While I go back
    To bring more from his homeland, thrust him below.
    His city gives us an abundant stock:

Every citizen there except Bonturo
    Practices barratry; and given cash
    They can contrive a *yes* from any *no*."

He hurled the sinner down, then turned to rush
    Back down the rocky crag; and no mastiff
    Was ever more impatient to shake the leash

And run his fastest after a fleeing thief.
    The sinner sank below, only to rise
    Rump up – but demons under the bridge's shelf

Cried: "Here's no place to show your Sacred Face!
    You're not out in the Serchio for a swim!
    If you don't want to feel our hooks – like this! –

Then stay beneath the pitch!"

CANTO XXXIII

"I don't know who you are that come here, or how,
    But you are surely Florentine to my ear.
    I was Count Ugolino, you must know:

This is Archbishop Ruggieri. You will hear
    Why I am such a neighbor to him as this:
    How, through my trust and his devices, I bore

First being taken, then killed, no need to trace;
        But things which you cannot have heard about –
        The manner of my death, how cruel it was –

I shall describe, and you can tell from that
        If he has wronged me. A slit in the Tower Mew
        (Called Hunger's Tower after me, where yet

Others will be closed up) had let me view
        Several moons already, when my bad dream
        Came to me, piercing the future's veil right through:

This man appeared as lord of the hunt; he came
        Chasing a wolf and whelps, on that high slope
        That blocks the Pisans' view of Lucca."

Gentucca di Lucca

from Dante: *Purgatory*
trans. Mark Musa

Gentucca di Lucca, Dante's lover here, had almost too apt a name.
Little is known about her, although she may have been Gentucca
Morla, wife of one Cosciorino Fondora. She is thought to have lived
in via Fillungo across from San Cristoforo (now used for art
exhibitions). The splendid merchant's house a little further down
via Fillungo called Casa Barletti-Baroni dates from the same period.
The thirteenth century Lucca poet Buonagiunta degli Orbicciani
(1220-1297) was acquainted with Dante's poetry and addressed a
few of his poems to him. He appears in Purgatory on the Mountain
of Purification, alluding to Gentucca.

CANTO XXIV

Often a face will stand out in a crowd;
        this happened here: I singled out the
        shade from Lucca, who seemed interested in me.

94

He mumbled something – something like "Gentucca"
  I heard come from his lips, where he felt most
  emaciating justice strip him bare.

"O, soul," I said, "you seem so much to want
  to talk to me; speak up so I can hear;
  that way your words can satisfy us both."

"A woman has been born," he said, "and she
  is still unmarried, who will give you cause
  to love my city, which all men revile."

from Maurice Hewlett: *The Road in Tuscany*

Dante was in Lucca in 1314, being a year short of his fiftieth; Gentucca may have been anything between seventeen and one-and-twenty. I know – the learned know – no more about her: the girl was an episode, as women must be content to be for poets. Fortunate for her that her name gave a rhyme for *Lucca!* She has made great sport for the scholiasts. Was she married? Was she a baggage? Did she, on the other hand, illume a Platonic candle? What does it matter? She was fair, her name was Gentucca, and so were her deeds. She made Lucca sweet for Dante; he tossed her lightly in a terzet. What more can woman do for poet, or poet for woman? I hope she is in Santa Zita's bosom by now.

1281-1328

Castruccio Castracani

The best known figure in medieval Lucca, Castruccio Castracani degli Antelminelli, was instrumental in consolidating much of Tuscany. He rose to power in Lucca in 1316 after the revolt of Lucca against its domination by Pisa and its tyrant Uguccione della

Faggiola. He fought successfully for the Ghibelline side and was named Duke of Tuscany by Louis the Bavarian. Castruccio celebrated his victory over the Florentines at Altopascio in 1325 by a triumphal return to Lucca in the style of a Roman general. Wearing a laurel wreath and dressed in purple and gold, he stood in a chariot drawn by four white horses, with captive soldiers in chains before him. Had he not died of malaria after the siege of Pistoia, he might have made Lucca the central power in Tuscany. Castruccio is buried in the church of San Francesco. A plaque there reads:

EN VIVO VIVAMQUE

FAMA RERUM GESTARUM

ITALAE MILITIAE SPLENDOR LUCENSIUM

DECUS ETRURIAE

ORNAMENTUM CASTRUTIUS GERII ANTELMINELLORUM STIRPE

VIXI PECCAVI DOLUI

CESSI NATURAE INDIGENTI ANIMAE PIAE BENEVOLI

SUCCURRITE BREVI MEMORES ET VOS MORITUROS

Behold: I live and will continue to live in the fame of my deeds, noble in Italian military exploits, the glory of Luccans and ornament of the Tuscans, Castruccio son of Ruggieri of the family of the Antelminelli. I have lived, I have sinned, I have sorrowed, I have yielded to the necessity of nature. Wellwishers of pious soul, support me, mindful that you will shortly die.

Inspires: a biography by Macchiavelli

from Niccolò Macchiavelli: *The Life of Castruccio Castracani*

Macchiavelli's biography is mostly fictitious, using Castracani's life as a model for various virtues he was supposed to have exemplified. It points out that Castruccio died at the same age (44) as Philip of Macedonia and Scipio, and would have been superior to them both had he had the power of Macedonia or Rome, instead of that of Lucca. Niccolò Macchiavelli (1469-1527) the statesman and Florentine author of The Prince, *visited Lucca in 1520, staying two months to sort out Michele Guinigi's bankruptcy. Guinigi's Florentine creditors wanted their loans and invoices repaid; an account of Macchiavelli's role says he was reduced to a* commercialista (*a rather low level economic consultant*). *Letters sent to him in Lucca still exist. Here is one of the many anecdotes of Castracani's life as reported by Macchiavelli.*

Castruccio was invited to dinner by a wealthy Luccan, who had just had his house redone in the most showy and sumptuous manner, with rich hangings and a tessellated floor, vari-coloured, having a flower-and-leaf motif; looking about him, Castruccio suddenly spat in his host's face and explained himself by saying that he did not know where else to spit without damaging something.

a novel by Mary Shelley

from Mary Shelley: *Valperga*

Shelley's wife Mary wrote the novel Valperga *based on the life of Castruccio. This is an excerpt describing his (actual) stay in England, when he was in the circle of Edward II.*

A strict friendship was established between Gavaston and Castruccio. Piers had not learned moderation from adversity; his wealth and luxury were increased, and with these his vanity and insufferable presumption. Atawel in vain endeavoured to win Castruccio from his society; but, if the deportment of Gavaston was arrogant towards the English lords, it was so much the more affable and insinuating towards Castruccio. The king also loved the Italian; and, not examining the merits of the case, he allowed himself to be entirely led away by the personal attachment that he bore to Edward and Piers.

Gavaston had wealth and rank; and, although he was considered an upstart, yet the possession of these gave him a consequence in the eyes of the nobles, of which Castruccio was wholly divested. They looked on the latter as one may regard a stinging insect, whose insignificance is not to compound for his annoyance. They endured the insolence of Gavaston with the sullenness of men who look into the future for revenge; but they bore the far slighter pain which Castruccio inflicted upon them, with the impatience one feels at an injury, however slight, for which we are by no means prepared. And, if Castruccio himself manifested few symptoms of insolence, yet he was supported by that of Gavaston; and they felt that, though for the present they could not injure the favourite personally, yet they might wound him through his Italian friend. This latter also was not unfrequently provoked beyond his usual courtesy by the pride and taunts of his enemies; and, if ever he dared reply, or when Gavaston replied for him, the nobles felt a rage they would ill smother at what they deemed so despicable an offender. The indications of mischief which had before slightly manifested themselves, broke out one day with a violence that suddenly terminated Castruccio's visit to England.

He accompanied the king, who went with a train of the first nobility on a hawking party, to Chelsea. The exercise excited Castruccio's blood, and inspired him with an exaltation of spirits which might have exhausted itself in gaiety alone, had not a quarrel, that arose between him and one of the nobles, urged him to a fury he could ill control. The contention began concerning the comparative flight of their birds; and, heated as they were by personal animosity, it became loud and bitter. Edward in vain endeavoured to appease them; but when, seconded by his friends, the English nobleman established his triumph in the contest, Castruccio replied by a sarcasm which so irritated his antagonist, that, no longer restraining his indignation, he darted forward, and struck Castruccio. The fiery youth, crying in Italian, "By blood, and not by words, are blows to be avenged" – drew his stiletto, and plunged it into the bosom of his adversary. A hundred swords immediately flashed in the air; Edward threw himself before his friend to protect him: Gavaston, Atawel and others who loved him, hastily withdrew him from the crowd, made him mount his horse, and without a moment's delay they rode to the river's side below the Tower, where they fortunately found a vessel on the point of sailing for Holland. Without waiting to see his other friends, without going to the house of Alderigo for money or equipment, they hurried him on board the vessel, which immediately got under weigh, and dropt down with a favourable wind towards the Nore.

The barons, burning with revenge, had sent archers to the house of Alderigo, who, not finding Castruccio, seized upon his kinsman, and threw him into prison. A law then existed in England, that if a foreigner killed a native and escaped, those with whom he resided became amenable for the murder. Alderigo was therefore in the most imminent peril; but Edward, as the last act of friendship that he could bestow upon Castruccio, saved the life and fortune of his kinsman. And thus, after a year's residence in this island, did the youth bring to a disastrous conclusion all the hopes and expectations which had led him thither.

a poem by Elizabeth Barrett Browning

Elizabeth Barrett Browning saw Castruccio as a symbol of mid-nineteenth century Italian unity.

THE SWORD OF CASTRUCCIO CASTRACANI
"Questa è per me" – KING VICTOR EMANUEL

I.

When Victor Emanuel the King
 Went down to his Lucca that day,
The people, each vaunting the thing
 As he gave it, gave all things away, –
 In a burst of fierce gratitude, say,
As they tore out their hearts for the King

99

II.

– Gave the green forest-walk on the wall,
   With the Apennine blue through the trees;
Gave the palaces, churches, and all
   The great pictures which burn out of these:
   But the eyes of the King seemed to freeze
As he gazed upon ceiling and wall.

III.

"Good," said the King as he passed.
   Was he cold to the arts? – or else coy
To possession? Or crossed, at the last
   (Whispered some), by the vote in Savoy?
   Shout! Love him enough for his joy!
"Good," said the King as he passed.

IV.

He, travelling the whole day through flowers
   And protesting amenities, found
At Pistoia, betwixt the two showers
   Of red roses, the "Orphans" (renowned
   As the heirs of Puccini) who wound
With a sword through the crowd and the flowers.

V.

"'Tis the sword of Castruccio, O King, –
   In that strife of intestinal hate,
Very famous! Accept what we bring,
   We who cannot be sons, by our fate,
   Rendered citizens by thee of late,
And endowed with a country and king.

VI.

"Read! Puccini has willed that his sword
   (Which once made in an ignorant feud
Many orphans) remain in our ward
   Till some patriot its pure civic blood
   Wipe away in the foe's and make good,
In delivering the land by the sword."

VII.

Then the King exclaimed "This is for *me!*"
   And he dashed out his hand on the hilt,
While his blue eye shot fire openly,
   And his heart overboiled till it spilt
   A hot prayer, – "God! The rest as Thou wilt!
But grant me this! – *This* is for *me.*"

VIII.

   Victor Emanuel, the King,
   The sword is for *thee*, and the deed,
And nought for the alien, next spring,
   Nought for Hapsburg and Bourbon agreed –
   But, for us, a great Italy freed,
With a hero to head us, – our King!

Enemies in the Barga hills

from Linda Villari: *On Tuscan Hills and Venetian Waters*

The beautiful Garfagnana hill town of Barga lies 25 kilometres north of Lucca up in the Serchio Valley. It is worth visiting for the early austere cathedral alone (where the pulpit is supported by a stone lion eating a Christian), but also for its setting in the Apennine foothills and the drive along the Serchio.

The Barghigiani never seem to have been an aggressive people, and reserved their valour for the defence of their rights and the maintenance of their boundaries. Their bitter hatred of the Lucchese, their often-recurring struggles against them, were always on this question of frontier. When Lucca wanted an excuse to attack Barga, it was her custom to stir up neighbouring districts to boundary quarrels with the place. It was on one such occasion that, as far back as 1298, the Potesta of Lucca, one Gonzelino, marched on Barga with 2,700 men, besieged it, carried it by storm, and demolished both its walls and its citadel.

But the town seems to have recovered its pristine strength with considerable rapidity, since in less than half a century Barga had become a place of refuge for the whole country round; its church became virtually the *chiesa maggiore* in consequence of the desecration of the Loppia fane and destruction of the village and outlying fortresses by the unrelenting Lucchese.

In fact, from the middle of the thirteenth to the second half of the fourteenth century, Barga was almost continually engaged in efforts to shake off the yoke of Lucca. The longest interval of tranquillity was during the latter years of Castruccio's reign, when that sagacious tyrant saw fit to pursue a policy of reconciliation. His death, in 1328, was the signal for a fresh revolt of the Barghigiani, who opened secret negotiations with Florence. But the plot was betrayed, and Lucca instantly sent a considerable force to reduce the town to obedience. Florence, on her side, hastily despatched Amerigo Donati at the head of 400 men, but the succour was ineffectual; other Florentine expeditions also failed, and the men of Barga had to rely on themselves alone. For a time they were subdued, but in 1331, by means of one of the Rolandinghi (the dominant family in the district) and another noble, they again threw off their allegiance to Lucca. Coppo di Medici came from Florence to take possession of the town, and on his departure left a small force behind to prevent it from being carried as before by some sudden *coup de main* of the Lucchese. But Lucca was on the alert to regain the coveted territory, and the following year besieged the town in junction with the troops of King John of Bohemia. The Florentines, although aided by Spinetto Malaspina, failed to relieve the place; Barga was again compelled to come to terms and open her gates to the attacking army. The chroniclers are silent as to the duration of this siege, but there is reason to suppose that it lasted about six weeks. The citizens' lives were spared, but the four principal personages in the town were made to take the oath of obedience barefoot and with every display of abject repentance.

1322

Giotto paints in Lucca

from Giorgio Vasari: *Lives of the Artists*

Despite this report, no trace of Giotto can be seen in Lucca.

Giotto also worked in Lucca, where he went in 1322 (his very dear friend Dante having, to his great sorrow, died the year before), and at the request of Castruccio, who was then ruler of his native city, he painted a panel picture for San Martino; this showed Christ above and the four patron saints of the city, namely, St Peter, St Regulus, St Martin, and St Paulinus, recommending a Pope and an Emperor, these, it is commonly believed, being Frederick of Bavaria and the anti-Pope Nicholas V. It is also believed by some that Giotto designed the impregnable castle and fortress of Augusta at San Frediano in the same city.

Hawkwood is bribed with an honorary citizenship and a house

Sir John Hawkwood (c. 1320-94) was the best known foreign mercenary leader in Italy in the fourteenth century. These adventurers, somewhat akin to modern mercenary soldiers today, were paid by various Italian city states to lead marauding armies with much cavalry against their rivals. Without much loyalty or scruple, the mercenaries would switch sides to the highest bidder, and were greatly feared. Hawkwood – Giovanni Acuto (sharp) in Italian – became the leader of a roving band of English, French and German soldiers known as the White Company. He wound up as commander of the Florentine armies, and is commemorated by a splendid portrait on horseback by Paolo Uccello in Florence Cathedral.

On October 18, 1375, the Comune of Lucca granted Hawkwood honorary citizenship and monetary awards; Lucca's grant of honorary citizenship was a special favour. Six years later they gave him an annuity and a house in the city (the mercenaries were usually kept outside the walls).

1384

The plague comes to Lucca

from Giovanni Sercambi: *Le Croniche*

Giovanni Sercambi (1348-1424) was a Lucca chronicler, who lived through many exciting events such as the plague, papal visits and constant small wars between the city-states.

The divine Goodness, seeing that the citizens and peasants of Lucca were in increasing great discord, and not wanting to give an arbitrary exemption to the educated personages, letting them discuss the good which can come from bad, and seeing how discord was growing in Lucca and how little ancient customs were respected, decided from his Wisdom that there was nothing to do, at least from fear of God, but to show them His displeasure. And therefore it happened, at His wish, that first in Lucca and then in the countryside the plague came, from which many citizens left Lucca in the month of October, some going to Pietrasanta and some elsewhere; and many citizens died and there were many great losses.

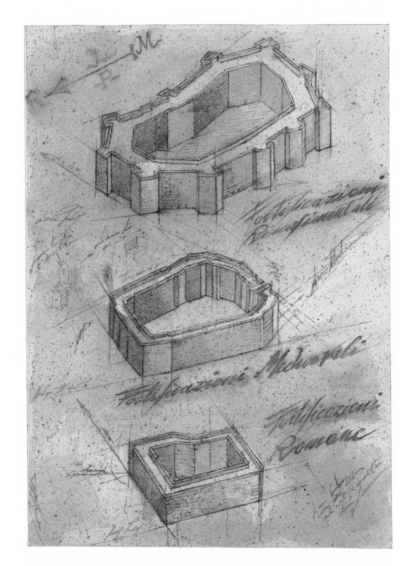

The walls

RENAISSANCE LUCCA

The Walls

It took more than 6,000,000 bricks to build the great rampart which is the outer face, symbol and image of our city. The bricks were made in the famous brick-kilns of Lucca during the century or so that it took to build the walls.

It was the fourth set of walls to encircle the city. Shortly after 180 BC, Roman architects laid the foundations of the colony and its first defences, and traces of these can still be seen in various places today. Roman Lucca was almost square, each side about 500 metres long, and almost corresponding to Plato's dimensions for the ideal city where you could shout and be heard from one side to the other.

The sixteenth century walls are still intact and, at 4.2 kilometres, almost twice the length of the Roman walls. They form a fortification which has few equals in the world for state of preservation, beauty and immensity. In order to build them, the little aristocratic oligarchic Republic passed laws forcing brick makers to supply bricks and mortar at fixed prices. Builders and master builders worked for fixed rates and were not allowed to work for anyone else. Workmen had to be brought in from outside the city, and architects and civil engineers came from almost all over Europe. For decades, the well-to-do were called upon to bequeath a portion of their wealth to pay for stones, bricks and labour.

The great work began in 1544 and was not completed until 1650. The question, however, is why the city built such imposing fortifications at a time when it was already clear that, as far as war was concerned, the name of the game was now gunpowder, and the game was no longer being played at a local level but on the great international chessboard. What's more, the decision was made in a city where it had always been diplomacy and not guns that had the fire-power, and peace had been maintained at the cost of millions of *scudi*.

Not long before construction work began, the well-informed

Charles V visited the city and its existing defences, and judged it "difficult to take". So there was no real urgency regarding fortification, even though Lucca was living under the threat of Cosimo the Great and his Florentines. On the other hand, it was obvious that such massive walls would serve as a deterrent and have a certain weight in any negotiations, especially in a city accustomed to buying its privileges and freedom. But Lucca was small, introverted and notoriously and traditionally thrifty – there must have been other factors involved to make it commit itself to something so enormous and protracted.

Perhaps the ruling class realised, subconsciously or not, that building walls so completely out of proportion to their existing and future needs would safeguard their community and ensure its continuance. And time has proved them right, though not in a military sense, since the walls of Lucca never frightened anyone. The only siege they ever underwent was during the flood of 1812, when the gates were closed and plugged with mattresses, and the city was saved from two metres of water from the Serchio.

In any case, the fact is that the walls were built and completed at a time when every scenario had changed and they had no real usefulness except as a customs barrier and for collecting tolls. What they did, however, was set a fundamental geographical limit to the city's development. Cities which were foolhardy enough to demolish their walls – Florence, for example, when it became the capital of Italy in the nineteenth century – lost their identity irrecoverably. Forever.

In Lucca there were, and even quite recently have been, proposals to do the same, but fortunately nothing was done and the survival of the walls has assured the continuity of a cultural identity which could almost be described as tribal. There are those who talk about a "walls mentality", but perhaps this is what makes Lucca so fascinating in a world that is changing with the speed of Internet. The walls built to face the outside world have come to represent the internal order of the city. They were built by the descendants of merchants who visited and traded in every part of the world but who knew how to protect their own way of life, with a farsightedness which deserves some thought. The Lucchesi were only really happy when they felt themselves protected by these walls.

108

They made a peaceful place here. Beyond the walls, beyond the hills of Montecarlo and the Quiesa, further inland and towards the sea, there are spots where the Lucchesi love to go to enjoy themselves. Fifteen kilometres away they have one of the most beautiful beaches in the world, and a little more than twenty kilometres away the thermal baths at Montecatini. But night-clubs and casinos have no place within the walls. When the shop shutters fall in the evening, then silence and peace fall too. Lucca enjoys one of the lowest crime rates in the world, there is almost no prostitution on the streets, and for years there has been only one madam for generations of Lucchesi. As the saying goes, when the Lucchesi want to misbehave, "they go over the mountains".

As for the walls, they have become a hanging garden, twelve metres high, and they live on in this new dimension. If you want to know (that is to say, love) Lucca, you must go and walk there for a long time, and if possible, in different seasons. Thousands of tourists from all over the world stroll on the walls while joggers in track suits dodge round and about them. They trot along between plane trees and oaks, without a thought for the defence problems of long ago. The walls were created for war but these people have turned them into the most beautiful gym in the world. (Daniele Vanni)

⌇⌇⌇⌇

1431

Brunelleschi tries to drown the town

from Niccolò Macchiavelli: *History of Florence*

Filippo Brunelleschi (1379-1446) started the revival of the Roman or Classical style in Italy. He is best known for the cupola of Florence Cathedral, the Pitti Palace and the churches of San Lorenzo and Spirito Santo, as well as the beautiful crucifix in Santa Maria Novella, all in Florence. Renaissance architects turned their hand to many projects: religious, noble or civil architecture, sculpture, painting and warfare.

At that time there lived at Florence a very distinguished architect, Filippo di Ser Brunelleschi, of whose works our city is full, and whose merit was so extraordinary, that after his death, his statue in marble was erected in the principal church, with an inscription underneath, which still bears testimony, to those who read it, of his great talents. This man pointed out, that in consequence of the relative position of the river Serchio and the city of Lucca, the waters of the river might be made to inundate the surrounding country, and place the city in a kind of lake. His reasoning on this point appeared so clear, and the advantages to the besiegers so obvious and inevitable, that the Ten were induced to make the experiment. The result, however, was quite contrary to their expectations, and produced the utmost disorder in the Florentine camp; for the Lucchesi raised high embankments in the direction of the ditch made by our people to conduct the waters of the Serchio, and one night cut through the embankment of the ditch itself, so that having first prevented the water from taking the course designed by the architect, they now caused it to overflow the plain, and compelled the Florentines, instead of approaching the city as they wished, to take a more remote position.

mid-15th century

Prostitutes and Russian slaves in Lucca

from Chapin: *The Economy of fifteenth century Lucca*

Markets of a different kind.

In August 1440 the law that prostitutes might only leave the brothel on Saturdays was amended to permit them to pass freely, and justice before the courts according to the statutes was guaranteed to them. In 1448, in response to the petition of the local *stufaiolo* – German by birth, like so many of his clients – it was conceded that prostitutes might freely accompany men to the public baths. Prostitutes, as might be expected, appear frequently in the court records in cases involving assault and verbal abuse; a very large number of them were foreigners. Perhaps the most enterprising of all Lucchese prostitutes was Pellegrina of Milan who was engaged in a small way in 1459 in the trade between Siena and Bologna via Lucca. From prostitutes to slaves is not a meaningless juxtapositioning. Exclusively female, drawn largely from Russia, often acquired in the markets of Pisa, slaves were most likely to achieve historical record either when bearing the children of their masters or when attracting the sexual attentions of their master's neighbours. It may be noted that when a slave was assaulted and lost a tooth, the damage was adjudged to be to her; when made pregnant, the damage was to her owners. Acknowledgement that "Our Redeemer took flesh that we might be restored to pristine liberty" resulted in frequent acts of manumission, especially when the owner's mind was concentrated by the approach of death. Freed slaves might receive dowries and the consequent possibility of marriage with local artisans. Others might receive their freedom only on harsh conditions, which could include a commitment to long-term future service. Traces of tension are suggested by occasional acts of theft, and more overtly by the murder of Bartolomeo Testa by his slave Caterina.

1493
Savonarola advises the Signoria to take in Jewish moneylenders

from a letter in the Archivio di Stato di Firenze
trans. Peter Lambert

Girolamo Savonarola (1452-1498) is an incandescent figure of the Italian Renaissance. A Dominican monk, he became the prior of San Marco in Florence (where Fra Angelico painted frescoes in each of the monks' cells, still one of the most striking sights in Florence). For a short time he was the effective head of state of Florence after

Lorenzo de' Medici's death in 1492. Constantly trying to make the pleasure-loving Florence become a true Christian city, his impassioned sermons for a while found enormous resonance in the Florence citizenry. In 1497 he instigated the "Bonfire of the Vanities" in the Piazza della Signoria there, into which the wealthy threw their books, lewd pictures and jewellery. But he had many enemies, including the Arrabbiati (the enraged). He was convicted of religious error and sedition and burned at the stake in the same piazza a year later. The following letter from Savonarola to the City Council in Lucca was in response to their question whether Jewish moneylenders should be admitted to the town.

Great and distinguished Lords. Whereas the Jews are witnesses of our faith, as S. Thomas writes, they should not be banished from Christian communities: as the Psalmist say, "Slay them not, scatter them lest my people forget." Hence, Christians are able, without indulging their consciences, to let out houses to the Jews and associate with them, looking after each other. So clearly this living among them and employment of them is not contrary to natural or divine law, and is in accordance with remaining laws and apostolic regulations, which this bull of Nicolas does not diminish. Therefore, although this bull grants permission to consort with Jewish moneylenders, it does not however actually say "for the purpose of money lending", and the supreme pontiff saves himself from contradictory divine and natural law. For I don't think it can be possible for the Pope to give dispensation for employment of Jews to collect taxes for the purpose of usury since, as the relevant rule states, that which has an evil end is also evil in itself. Therefore, as usury is contrary to divine and natural law, which is above the Pope's authority, it is an evil in itself: therefore it cannot be made good by any means, for something that is in its nature evil can in no way be made good.

The Jews, however, can be employed, not to practise their usury but so that they may stay in the community because of other benefits to the community: and if afterwards they want to practise their money-lending trade, the elders of the community can allow it. Just as it is not possible for anyone to employ a prostitute to ply her trade as a prostitute, but it might be possible to employ a woman, who if she wanted to be a courtesan later, could be permitted because of the lesser evil. However, the temporal rulers ought to restrain the rate of interest as far as they can, so as to keep the lenders clearly to a lower rate than they themselves would like: however, they cannot forbid them this privilege so as to prevent them exacting extortionate interest, since this would clearly be contrary to justice, the essence of which is to return to each individual that which is his own right.

It may be that this bull could provide some with an opportunity of deceiving their conscience by saying, "We will employ them, not for this purpose but so that they can stay in the community", knowing, however, and consciously reckoning with themselves that this action is really for no other reason than usury: and I don't believe this possible without risk to their consciences.

My Lords, it seems to me these comments should be addressed to your uncertainty, for which you requested an immediate reply: and I, without having looked anything up, so that I may meet your demands, responded as soon as possible with the thoughts that immediately occurred to me. Perhaps I should have made a better response if I had been able to consider for longer. If, however, I have made an error in my reply I am ready to correct it.

Goodbye: remember both me and our monastery.

From our monastery of S. Mark, 18 May 1493.

Your servant

Father Hieronymus de Ferraria.

1495

and is ordered to preach in Lucca at Lent by Pope Alexander VI

from Hubert Lucas: *Fra Girolamo Savonarola*

This was part of a plot to remove him from Florence: Savonarola made many enemies both through his rigorous discipline and his claim to the gift of prophecy. In 1495 he was charged with heresy and summoned to Rome, but failed to appear. Many groups in

Florence were increasingly antagonistic to both the reformer and his ideas.

Operated upon by influences such as these, and induced further by the discontents of the Lombard congregation, Alexander VI determined to take up the challenge tendered by Savonarola. A papal brief accordingly arrived in Florence, directing Savonarola not to preach, as appointed, at Florence during the Lent of 1495, but at Lucca. It was the Pope's policy therefore to remove him from Florence. Savonarola penetrated at once the cunning of his enemies in this ostensible estimation of his oratorical powers; but yet, because he thought he had done the State as much good service as could be expected from an individual, and might now for a while safely leave the City to itself, he prepared to obey the command of his holiness, though not without expressing publicly his reluctance, and chiding the Florentines for their frequent disobedience, adding tauntingly, that when he was absent they might manage matters in their own way. "I", he exclaimed, "will no more trouble myself about anything. Send not to me – though the king of France or the Emperor come, I will not. Do in your Council what your spirit may prompt! Now I will give place to anger. Must I then go to Lucca to preach, and thence perhaps further? Pray God that it may be permitted me to preach the Gospel to the unbelieving. But we commend our bark to God, that He may come to its aid if it strike on rocks."

The mortification these words express, was that of a man who loved Florence to his soul, and could not leave her without the passionate reproaches of an affection that had been often offended, and had as often forgiven. It found an echo in popular sympathy – the magistracy interfered, and, to allay the restlessness of the general mind, wrote to the Pope, praying him to withdraw his direction. The Signory, likewise, sent a letter expressing their astonishment, that the authorities in Rome should be incautious enough to believe, or men be found bold enough to utter such calumnies of such a man, assuring the pontiff that Savonarola had never in his preaching put out of sight the claims of duty and the rights of office, but had only, in a general manner, denounced equally the failings and vices of the great and of the people.

This manifestation in his favour, however gratifying to

Savonarola's feelings, incurred his censure. "My children," he said, "you have done wrong, in being so zealous about my honour. Do not so – for it is not well that all things should always go smoothly – lest conceit should come of it. Strokes of fate are good – for they make us better. Leave only to God to provide!"

The solicitation, however, of the magistracy and the Signory, was effectual with the Pope. He consented to recall his brief, permitted Savonarola to preach during the Lent in Florence, and promised that he should not be compelled to quit it before.

1497

Michelangelo receives safe passage through Lucca to Carrara to get marble for the Pietà

from George Bull: *Michelangelo*

The great marble quarries of Carrara have been worked since Roman times. Sculptors would (and still do) go there to select marble for specific works. In this case, Cardinal Jean Bilhères du Lagraulas, Abbot of St Denis and French envoy to the Pope, wished to place a statue of the dead Christ and his Mother in St. Peter's in Rome for his own tomb. In 1497 the Cardinal and Michelangelo agreed on the commission. Bilhères, following the practice of supplying artists with safe-conduct papers or letters of recommendation, wrote this letter to the Signoria of Lucca.

We have recently agreed with master Michele Angelo di Ludovico Florentine sculptor and bearer of this, that he make for us a marble tombstone, namely a clothed Virgin Mary with a dead Christ naked in her arms, to place in a certain Chapel, which we intend to found in St. Peter's in Rome on the site of Santa Petronilla; and on his presently repairing to those parts to excavate and transport here the marbles necessary for such a work, we confidently beg your Lordships out of consideration for us to extend to him every help and favour in this matter, as will be expounded by him at greater length: and this we will reckon as having been done for us ourselves, as it will indeed have been; and we shall not forget this good deed: and if it so happens that we can ever serve your Lordships in practice, you will understand how acceptable and understanding this will be. Farewell.

1513

Sir Thomas More writes to Antonio Buonvisi on the eve of his execution

from Olive Hamilton: *Paradise of Exiles: Tuscany and the British*

Antonio Buonvisi (1484-1559), from a famous Lucca family, settled in England for many years, where his name was anglicised to Bonvisi. The Buonvisi Chapel can be seen in San Frediano, with its memorials to three Buonvisi who became cardinals.

A visit we paid to Lucca on a New Year's Day provided the opportunity to find out about the family of Antonio Bonvisi, whose friendship for St Thomas More was one of the most touching in the history of Anglo-Tuscany. I knew that Bonvisi was a merchant banker from a cultured family of Lucca; and that he had settled in London buying Crosby Hall from More in 1513. When Sir Thomas, Henry VIII's Chancellor, was imprisoned in the Tower by the King, Antonio kept him supplied with meat and wine, and at the end sent him "a warm camelot gown", soft and silky for his skin, to wear for the execution. Apparently More would have worn it but for the dissuasion of the Lieutenant of the Tower.

Just before his trial he sat down to write to Antonio in Latin, and his words are so vivid and human that they sound across the centuries:

"Sith my mind doth give that I shall not have long liberty to write unto you by this little epistle of mine how much I am

116

comforted with the sweetness of your friendship ... when I consider in my mind that I have been almost this forty years not a guest, but a continual nursling in Master Bonvisi's house ... now I comfort myself with this, that I never had occasion to do you pleasure. For such was always your great wealth that there was nothing left in which I might be unto you beneficial.

"... I therefore my dear friend of all mortal men dearest do ... earnestly ... pray that for his mercy sake he will bring us from this wretched and stormy world into his rest, where shall need no letters, where no wall shall dissever us, where no porter shall keep us from talking together ... and as I was wont to call you the apple of mine eye, right heartily fare ye well. And Jesus Christ keep safe and sound and in good health all your family which be of like affection toward me as their master is."

A visit to the State Archives of Lucca revealed that Antonio, born in 1484, was the eldest of four brothers, and that he did not marry but left his estate to a nephew, according to a copy of his will which had been sent from Louvain, where he died in 1559. He was driven out of England in 1544 in a period of Catholic persecution, and Crosby Hall was seized.

1536

Charles V visits and is surprised by Lucca's size and potential strength

from Janet Ross and Nelly Erichsen: *The Story of Lucca*

Charles V (1500-1558) was the son of Philip of Burgundy and Johanna, third child of Ferdinand and Isabella. After a visit to Henry VIII and his aunt Catherine in England, he was crowned Holy Roman Emperor in 1520, as his grandfather Maximilian had intended. A very conservative Catholic, he dealt harshly with the rise of Protantism. The Diodati baby mentioned was the grandfather of Milton's schoolboy friend. Civil marriages in Lucca

117

are now performed in the beautiful mirrored hall of Palazzo Diodati, which houses the City offices. An elegant edition of the Diodati Bible was published in London in 1808, in Italian.

In 1536 Charles V was in Lucca, and one of her historians notes with pride that as the Emperor rode round the walls he exclaimed, "This is not the small town that has been described to me, but one so strong that if well-furnished with men and provisions a large army would be needed to reduce it." Six years later the Emperor was again at Lucca to meet Paul III. "Immense was the concourse of great and noble people," exclaims an eye-witness. "The Dukes of Florence and of Ferrara, the Duke of Alva and the Viceroy of Naples, and sixteen Cardinals in attendance on the Pope." Paul received the Emperor first in the cathedral, and next day they were closeted together for some hours in the archiepiscopal palace. The Emperor was lodged in the Diodati palace, and during his visit the mistress of the house gave birth to a son, who was christened by the Pope, whilst Charles V stood sponsor. Not many years afterwards the boy who entered life under such august auspices was a wanderer on the face of the earth, his parents being among the Reformers who fled for their lives to Geneva in 1555. His son was Giovanni Diodati, Oriental scholar and Professor of Hebrew at the University of Geneva, whose translation of the Bible into Italian is well-known.

mid-16th century

The Protestant movement in Lucca

from Thomas McCrie: *History of the progress and suppression of the Reformation in Italy*

The Protestant movement in Lucca arose in part from the influence of Lucca merchants living in France or Switzerland. While some converts may have been tortured, the Inquisition in Lucca was moderate. Records of the Inquisition are held in the Archivio di Stato; they were disguised to conceal them from Napoleon's agents. The Peter Martyr referred to is Pietro Martire Vermigli (1500-1562), an Italian divine who rejected Roman Catholicism. After falling out with the authorities and his own Augustinian order, he escaped to Switzerland. Cranmer invited him to England in 1547, where he became Regius Professor of Divinity at Oxford.

Hard as was the fate of the Locarnese protestants, it was mild, compared with that of their brethren in the interior of Italy, who had no friendly power to save them from the vengeance of Rome, and no asylum at hand to which they could repair when refused the protection of their own governments. To retire in a body was out of the question; they were obliged to fly singly; and when they ventured to return for the purpose of carrying away their families or recovering the wreck of their fortunes, they were often seized by the familiars of the inquisition and lodged in the same prisons with their brethren whom they had left behind them. While the profession of the truth exposed persons to such hardships and perils, we need not wonder that many were induced to recant, while still greater numbers, with the view of avoiding or allaying suspicion, gave external countenance to a worship which they inwardly detested as superstitious and idolatrous. This was the case at Lucca. Averse to quit their native country, and to relinquish their honours and possessions, trusting in their numbers and influence, and deceived by the connivance of the court of Rome at their private meetings for a course of years, the protestants in that republic became secure, and began to boast of their superior resolution in maintaining their ground, while many of their brethren had timidly deserted it, and suffered the banner of truth which had been displayed in different quarters of Italy to fall. But this pleasing dream was soon to be dissipated. Scarcely had Paul IV mounted the papal throne when orders were issued for the suppression of the Lucchese conventicle; according to a preconcerted plan, its principal members were in one day thrown into the dungeons of the inquisition; and at the sight of the instruments of torture the stoutest of them lost their courage, and were fain to make their peace with Rome on the easiest terms which they could purchase. Peter Martyr, whose apology for his flight

119

they had with difficulty sustained, and whose example they had refused to follow when it was in their power, felt deeply afflicted at the dissipation of a church in which he took a tender interest, and at the sudden defection of so many persons in whose praises he had often been so warm. In a letter which he addressed to them on the occasion, he says, "How can I refrain from lamentations, when I think that such a pleasant garden as the reformed church at Lucca presented to the view, has been so laid waste by the cruel tempest as scarcely to retain a vestige of its former cultivation. Those who did not know you might entertain fears that you would not be able to resist the storm; it never could have entered into my mind that you would fall so foully. After the knowledge you had of the fury of antichrist, and the danger which hung over your heads, – when you did not choose to retire, by availing yourselves of what some call the common remedy of the weak, but which, in certain circumstances, I deem a prudent precaution, – those who had a good opinion of you said, 'These tried and brave soldiers of Christ will not fly, because they are determined, by their martyrdom and blood, to open a way for the progress of the gospel in their native country, emulating the noble examples which are given every day by their brethren in France, Belgium, and England.' Ah, how much have these hopes been disappointed! What matter of boasting has been given to our antichristian oppressors! But this confounding catastrophe is to be deplored with tears rather than words." The seeds of the reformed doctrine were not however extirpated in Lucca. We find the popish writers complaining that, in the year 1562, the heretics in that city kept up a correspondence with their brethren in foreign countries, by means of merchants, who imported protestant books from Lyons and Geneva.

The Senate of Geneva asks the Senate of Lucca to withdraw their
edict against Calvinist exiles

from J.R. Hale: *England and the Italian Renaissance*

Magnificent Lords, six months have passed since some of your
citizens have come to our city for reasons you know very well; we have
received them with kindness and friendship. And after we recognised
their style of life and honest ways, we took them in as inhabitants.

And further, we allowed a number of these people to enjoy and
to participate with us in all the privileges and prerogatives of our city
and its citizens. Now, however, we have learned that since the month
of last January you have passed a new edict against these people,
declaring them rebels against you, and that anyone who kills one of
them, not only in your own territory, but also in Italy, France, Flanders
and Spain, will receive a reward of 300 scudos. We are very displeased
with this and saddened greatly by a matter contrary to the civic
protection and safeguard with which we have received them, believing
that they were deprived by you of your courtesies, and received into
our domination, per the means of your edict we are harmed in our
liberty because they are deprived of the means of trade and commerce
in countries which are not under your domination.

For these reasons we have sent the present messenger, one of
our subjects, to ask you affectionately to revoke that edict to maintain
and conserve the friendly relations which have existed between us
for a long time to your great profit and joint utility, also that it is
necessary and useful for the liberty of your and our republic that
there is mutual affection and decency in all civil and commercial affairs.

And in doing this as we hope that you will, you will do
something agreeable to us.

And we will do something similar for you when the occasion
arises. Otherwise we can do no other but to conserve our liberty
and provide the security of our subjects to which they are entitled.
And we will do this in such time and place by the methods of law
and reason which you can judge for yourselves. Praying that the
Saviour will preserve your signory.

XXVII Feb. 1562

Montaigne disapproves of Lucca's protection by the Holy Roman Empire

from Montaigne: *Journal de Voyage en Italie*

The renowned French writer Michel Eyquem de Montaigne (1533-92) came to Bagni di Lucca to take the waters. His Journal *of the trip mixes comments about politics, women and his bowels.*

At the end of twenty miles we came upon Lucca, situated in the plain aforesaid, a town about one-third smaller than Bordeaux, and free, except that by reason of its weakness it has put itself under the protection of the Emperor and the house of Austria. It is well walled and strengthened with bastions, but the ditches are shallow, and only a scant stream of water flows through the same. Moreover, at the bottom they are full of green plants with wide flat leaves. All round the walls, on the level ground within, are planted two or three rows of trees which afford shade, and would serve, according to what I heard, for fascines in case of need. Viewed from without the place looks like a wood, for the houses are concealed by the trees aforesaid. A guard of three hundred foreign soldiers is always kept.

The town is well peopled, principally by silk workers; the streets are narrow but handsome, with fine lofty mansions on all sides. They were then constructing a small canal whereby to bring into the city the water of the Serchio, and building a public palace, at a cost of a hundred and thirty thousand crowns, which is almost completed. Besides the townsfolk they claim a population of a hundred and twenty thousand subjects, several small villages, but no other town lying within their jurisdiction. The gentlefolk and warriors of the place are all of the merchant class, the Buonvisi being the most wealthy, and strangers are allowed to enter only by one gate, where there is always a strong guard. I never saw a town in a more pleasant site, surrounded as it is by a most beautiful plain two leagues in extent, and beyond this the lovely mountains and hills, which for the most part are cultivated to the tops. The wines are only passable, and living costs about twenty soldi per diem, the inns being, after the manner of the country, indifferent. Many gentlemen of the city paid me courteous attentions, sending me wine and fruit, and even offering to accommodate me with money.

1581
Ammannati complains to the Town Council about his commission

from a letter in the Archivio di Stato di Lucca

Bartolomeo Ammannati (1511-1592) was a prominent Florentine architect; his most important works were the enlargement of the Pitti Palace and the Boboli Gardens, and the graceful Ponte Santa Trinita over the Arno. In Lucca he rebuilt most of the Palazzo della Signoria after a design accepted in 1577. Now the Palazzo Pubblico or Palazzo Ducale, it is the provincial seat and stands on the site of Castruccio's Augusta fortress. The Swiss courtyard and loggia can be reached through the main doors on to Piazza Napoleone. A number of his letters to the Lucca authorities exist in the Archivio di Stato; many promise that he intends to come shortly, indicating that he was something of an absentee architect.

To my esteemed Lords, always devoted.
To the letter of your excellencies I will respond briefly, saying that I am resolved to come there soon, but after I am freed of a certain eye trouble, which has vexed me for eight days already, and I hope in God to be cured; anyway I have certainly not hesitated a single day, not a moment, to come to Lucca, although you haven't paid me my commission without any reason; it remains as I have written, about the commission granted by the Great Duke, my Lord, and it is true that these strange methods displease me.

This has been authorised several times to be drawn, which seems a matter outside my own duties and I cannot help but be disturbed. I protest with much feeling against such mechanisms against me, since I have had much satisfaction in carrying out my professional duties; otherwise I kiss the hands of your excellencies, whom God preserve.

Florence, 25 November 1581

1582

A Nuremberg merchant sends a lonely letter home

from Steven Ozment: *Magdalena and Balthasar*

Lucca also attracted merchants from abroad; enough German traders had come to Lucca by the sixteenth century for there to be a recognised "German Quarter". One such merchant was Balthasar Paumgartner (1551-1600) of Nuremberg; he used Lucca as a collecting point for products of north central Italy, which he exported to his home city and the trade fairs in Frankfurt. One hundred and sixty-nine letters between Balthasar and his wife Magdalena, written 1582-1598, still exist, describing his travels and residence in Lucca, with her responses. One of Magdalena's letters contains recipes for his Lucca cook.

Most dearest love, I will await your answer to this letter here. Thereafter, you need not write to me again in Lucca, for around the end of January I will have to travel on business to other places and towns en route to Modena and Reggio, and for this reason your letters may no longer find me here. Too much is presently unsettled in our business to know for sure if I will depart so soon. I desire to go, but all too often and for too long I am prevented by many things beyond my control. If I could now complete one most important matter in which our firm has not a little invested, how quickly I would turn the other matters over to my brother and the staff here and be on my way! I am trusting and hoping in Almighty God that next January nothing will prevent my planned departure.

... Meanwhile there is plenty for me to do here. Over the holiday I am going to Florence, which is forty miles away, but I will be returning here in three or four days. Meanwhile, trust that on my return from Florence my health may, praise God, be good and that I will have recovered from my wearisome journey, for I will return here beaten and exhausted. Take care not to let yourself be tormented by many vain worries over things which in the end you can do nothing about. You may be sure that as soon as my affairs here are settled, I will not tarry here one hour, but (God willing) may hope to be with you there even sooner than you and I now think. May dear God grant that hope soon and happily!

I am certainly distressed to hear about the long, grievous pestilence you are having. Others there have written to me that it has abated somewhat and that cold weather is on the doorstep. I hope to almighty God that it has not posed any further danger. Here we have had almost beautiful bright weather for five weeks. Many others would not say so, as at this time of the year it customarily mostly rains (presently the rain is steady) and many are surprised by the beautiful weather.

... When you see Frau Lochner, indicate to her that I will do my best to get the crimson satin lining and the bicolored double taffeta. I had already ordered the lining before I got your letter.

Otherwise, apart from my work, I lead a truly boring life without any diversions whatsoever, save for a two-week visit here of players who performed every evening for four hours after sunset into the night. Among them was a woman who could (as one is accustomed to say) "speak and ride". I wish to God you could have seen her, for you would certainly have marveled. I passed some time watching the plays, but such things come to an end. After the Christmas holidays other players will come, but they are no match for the plays you have in St. Martha's and the Dominican cloister there. But I cannot sufficiently describe how eloquent and skilful the women in such plays here are, especially the one who was just here. If you have not seen it for yourself, you cannot believe it. Without doubt, they have studied many storybooks and must be well taught.

Lucca women are the most constant

from Fynes Moryson: *An itinerary concerning his 10 years travel*

Northern visitors to Italy sometimes categorised the various cities they saw in proverb form. Fynes Moryson (1566-1630) heard the proverb: "Merchants of Florence are crafty, those of Lucca greedy, those of Venice bold." When it came to choosing a wife, the Milanese were said to be "little jealous and to hate fast women. The Mantuans love women that can dance, the Florentines those who are modest and love home. The Lucchese women are the most constant". Moryson served as a lord-deputy in Ireland, and helped his brother, the Governor of Dundalk, suppress the Tyrone rebellion. He travelled widely in Europe and wrote a history of the twelve countries he visited, which was so bulky that, with what the Dictionary of National Biography calls "a consideration rare in authors", he destroyed it. The herbs mentioned in the last sentence are still prized and collected today.

    The next morning I walked one mile to Lucca; the Emperor Charles the fourth made this City free, which hath kept the libertie to this day, governed by Senators, but lives in perpetual fear of practises against this libertie from the great Duke of Florence. It is seated in a plain, and strongly fortified, and compressed with mountains on all sides, but somewhat distant, and onely lies open on the side towards Pistoia, being two miles in compass and having about thirtie four thousand Inhabitants. The streets are narrow, and paved with broad free stone, most easie to walke upon. The pallaces of the chiefe Gentlemen are built of free stone, with a low roof after the Italian fashion, and they have many pleasant Gardens within the walls. In the corner towards North-west by North is a strong castle, neere which lies the Cathedrall Church, stately paved with Marble, but very darke, as most of the Papists Churches are built, either because they think darknesse increaseth Religion, or to make it an excuse for their burning candles in the day. There also lies the Senate house; and al the Innes are in one street, that they may more easily look into strangers, for any practise against their liberty; for which cause no man may weare any weapons in the city, not so much as a knife, except the point be blunt. These Citizens first spread through Italy the Art of making silk, and weaving it into clothes, and from this traficke they have very rich families. Here I paid (at an Ordinarie) six reali for my dinner and supper. From here I walked five miles through a pleasant Plaine to the Mountain of Pisa, which divide[s] the territories of these two Cities, and it is very high and stoney, yet is full of Rosemary, Time and sweet smelling hearbs.

1625

An early German guidebook

from George Kranitz von Wertheim: *Paradisus Deliciarum Italiae*

This is the first German guidebook to Italy, written for Germans on the Grand Tour. Its title continues: "Which is my own description of what is worth seeing in all of Italy, with supplements on how to travel, currency and useful vocabulary."

It has many beautiful and imposing houses within, also Palaces; the streets are charming, paved with great square stones. And it has many beautiful churches, for example San Martino, with a large wonderful market, where you can get for money whatever your heart desires.

You won't have seen any other city like this, with such impressive walks all around; here there are the guns and under the towers a strict watch is held. In sum, it is fine to live there.

Milton visits Lucca to see the ancestral home of his schoolboy friend

from David Masson: *The Life of John Milton*

John Milton (1608-1674) visited Italy in 1638-9 and was enthusiastically received by scholars and writers in Florence. He made a famous trip to Pisa to see Galileo at the same time. From Florence he also made a brief excursion to Lucca, based on his desire to see the ancestral home city of Charles Diodati, his best friend at St. Paul's School in London.

Usually, however, an ingenuous boy has friends and acquaintances of his own age, with whom he exchanges confidence. Doubtless Milton had such among his school-fellows at St. Paul's. His brother Christopher had entered the school, a boy of nine or ten, before he left it. Among his schoolfellows nearer his own age was Robert Pory or Porey, who became a clergyman, and was one of the prebendaries of St. Paul's in the year of the Restoration. He was probably Milton's form-fellow, for he left St. Paul's School for College along with Milton. But the schoolfellow between whom and Milton there existing the most affectionate intimacy was a youth named Charles Diodati.

As the name indicates, Diodati was of Italian extraction. The family had migrated originally from Lucca to Geneva on account of their Protestant opinions. Of two brothers born in Geneva, the younger, named Giovanni, remained there and became eminent as a Reformed preacher and theologian. He was Professor of Hebrew in the University of Geneva and one of the pastors of the city; and he was the author of theological writings much admired in their day by the Calvinists of different countries, and still found in theological libraries. He was one of the leading foreign members of the Synod of Dort. His name is now best remembered in association with the Italian version of the Scriptures published by him in 1607, and known as Diodati's version. The elder brother of this Genevese divine, born in 1574 and named Theodore, had adopted the medical profession, and, coming over to England in early life, had there married an English lady of some fortune, and obtained good practice and considerable reputation as a physician. About the year 1609 he had a house at Brentford, and was in professional attendance on the heir-apparent, Prince Henry, and his sister the Princess Elizabeth, afterwards Queen of Bohemia; and a successful case of extraordinary phlebotomy which occurred there in his practice – 60 ounces of blood drawn from a patient over seventy in three days – attracted much attention, and was afterwards thought worthy of scientific record. But London was his usual place of abode; and there his son Charles was born in or about 1608. He was, therefore, almost exactly of the same age as Milton, or only a little older. In the routine of scholastic study, however, he had somewhat the start of Milton. He was sent at a very early age to St. Paul's School, whence he removed, in February 1621-2, to Trinity College, Oxford – the College to which the younger Gill belonged, and which he had only recently left. Notwithstanding this disparity, an intimacy had sprung up between the two youths much closer than is common even between lads of the same form. Milton's allusions to their friendship in some of his subsequent letters show on what familiar terms it rested. He calls him "*pectus amans nostri, tamque fidele caput*" ("a heart attached to his, and his so faithful one"); also his "*lepidum sodalem*" ("sprightly companion"); and once, when Diodati, sending him some verses, asks for some in return in proof of continued affection, Milton protests that his love is too great to be conveyed in metre. From the tone of these allusions one fancies Diodati as a quick, amiable, intelligent youth, with something of his Italian descent visible in his face and manner.

129

Elisa Buonaparte dallies with Paganini

LUCCA DURING THE GRAND TOUR

The Grand Tour

from Ernest O. Hauser: *Italy: A Cultural Guide*

A loose term, first heard in English towards the end of the seventeenth century, designating a gentleman's leisurely circuit of the European continent, institutionalised by the British upper class in the seventeen hundreds, its beginnings reach further back. We hear of a Prince of Julich and Cleeves, in the northern Rhineland, who went to look at Italy in 1575 with an escort of sixty horse, and died in Rome. But Europe did not really open up to peaceful travel until 1648, when the end of the Thirty Years' War made the main highways relatively safe; and the movement of sightseers, thereafter, fluctuated with the continent's political vicissitudes. A blend of motives lay behind the Tour. It was, for one thing, a status symbol – back home again, you would be able to talk about narrow escapes from robbers, a duel or two, your impressions of the Laocoon statue at the Vatican. It also meant keeping up with the Lord Joneses, who were doing the same thing. But the Grand Tour was, primarily, a way for the young Englishman of "good birth" and ample means to round out his education, polish his social manners, improve his dress, and absorb "culture". He'd spend a year or more visiting the major centers of civilization and enjoyment, lingering at Paris, perhaps at Vienna, seeing the mighty Rhine, crossing the frozen Alps, and making sunny Italy the main dish of his varied menu. Germans, too, hit the southward trail, impelled by a romantic longing to "know the land where the lemon trees bloom; where gold oranges glow among dark foliage", as Goethe wrote. (The German poet went to Italy in 1786-88 in order to escape from his administrative chores at the provincial court of Weimar and in vain hopes of finding the *Urpflanze*, ancestor of all vegetation.) But the Americans were latecomers, arriving – not counting a few early scouts – in the mid-nineteenth century, when the tour was no longer "grand".

The typical English Grand Tourist was eager to see, with his

131

own eyes, the ancient monuments he had read so much about. He had studied the Latin classics, at Oxford or Cambridge, and would recite them at the drop of a hat. James Boswell (1740-95) – best known for his *Life of Samuel Johnson* – who made the Grand Tour in his mid-twenties, could rattle off forty of Horace's 102 *Odes*. Edward Gibbon (1737-94) visited "each memorable spot where (he fancied) Romulus stood, or Tully [Marcus Tullius Cicero] spoke." He conceived the idea for his monumental *Decline and Fall of the Roman Empire* while brooding among the ruins of the Capitol in Rome. But though the "milords", as the Italians called all Englishmen, dutifully toured art galleries and churches (where Catholic pomp troubled their Protestant consciences), few of them knew what to make of Italian art, especially that of the Middle Ages and of the Baroque. They did enjoy the social life, however, so much less hidebound than at home. Many of them were armed with introductions to noble families and were readily welcomed at their palaces and villas. If they were travelling with a tutor, they did their best to get away from him, timing their itinerary so as to abandon themselves, in early spring, to the "frantic, bacchanalian", and delightfully un-English, carnival. Sex was predominantly on their minds. Italian women, known for their dark-eyed beauty, were reputed to be easy game, and Boswell claims that, whenever he admired a lady, married or not, he was told, "Sir, you can have her. It would not be difficult." Nevertheless, as he wrote to Jean-Jacques Rousseau (1712-78), he had "no success at all with the ladies of Piedmont", perhaps because his approach was too direct. But he did indulge his passion in Naples, where "the ladies resembled country chamber maids." And carried on a serious love affair with the wife of the *capitano del popolo* (roughly, "mayor") of Siena, Girolama ("Moma") Piccolomini, a woman considerably older than himself. He lingered in her arms until his pa, Lord Auchinleck, ordered him back to Scotland. Freedom from puritan morality seems to have been one of the reasons why British fathers sent their sons to Italy, where they would "learn how to live", and where their amorous adventures could safely be left behind. There was an odor of wild oats, and of a corresponding guilt feeling, about the journey south. "Whore-hunting among groves of myrtles," Scotland's national poet, Robert Burns (1759-96), called the Italian leg of the Grand Tour.

The more mature milords stopped at cultural way stations they had heard about at their clubs. In Rome, they visited the printshop of Giambattista Piranesi (1720-78) and, later in the century, the sculptor's studio of Antonio Canova (1757-1822); carried on earnest literary and artistic conversations – in poor Italian or fair French – in the salons of countesses and at coffee houses, and, if they were lucky, made the rounds of ancient monuments with the great Winckelmann (1717-68) himself as their cicerone. From Naples, they went on excursions to Pompeii, partly excavated since 1748, and climbed Mount Vesuvius whose A.D. 79 eruption had buried it, to enjoy one of Europe's most celebrated views. In Florence, they bought antiques, fake or authentic, and might pick up a Botticelli or a Raphael that is, today, the pride of a museum in England or the United States. In Venice, they forgathered at the house of the British consul, Joseph Smith – "the Merchant of Venice" – to inspect his remarkable collection of rare books and paintings (among the latter, Vermeer's *Lady at the Virginal*), which he later sold to King George III. What one too easily forgets is that these travelers were willing to undergo considerable hardships in order to see Italy. The two-day trip across the Alps, usually by way of Mont Cenis, was a hair-raising experience. Milord's carriage, unless he wished to take another one on the other side, was dismantled and carried across piecemeal. He himself sat in a rope chair suspended from two parallel poles and was lifted over icy heights by a team of six bearers. Horace Walpole (1717-97) novelist, antiquarian, and collector – who on occasion wore a limewood necktie sculpted by the master wood carver, Grinling Gibbons (1648-1721) – had his lapdog snatched from him by a wolf during the ride. Once in Italy, the tourist found bad roads, dirty inns, and, frequently, poor food. Unless he traveled, like Lord Byron (1788-1824), with a train of five carriages, seven servants, and livestock of his own, could he be really comfortable? Brigands were lurking in romantic ruins. The foreigner was cheated, or thought he was, at every turn. To top it all, a noxious miasma, hanging in the warm night air, brought on malaria, or "Roman fever". (The female anopheline mosquito was not identified as the sole carrier of the disease until 1898 – by three Italians: Bignami, Grassi, and

Bastianelli). No wonder, then, that many visitors took an ill-humored view of Italy and its inhabitants.

1645

Evelyn hears the purest Italian

from John Evelyn: *Diary*

John Evelyn (1620-1706), the great diarist, was on the Grand Tour between 1643 and 1647, marrying the daughter of Charles I's Ambassador to Paris along the way. He let Peter the Great use his London house during Peter's stay in 1698. The Russian Emperor and his crew were poor tenants: they wrecked his garden by their wheelbarrow races across Evelyn's flowerbeds and favourite holly hedges. Many believe the Italian spoken in Lucca is still the purest.

The next day I came to Lucca, a small but pretty territorie and state of itselfe. – The Citty is neate and well fortified, with noble and pleasant walkes of trees on the workes, where the gentry and ladies use to take the aire. 'Tis situate on an ample plaine by the river Serchio, yet the country about it is hilly. The Senate-house is magnificent.

... Next to this we visited St. Crosses, an excellent structure, all of marble both without and within, and so adorn'd as may vie with many of the fairest even in Rome; witness the huge Crosse valued at £ 15,000, above all venerable for that sacred volto which (as tradition goes) was miraculously put on the image of Christ, and made by Nicodemus, whilst the artist, finishing the rest of the body, was meditating what face to set on it. The inhabitants are exceedingly civill to strangers, above all places in Italy, and they speake the purest Italian. 'Tis also cheape living, which causes travellers to set up their rest here more than in Florence, tho' a more celebrated Citty; besides, the ladys here are very conversable, and the religious women not at all reserv'd; of these we bought gloves and embroidered stomachers generaly worn by gentlemen in these countries. The circuit of this state is but two easy days journey, and lies mixed with the Duke of Tuscany's, but having Spain for a Protector (tho' the least bigotted of all Roman Catholics), and being one of the best fortify'd Citties in Italy, it remains in peace. This whole country abounds in excellent olives.

Addison learns that one Lucchese can beat five Florentines

from Joseph Addison: *Remarks on Several Parts of Italy*

Joseph Addison (1672-1719) was the son of the Dean of Lichfield Cathedral. He went abroad in 1699, returning in 1703 to a prominent government and literary career, creating the Spectator *with Steele. The two month period of office mentioned here gave rise to the appellation "Gonfaloniere of the sixty soups".*

It is very pleasant to see how the small territories of this little republic are cultivated to the best advantage, so that one cannot find the least spot of ground, that is not made to contribute its utmost to the owner. In all the inhabitants there appears an air of cheerfulness and plenty, not often to be met with in those of the countries which lie about them. There is but one gate for strangers to enter at, that it may be known what numbers of them are in the town. Over it is written, in letters of gold, *libertas*.

This republic is shut up in the Great Duke's dominions, who at present is very much incensed against it, and seems to threaten it with the fate of Florence, Pisa, and Sienna. The occasion is as follows.

The Lucquese plead prescription for hunting in one of the Duke's forests, that lies upon their frontiers, which about two years since was strictly forbidden them, the prince intending to preserve the game for his own pleasure. Two or three sportsmen of the republic, who had the hardiness to offend against the prohibition, were seized, and kept in a neighbouring prison. Their countrymen, to the number of threescore, attacked the place where they were kept in custody, and rescued them. The Great Duke redemands his prisoners, and, as a further satisfaction, would have the governor of the town, where the threescore assailants had combined together, delivered into his hands; but receiving only excuses, he resolved to do himself justice. Accordingly, he ordered all the Lucquese to be seized that were found on a market-day in one of his frontier towns. These amounted to fourscore, among whom were persons of some consequence in the republic. They are now in prison at Florence, and, as it is said, treated hardly enough, for there are fifteen of the number dead within less than two years. The king of Spain, who is protector of the commonwealth, received information from the Great Duke of what had passed, and approved of his proceedings, with orders to the Lucquese, by his governor of Milan, to give a proper satisfaction. The republic, thinking themselves ill used by their protector, as they say at Florence, have sent to Prince Eugene to desire the emperor's protection, with an offer of winter-quarters, as it is said, for four thousand Germans. The Great Duke rises on them in his demands, and will not be satisfied with less than a hundred thousand crowns, and a solemn embassy to beg pardon for the past, and promise amendment for the future. Thus stands the affair at present, that may end in the ruin of the commonwealth, if the French succeed in Italy. It is pleasant, however, to hear the discourse of the common people of Lucca, who are firmly persuaded that one Lucquese can beat five Florentines, who are grown low-spirited, as they pretend, by the Great Duke's oppressions, and have nothing worth fighting for. They say they can bring into the field twenty or thirty thousand fighting men, all ready to sacrifice their lives for their liberty. They have a good quantity of arms and ammunition, but few horses. It must be owned these people are more happy, at least in imagination, than the rest of their neighbours, because they think themselves so; though such a chimerical happiness is not peculiar to republicans, for we find the subjects of the most absolute prince in Europe are as proud of their monarch as the Lucquese of being subject to none. Should the French affairs prosper in Italy, it is possible the Great Duke may bargain for the republic of Lucca, by the help of his great treasures, as his predecessors did formerly with the emperor for that of Sienna. The Great Dukes have never yet attempted anything on Lucca, as not only fearing the arms of their protector, but because they are well assured, that should the Lucquese be reduced to the last extremities, they would rather throw themselves under the government of the Genoese, or some stronger neighbour, than submit to a state for which they have so great an aversion. And the Florentines are very sensible, that it is much better to have a weak state within their dominions, than the branch of one as strong as themselves. But should so formidable a power as that of the French king support them in their attempts, there is no government in Italy that would dare to interpose. This republic, for the extent of its dominions, is esteemed the richest and best peopled state of Italy. The whole administration of the government passes into different hands at the end of every two months, which is the greatest security imaginable to their liberty, and wonderfully contributes to the quick despatch of all public affairs: but in any exigence of state, like that they are now pressed with, it certainly asks a much longer time to conduct any design, for the good of the commonwealth, to its maturity and perfection.

≈≈≈

1721

The foreign residents sing and play in the Volto Santo festivities

from V. Marchiò: *Il Forestiere informato delle cose di Lucca*

Every foreigner, who comes to Lucca, can tell for himself which are the ancient, and which the modern, buildings of the city; can take for his pleasure a stroll on the walls; can admire the architecture of the churches; and in the same way he can worship the miraculous images, especially the more than seventy bodies of Christ crucified. If he needs archives, manuscripts and important contracts, we have thousands, and he can satisfy himself by

137

perusing those protected by the canons of the Cathedral, or at the Abbey of San Ponziano, or at the church of San Giovanni, or at the Palace of the Archbishop. If he wishes to see the Armoury, he can go to the Palace of the Great Lords, to which it has been transferred, through whose two courtyards one enters by gates guarded by a company of Swiss guards. Walking under the porticos, three gates lead into the Armoury, kept in good order and in the highest maintenance. It is full of various kinds of weapons and capable of arming many soldiers.

Many places in the city are full of gunpowder, which for good order's sake are kept far away from each other – the great powder magazines are controlled diligently, as are the cannons of various kinds, which are increasing and constantly renovated by the Foundry. These have been remounted and put in position on the walls, or inside the covered bastions.

There are also festivals in Lucca, accompanied by solemn ceremonies, particularly that of the Volto Santo on the 14th of September, and that of Liberty, celebrated on the Sunday after Easter. These are greeted with cannonades from the Swiss guards, and from the towers and walls; out of the Palace, dressed magnificently, comes the Gonfaloniere with two Anziani (elders), in decorous livery.

The same cannonade, with perhaps more cannons, is given at the morning of the festival, and the evening before, coinciding with the celebration of the Volto Santo, to which occasion all the foreigners residing in the Republic come; they voluntarily sing or play instruments in the first and second Vespers, in the Mass and in the Luminara procession.

Montesquieu describes Lucca's government and finances

from Montesquieu: *Voyage en Italie*
trans. Charles Nicholl

Baron Charles Louis de Montesquieu (1689-1755) went on tour in Europe just after his election to the Academie Francaise in 1728 to study other countries' political and economic systems. He stayed nearly a year in Italy; the result was the Voyage en Italie *from which this extract is taken. He also wrote* Considerations on the causes of the Grandeur and the decadence of Rome.

Lucca is a city of some 22,000 souls. Commercially it is rather in decline because its silk products are not selling so well in Germany, and because the Princes, in particular the Emperor, are making business so difficult. Some of the city's silk is produced within its own State, which is part of Romagna.

Signor Colonna tells me that there are about 5,000 silk-workers in Lucca. This is a lot considering the city is so underpopulated.

There are four or five hundred families in the city who are of the nobility, that is to say part of the government. Titles can be purchased here, as in Venice; the cost is about 12,000 écus, in other words about 10,000 piastres. In contrast to the Genoese, the Lucchesi are poor but their public treasury is quite rich. They have hardly any expenses, other than what they must spend, like all the minor powers in Italy, on purchasing their peace and liberty from the Emperor. There are no public entertainments in Lucca.

The Republic's revenues are considerable. Tax on tobacco and liquor brings in 12,000 scudi; there is no tax on salt. Altogether, including entry and exit tolls and property taxes, the revenues amount to some 200,000 écus ... of which the city contributes 150,000 écus and the countryside 50,000. (These figures should be viewed with caution, however. This is what Colonna told me, but the sum of 200,000 écus seems impossibly high. I think half of that is more likely.)

The Republic maintains at its own cost 500 soldiers, who form the guard of the city; plus 80 Swiss, who are the Prince's bodyguard; and 44 artillery men: all this for the defence of the city. In addition there are about 200 men in the smaller towns of the State, which are Castiglione, on the border with Modena; Viareggio, which is their seaport (it is actually no more than a harbour, which nothing bigger than a galliot can enter); and Montignoso, near the Massa border. A tour through the State covers 28 or 30 miles.

The city's fortifications are good: there are eleven bastions, each one mounted with ten cannon; the curtains are protected by demi-lunes. The ramparts are planted with trees: this gives a very pleasing effect. It is the promenade of the city: tranquil princes have no need to be jealous of their fortifications. There are always enough provisions in the city to last for three years, and when the stored corn is in danger of spoiling it is distributed to the countryside, to add to the harvest. In the arsenal (it is claimed) there are arms sufficient for 22,000 men. It is certainly true that there are two very large rooms well-stocked with weapons. On top of this every citizen is obliged to carry a firearm.

The Archbishopric of Lucca (this title has been given to the current prelate) is worth 9,000 écus. The Pope nominates the canons of the Cathedral and San Giovanni, the Prince nominates those of San Michele and San Paolino (though at present it is the Gonfalonier who nominates for San Paolino.)

The Gonfalonier has nine elders who act as councillors; these are changed every two months. According to the law, they cannot leave the confines of the palazzo which is set aside to accommodate them, not even to go to their own houses. They sometimes slip out, however, in the evening, furtively. Many government offices are distributed among these men. There is another magistrate appointed by the Gonfalonier, which changes every two months, and three others who are changed every year. These have the authority to imprison, and to bring anyone to trial, but after the case has been heard it is the council which delivers judgement.

There is no Inquisition at all in Lucca.

Boswell writes to Jean Jacques Rousseau

from James Boswell: *Diaries*

James Boswell (1740-1795) was the son of Lord Auchinleck and friend and biographer of Samuel Johnson. He was at first a Jacobite, and prayed for King James until an uncle gave him a shilling, whereafter he prayed for King George. He was a compulsive diarist, and kept up an extended correspondence with Rousseau during his Italian trip in 1765-6.

Lucca, 3 October 1765

If it were possible, illustrious philosopher! to write to you without that respect which hinders the imagination by introducing a degree of fear, I should flatter myself that I could entertain you with an account of my tour of Italy. I shall do my best; and if I am not successful you will know what to ascribe my failure to.

You were indeed right to congratulate me when my father gave me permission to travel in Italy. Nine months in this delicious country have done more for me than all the sage lessons which books, or men formed by books, could have taught me. It was my imagination that needed correction, and nothing but travel could have produced this effect.

I carried over the Alps ideas of the most rigorous morality. I thought of myself as a penitent who must expiate the sins which he had confessed to you in your sacred retreat; I felt like a hero of austerity in a dissolute age. But the ladies of Turin were very beautiful, and I thought that I might allow myself *one* intrigue in Italy, in order to increase my knowledge of the world and give me a contempt for shameless women. So I made myself into a gallant; but I was too modest a gallant to succeed with ladies who scorned the detours of delicacy, and who thought anyone a peasant or an imbecile who did not head straight for the main chance. Moreover, I had a heart. I was seized by passion, I could not hide it; and that was not reconcilable with the decorum which had to be maintained in public. In short, I had no success at all with the ladies of

Piedmont. A French officer who was my instructor in gallantry, mortified by finding me *so young*, consoled me by procuring willing girls.

Thus, Sir, did I carry out the good resolutions I had made at Môtiers. I wrote on a piece of paper, "O Rousseau! How am I fallen since I left you!" Yet my principles remained firm. I considered that I had done wrong. I summoned my inclinations back to virtue, and at Parma M. Deleyre strengthened me in my resolutions. I was charmed by the fine mind and the finer soul of that amiable Frenchman; and the sincere evidence which he gave of his attachment to me brought me back again to the opinion that I was something above the crowd of mankind. You told me when I was about to leave you, "Sir, all you lack is a knowledge of your own worth." Believe me, illustrious philosopher! There is a great deal in that remark. I know my worth sometimes, and I think and act nobly. But then melancholy attacks me, I despise myself, and it seems to me a waste of time to try to improve so petty a thing.

1768

Smollett toils through Tuscany

from Tobias Smollett: *Travels through France and Italy*

Smollett wrote that he had "a great desire to see Lucca" during his Italian trip. Unfortunately the English novelist died in Livorno first; he is buried in the Foreign Cemetery there. Smollett's usually jaundiced views of his experiences caused Laurence Sterne to model Smelfungus after him in Sentimental Journey.

At the post-house in Lerici, the accommodation is intolerable. We were almost poisoned at supper. I found the place where I was to lie so close and confined, that I could not breathe in it, and therefore lay all night in an outward room upon four chairs, with a leathern portmanteau for my pillow. For this entertainment I payed very near a loui'dore. Such bad accommodation is the less excusable, as the fellow has a great deal of business, this being a great thoroughfare for travellers going into Italy, or returning from thence.

I might have saved some money by prosecuting my voyage directly by sea to Leghorn: but, by this time, we were all heartily tired of the water: the business then was to travel by land to Florence, by the way of Pisa, which is seven posts distant from Lerici. Those who have not their own carriage must either hire chaises to perform the whole journey, or travel by way of *cambiatura*, which is that of changing the chaises every post, as the custom is in England. In this case the great inconvenience arises from your being obliged to shift your baggage every post. The chaise or *calesse* of this country, is a wretched machine with two wheels, as uneasy as a common cart, being indeed no other than what we should call in England a very ill-contrived one-horse chair, narrow, naked, shattered and shabby. For this vehicle and two horses you pay at the rate of eight *paoli* a stage, or four shillings sterling; and the postilion expects two *paoli* for his gratification: so that every eight miles cost about five shillings, and four only, if you travel in your own carriage, as in that case you pay no more than at the rate of three *paoli* a horse.

About three miles from Lerici, we crossed the Magra, which appeared as a rivulet almost dry, and in half a mile farther arrived at Sarzana, a small town at the extremity of the Genoese territories, where we changed horses. Then entering the principalities of Massa and Carrara, belonging to the duke of Modena, we passed Lavenza, which seems to be a decayed fort with a small garrison, and dined at Massa, which is an agreeable little town, where the old dutchess of Modena resides. Notwithstanding all the expedition we could make, it was dark before we passed the Cerchio, which is an inconsiderable stream in the neighbourhood of Pisa, where we arrived about eight in the evening.

The country from Sarzana to the frontiers of Tuscany is a narrow plain, bounded on the right by the sea, and on the left by the Appenine mountains. It is well cultivated and inclosed, consisting of meadow-ground, corn fields, plantations of olives; and the trees that form the hedge-rows serve as so many props to the vines, which are twisted round them, and continued from one to another. After entering the dominions of Tuscany, we travelled through a noble forest of oak trees of a considerable extent, which would have appeared much more agreeable, had we not been benighted and apprehensive of robbers. The last post but one in this day's journey, is at the little town of Viareggio, a kind of sea-port on the Mediterranean, belonging to Lucca. The roads are indifferent, and the accommodation is execrable. I was glad to find myself housed in a very good inn at Pisa, where I promised myself a good night's rest, and was not disappointed.

1789

Mrs Piozzi finds a fairy commonwealth

from Hester Piozzi: *Observations and reflections made in the course of a journey through France, Italy and Germany*

Hester Lynch Piozzi (1741-1821) was, as Mrs Thrale, a close friend of Dr Johnson, who was "almost domesticated" at her country home Streatham Park. She published Johnson's letters and a volume of anecdotes about him, but eventually broke off contact. She came to Lucca on honeymoon after her wedding to Gabriel Piozzi, an Italian musician.

From the head-quarters of painting, sculpture, and architecture, then, where art is at her acme, and from a people polished into brilliancy, perhaps a little into weakness, we drove through the celebrated vale of Arno, thick hedges on each side us, which in spring must have been covered with blossoms and fragrant with perfume, now loaded with uncultivated fruits – the wild grape, raspberry, and azaroli – inviting to every sense and promising every joy. This beautiful and fertile, this highly-adorned and truly delicious country carried us forward to Lucca, where the panther sits at the gate, and liberty is written up on every wall and door. It is so long since I have seen the word that even the letters of it rejoice my heart; but how the panther came to be its emblem, who can tell? Unless the philosophy we learn from old Lilly in our childhood were true – nec vult panthera domari [that the panther will never be tamed].

That this fairy commonwealth should so long have maintained its independency is strange; but Howel attributes her freedom to the active and industrious spirit of the inhabitants, who, he says, resemble a hive of bees for order and for diligence. I never did see a place so populous for the size of it; one is actually thronged running up and down the streets of Lucca, though it is a little town enough for a capital city, to be sure – larger than Salisbury, though, and prettier than Nottingham, the beauties of both which places it unites with all the charms peculiar to itself.

The territory they claim, and of which no power dares attempt to dispossess them, is much about the size of Rutlandshire, I fancy, surrounded and apparently fenced in on every side by the Apennines as by a wall – that wall a hot one on the southern side, and wholly planted over with vines – while the soft shadows which fall upon the declivity of the mountains make it inexpressibly pretty, and form, by the particular disposition of their light and shadow, a variety which no other prospect so confined can possibly enjoy.

This is the Ilam Gardens of Europe, and whoever has seen that singular spot in Derbyshire, belonging to Mr. Port, has seen little Lucca in a convex mirror. Some writer calls it a ring upon the finger of the Emperor, under whose protection it has been hitherto preserved safe from the Grand Duke of Tuscany till these days, in which the interests of those two sovereigns, united by intimacy as by blood and resemblance of character, are become almost exactly the same.

A Doge, whom they call the Principe, is elected every two months, and is assisted by ten senators in the administration of justice.

Their armoury is the prettiest plaything I ever yet saw, neatly kept, and capable of furnishing twenty-five thousand men with arms. Their revenues are about equal to the Duke of Bedford's, I believe – eighty or eighty-five thousand pounds sterling a-year – every spot of ground belonging to these people being cultivated to the highest pitch of perfection that agriculture, or, rather, gardening (for one cannot call these enclosures fields), will admit; and, though it is holiday-time just now, I see no neglect of necessary duty. There were watering away this morning at seven o'clock, just as we do in a nursery-ground about London, a hundred men at once, or more, before they come home to make themselves smart and go to hear music in their best church in honour of some saint, I have forgotten who; but he is the patron of Lucca, and cannot be accused of neglecting his charge, that is certain.

This city seems really under admirable regulations. Here are fewer beggars than even at Florence, where, however, one for fifty in the states of Genoa or Venice do not meet your eyes; and either the word liberty has bewitched me, or I see an air of plenty without insolence, and business without noise, that greatly delight me. Here is much cheerfulness, too, and gay good humour; but this is the season of devotion at Lucca, and in these countries the ideas of devotion and diversion are so blended, that all religious worship seems connected with, and to me now regularly implies, a festive show. Well, as the Italians say, "Il mondo è bello perché è variabile." [The world is pleasant because it is various]. We English dress our clergymen in black, and go ourselves to the theatre in colours. Here matters are reversed; the church at noon looked like a flower-garden, so gaily adorned were the priests, confrairies, etc., while the Opera-house at night had more the air of a funeral, as everybody was dressed in black, a circumstance I had forgotten the meaning of, till reminded that such was once the emulation of finery among the persons of fashion in this city, that it was found convenient to restrain the spirit of expense by obliging them to wear constant mourning, a very rational and well-devised rule in a town so small, where everybody is known to everybody, and where, when this silly excitement to envy is wisely removed, I know not what should hinder the inhabitants from living like those one reads of in the Golden Age, which, above all others, this climate most resembles, where pleasure contributes to soothe life, commerce to quicken it, and faith extends its prospects to eternity. Such is, or such at least appears to me, this lovely territory of Lucca – where cheap living, free government, and genteel society may be enjoyed with a tranquillity unknown to larger states; where there are delicious and salutary baths a few miles out of town, for the nobility to make *villeggiatura* at; and where, if those nobility were at all disposed to cultivate and communicate learning, every opportunity for study is afforded.

Napoleon acknowledges his new subjects

Lucca fell into French occupation in 1799 and was garrisoned by French troops. The town wanted its freedom restored, or some semblance of it, after four centuries as a proud republic. Napoleon was appealed to, and in 1803 appointed the Lucca citizen Saliceti as his representative in Lucca, and withdrew the garrison. The local government under Saliceti was to consist of 300 citizens, two thirds from the landowners and one third from the merchants, scholars and artists. Schools were established, trade began to recover and a Chargée d'Affaires from Paris arrived in September. Lucca then sent an envoy extraordinary – Giuseppe Belluomini – to Paris asking for Napoleon's continued protection; he was treated courteously as the representative of a friendly power. The Emperor wrote the following reply to the government of Lucca:

Dear and good friends, I am sensible of the assurance you give me in your letter of June 7, of your interest in the events which have established my family in the hereditary government of this Empire. I am firmly resolved to use the power, with which Divine Providence has deigned to invest me, for the maintenance and improvement of the ties which bind together the two States. In accrediting my envoy to Lucca I charged him to repeat to you the assurance of my esteem and of my immutable sentiments.

He makes his sister Elisa Princess of Lucca

from Eugenio Lazzareschi: *Elisa Buonaparte Baciocchi*

The first sentence of Tolstoy's War and Peace *is, "Well, Prince, Genoa and Lucca are now no more than private estates of the Bonaparte family." The elderly lady who said this in July 1805 at a soirée in St. Petersburg was referring to Napoleon's formation of the principality of Lucca that year. His sister Elisa (1777-1820) was married to Felice Baciocchi, Prince of Piombino (ironically the mainland port for Elba) and Napoleon confirmed on them the titles of Prince and Princess of Lucca. Their faces appeared together on the new silver coinage. Elisa became Grand Duchess of Tuscany in 1808. The new sovereigns made a triumphal entry into Lucca on 14 July 1805 (coincidentally – or maybe not – Bastille Day), recorded by the Abbot Iacopo Chelini. He said "their entrance could not have been more brilliant or more magnificent" but also "nor more silent or more melancholy among the spectators, because we could not forget the sweet liberty which we were about to lose."*

The procession started with 100 cavalrymen of the Imperial Guard and four detachments of the guards of honour of the principal Italian cities. The carriage of their Serene and Imperial Highnesses was drawn by six horses, guided by six equerries, and followed by many other carriages of personages from the Court, Ministers or Counsellors of State. At the gate of Santa Maria they were presented with the symbolic keys to the city in silver, resting on a cushion of velvet, while artillery pieces were fired and all the church bells were unleashed. Felice alone descended from the carriage, put his left hand on the symbol of possession of the city and, loaded with decorations and medals, jumped agilely into the saddle, notwithstanding his 43 years and the beginnings of middle-aged spread. No-one in the thick crowd, which showed no expression of joy, had ever seen the Princess; but the ladies-in-waiting, who had offered their respects in the convent of San Vito, could say that Elisa was truly radiant with her iridescent diadem of diamonds, and majestic as a pale sovereign should be, under the weight of a cloak of velvet. "This was purple, embroidered with golden eagles" wrote the good priest Chelini, who, watching from one of the choir stalls of San Martino, and about to begin playing his viola, saw the greater part of the procession, which had crossed Lucca in silence, like a funeral.

The venerable Archbishop Sardi was under the portico of the Cathedral, waiting for the princely pair, in order to accompany them to the shadow of the altar canopy, and to offer them a blessing with holy water. And he himself, the poor old man in his seventies, who had to celebrate at this late hour a *Grand Mass* with songs and music, blessed after the reading of the Gradual the so-called "symbols of honour", consisting of a silver hand representing justice, two rings symbolizing fidelity, and the sword of power. The Prince received from the Archbishop the silver hand and a ring, the Princess the second ring and General Hedonville the sword, which he gave to Felice as a present from Napoleon. The sovereigns, thus invested with their powers and following an ancient medieval rite, sat down on a throne at the left side of the altar and listened to a speech by the same Ambassador Hedonville about the Emperor's guarantee to the Principality. He promised "with the help of God, to remove everything which is bad for the people of Lucca, for its independence, and for our dearly beloved sister and brother-in-law and their descendants."

She adorns the walls

from G. Barsotti: *Lucca Sacra*

Elisa Baciocchi was bright, dynamic and a lover of the arts and architecture. A story, probably apocryphal, says that once, when the Serchio flooded and the town gates were closed, she was winched up over the walls. She redesigned much of the town; this required razing older buildings, especially church properties, for Elisa was of secular bent. Schools and public welfare institutions were strengthened, and the walls laid out as public gardens. One priest expostulated in 1923:

There was a fury of abolition, alienation, suppression and wholesale destruction of church property ... A decree of 1808 closed as many as 60 churches and oratories and some of these were razed to the ground. None of this was in any sense for the benefit of the people but only for the rulers who had been forced on us. All done with the stroke of a pen.

and dallies with Paganini in the Lucchesia

from Jonathan Keates: *Tuscany*

The nobles of the ruling oligarchy followed the customary practice of quitting the town in summer for their country retreats scattered along the hillsides of the Lucchesia, the fertile valley of the River Serchio. These villas and their surrounding countryside are unlike anything regarded as typically Tuscan by visitors from beyond the Alps. For a start, the soil hereabouts is exceptionally fertile, and the roads from Florence are lined with nurseries and market gardens, so that even the humblest peasant plot is green and fecund to bursting. The whole landscape has a softness and diversity which the staring cornlands of the *crete senesi* or the lurid sunflower fields of the Val di Chiana notably lack.

Village houses in the Lucchesia have their own style, basically built as tall blocks of dwellings bonded together around a courtyard. Each has its *fienile*, or hay barn, with windows of zigzagged bricks to aerate the drying winter fodder. In between the various communities, especially around the heights of Le Pizzorne north-east of Lucca, lie the villas, each surrounded by an ornate park fusing both Italian and English garden features, and each far more self-consciously a town dweller's rustic resort than any of the farmhouse fortresses of the Florentines and Sienese.

150

You can visit several of them by taking the main road north out of Lucca up the left bank of the Serchio, turning right to Marlia. This, the grandest pile of them all, is open solely at the whim of its owners, and you can count yourself lucky to be able to view the garden, but the place deserves more than a nod as a symbol of the region's Napoleonic destiny. It was here that Elisa Bonaparte and her complaisant spouse Felice Baciocchi decided to turn the existing villa into a residence worthy of the vigorous, efficient and generally beneficent sway of the Princess of Piombino and her consort – as they had now become. Until chased away by a British expeditionary force, Elisa successfully played the *grande dame* here and dallied with the young Niccolò Paganini, whose legendary violin technique – at least according to him – used to make her swoon with emotion. As for poor Felice, he made the best of things, consoling himself with a sardonic play on his name, which in Italian means "happy". He had changed it from Pasquale, which in those days was synonymous with "fool", so he used to say: "When I was Pasquale then I was Felice: now I'm Felice, I've become Pasquale."

1805

Losing my heart to a nutcracker

from Ludwig Tieck: *Poems*

Ludwig Tieck (1773-1853) was a prominent and versatile representative of Romanticism in Germany. The son of a Berlin rope-maker, he began writing verse as a schoolboy. Tieck's Die Sommernacht *(1789) is a charming sketch of the boy Shakespeare's devotion to poetry, foreshadowing his lifetime preoccupation with (and translations of) Shakespeare. Tieck was in Italy in 1805-6 and wrote this witty poem called* Lucca.

A festival is gathered before the gate
where the lively population is gathered,

silk clothes shine
in the dusk on the green grass.
Happy tumult and children's glee,
youths wander about and look for a glance
from more beautiful eyes.
Ha! This noble figure in green silk,
promenading at the side of her enraptured bridegroom
shines brighter than all in her freshness,
    beauty and gleaming eyes,
how she sweetly opens her full lips with
a smile, when speaking softly.
The light of her pearly teeth flashes through the
    coral red
and everything about her, form, movement and voice
sounds like music and captures my heart
so that I, envying the groom, almost hate him.
    Then the heavenly one takes large walnuts
    from Lombardy out of her basket,
and cracks them loudly behind the red
    glow with her pearly teeth.
O groom! Most miserable of men!
So I called out, fleeing,
certainly one has heard of sirens, vampires
and other fantastic magical creatures,
who take over men's hearts demonically
    with changing shapes;
and I was near (how awful) to
    the dreadful danger
of losing my heart to a nutcracker.

Rev. Eustace bemoans Lucca's loss of liberty

from John Eustace: *A Classical Tour through Italy in 1802*

John Eustace (1762-1815) describes Lucca at length in his Classical
Tour through Italy. *He was a classical antiquary, trained as a
Benedictine monk, and close friend of Edmund Burke, whom he
comforted in his last illness. He died in Naples while collecting
material for a new volume of his* Tour. *Shelley didn't think much of
his work. He said, "Consult Eustace, if you want to know nothing
about Italy."*

One advantage the *Lucchesi* enjoy peculiar to themselves, an
advantage which, though highly desirable, was seldom attained
by the ancient commonwealths, whether Greek or *Roman*; – the
cordial and uninterrupted union of the people and their governors.
Public good seems at *Lucca* to be the prime, the only object of
government, without the least indirect glance at either private
interest or even corporate distinction. With motives so pure, and
conduct so disinterested, the nobles are justly considered as the
fathers of the republic, and are looked up to with sentiments of
gratitude and of reverence. One of the grand features of true
republican liberty, the constant and perpetual predominance of
the law, is here peculiarly visible. It protects all without distinction,
and deprives all alike of the means of attack or annoyance; hence
the noble as well as the plebeian is disarmed, and like the Romans
of old, obliged to look not to his sword but to the law for defence
and redress; the least deviation from justice meets with prompt
and rigorous punishment.

At *Lucca*, as in England, rank is no protection; it only renders
the offence and the punishment more notorious. Hence, though
the people have much of the courage, perhaps of the fierceness, of
liberty, yet crimes and deeds of violence are rare, and the quarrels
and murders that so often occur in other cities of Italy are here
unknown; a circumstance that proves, if proofs were wanting, that
the Italians owe their vices to the negligence, the folly, and
sometimes perhaps to the wickedness of their governments.
Another vice with which the Italians are reproached (unjustly in

my opinion), idleness, and its concomitant, beggary, are banished from *Lucca* and its territory. None even among the nobles appear exorbitantly rich, but none seem poor; the taxes are light, provisions cheap, and competency is within the reach of every individual.

The territory of *Lucca* is about forty-three English miles in length and sixteen in breadth; of this territory about two-thirds are comprised in the mountains and defiles, the remainder forms the delicious plain immediately round the city. Now this little territory contains a population of about one hundred and forty thousand souls, a population far surpassing that of double the same extent in the neighbouring provinces, though under the same climate, and blest with superior fertility. The difference so honourable to *Lucca* is the result, and at the same time the elogium, of republican government. But why should I enlarge upon the liberty and the prosperity of *Lucca*? The republic of *Lucca*, like Rome and Athens, is now a name. The French cursed it with their *protection*; at their approach, Liberty vanished and Prosperity withered away. These *generous* allies *only* changed the form of government, quartered a *few* regiments on the town, obliged the inhabitants to clothe and pay them, and cried out *Viva la Republica*.

◟◞

1817

On the necessity of Italian to a Traveller

from William Rose: *Letters from the North of Italy*

From a book of letters about Italy written to the historian Henry Hallam (1777-1859). Rose (1775-1843) was a poet and translator, who lived in Italy after the Napoleonic wars and married a Venetian lady.

After having expended so much fire on the Italian language, you will perhaps be inclined to reproach me, for having omitted a

154

point very interesting to the traveller, if not to the *philologist*: to wit, whether a knowledge of this language is necessary to the tourist in Italy. As to this; I should say, that it depends upon the object of the traveller; for, if he merely goes in search of monuments of art and antiquities, he may do very well with no other language but his own; for the Italian is so quick of understanding, that a sign or a look is enough to speak your meaning: and this is not thrown out at random; for I know an instance of an Englishman who travelled over a great part of the peninsula on foot without any knowledge of Italian, or even of French: but if the traveller's views are more extensive, and embrace the study of manners, Italian is absolutely necessary.

It is to be premised, in the first place, that though French is very general in Italy, there are many cultivated Italians, who cannot speak it with fluency; and, in the next place, that those who *do*, will merely address themselves in it to *you*, while all general conversation is carried on in Italian. But the Italian who *does* speak it becomes a different person, on varying his language. This apparent change of character may be observed in England. Let us suppose a foreigner, a German, for instance, not familiar with French phraseology, to be conversing with an Englishman who *is*, in French. The Englishman, speaking of a dish which pleases him, says "it is a dish to be eat on all fours," or talks of "fatiguing a sallad," or speaking of colours, raves about "the thigh-colour of an agitated nymph." The foreigner naturally sets him down either for a beast, or a fool; whilst, on the contrary, the man is neither the one nor the other, but merely adapts himself to the idiom of the language in which he speaks. We may therefore infer from what I have stated, that, let the Italian speak French well or ill, the rational traveller's object in conversing with him is in part defeated; for if he speaks it well, his natural character is seen through a doubtful medium; if ill, it is a fatigue to figure in a duet, where both are out of tune. The second case is by far the most frequent; for languages (though he is a better linguist than the Englishman) are not usually the strong side of the Italian.

The Statue of Marble

from Joseph von Eichendorff: *The Statue of Marble*

Joseph Baron von Eichendorff (1788-1857) was one of the great German romantic poets, and friend of von Brentano and Joachim von Arnim. Many of his poems were set to music by Robert Schumann and Hugo Wolf. The Statue of Marble *deals with a young man, Florio, who comes to Lucca, falls in love with a mysterious girl who resembles an ancient statue of Venus, in the park of an equally mysterious villa. Eichendorff never set foot in Lucca, yet chose it as the model of an idealised city split between reality and dreams. Here are the opening passages:*

It was a beautiful summer evening as Florio, a young nobleman, slowly rode towards the towers of Lucca, rejoicing in the fine air which trembled over the wonderful landscape and the towers and roofs of the city before him, also in the gay features of the graceful men and women who walked up and down both sides of the street under tall chestnut trees.

Hidden musicians played from all sides from out of the flowering bushes, under the high trees demure women wandered around and let their beautiful eyes gaze on the glistening pasture, laughing and gossiping and bowing with their bright plumes in the golden evening, like a flower bed that rocks in the wind. Further on, on a bright green square, a number of girls were enjoying games with balls. The brightly feathered balls flew like butterflies, making gleaming arches here and there through the blue air, while the girls below in the green fields made the sweetest picture. One in particular struck Florio with her delicate, almost still childlike face and the gracefulness of her movements. She had a full, colourful wreath of flowers in her hair, and looked just like a merry picture of Spring, as she flew along the grass, sometimes bowing, then soon again throwing her limbs up into the air. By a mistake of her opponent her feather ball took a false turn and fluttered down just in front of Florio. He picked it up and gave it to the approaching girl with her garland. She stood before him as if shocked and looked at him silently out of her beautiful eyes. Then she blushed, nodded and hurried back to her partners.

Byron moves to Lucca after a fight in Pisa

from Byron: *Letters and Journals*

George Gordon, Lord Byron (1788-1824) travelled extensively within Tuscany, often in the company of Shelley and Leigh Hunt. Byron was living in Pisa in 1822 and had two adventures concerning Lucca. Shelley heard that a man was to be burnt alive for sacrilege in Lucca the next day, and rushed to Pisa to tell Byron. He wanted to take a party of English to Lucca to rescue the man, but Byron wanted more information. He asked his friend Count Taafe to find out more, to "try the priests – a little cash to the church might perhaps save the man yet." In the event, the man escaped to Florence. More serious was an incident between an English riding party including Byron and Shelley, which was overtaken by an Italian who rushed through the group and knocked Shelley to the ground. A servant of Byron's stabbed the Italian, who turned out to be a soldier. Byron briefly moved to Lucca from Pisa after this; here is his account of the incident.

I have lately had some anxiety, rather than trouble, about an awkward affair here; but our minister has behaved very handsomely, and the Tuscan Government as well as it is possible for such a government to behave, which is not saying much for the latter. Some other English, and Scots, and myself, had a brawl with a dragoon, who insulted one of the party, and whom we mistook for an officer, as he was medalled and well mounted, &c.; but he turned out to be a sergeant-major. He called out the guard at the gates to arrest us (we being unarmed); upon which I and another (an Italian) rode through the said guard; but they

157

succeeded in detaining others of the party. I rode to my house, and sent my secretary to give an account of the attempted and illegal arrest to the authorities, and then, without dismounting, rode back towards the gates, which are near my present mansion. Half way I met my man, vapouring away, and threatening to draw upon me (who had a cane in my hand, and no other arms). I, still believing him an officer, demanded his name and address, and gave him my hand and glove thereupon. A servant of mine thrust in between us (totally without orders), but let him go on my command. He then rode off at full speed; but about forty paces further was stabbed, and very dangerously (so as to be in peril), by some *callum bog* or other of my people (for I have some rough-handed folks about me), I need hardly say without my direction or approval. The said dragoon had been sabring our unarmed countrymen, however, at the *gate, after they were in arrest,* and held by the guards, and wounded one, Captain Hay, very severely. However, he got his paiks – having acted like an assassin, and being treated like one. *Who* wounded him, though it was done before thousands of people, they have never been able to ascertain, or prove, or even the *weapon*; some said a *pistol*, an *air-gun*, a stiletto, a sword, a lance, a pitch-fork, and what not. They have arrested and examined servants and people of all descriptions, but can make out nothing. Mr. Dawkins, our minister, assures me that no suspicion is entertained of the man who wounded him having been instigated by me, or any of the party. I enclose you copies of the depositions of those with us, and Dr. Craufurd, a canny Scot (*not* an acquaintance), who saw the latter part of the affair.

The worst possible taste

from L. Simond: *A Tour in Italy and Sicily*

We left Pisa after dinner, and traversed a most fertile country, – healthy too I understand, although low and damp; the inhabitants were good-looking, and extremely well dressed, this being Sunday. Lucca itself, like the other Tuscan towns, formerly independent, and now merged in a comparatively large State, has its frowning ramparts, its stately palaces with prison-like walls and grated windows, its historical statues and monuments of departed statesmen, warriors and patriots. The churches are ornamented in a peculiar taste, costly and fantastic, with marbles of different colours in zebra stripes or chequered, and all in the worst possible taste. A dusty walk under fine trees on the ramparts swarmed with gay company, so that here we had a glimpse of the *beau monde* of the place. The whole population, we understood, amounts to thirty thousand.

Heine changes his first, poor, impression

1828

from Heinrich Heine: *The City of Lucca*

Heinrich Heine (1797-1856) is Germany's greatest romantic poet and a brilliant essayist and travel writer. His first prose work consisted of four volumes about his travels in Germany, Italy and England. He "sang on the peaks of the Apennines" and felt his five months in Lucca and Florence were the richest in his life. This extract may refer to the Luminara on 13 September, the night when the city indeed turns into light by the thousands of candles lit in the town windows. Heine also wrote – tongue in cheek – in his Lucca book that, "There is nothing more boring in the world than reading a travel description of Italy – unless it be the writing of it itself – and the writer can only make it somewhat bearable by writing as little about Italy as possible."

It was not till night that I reached the City of Lucca. How differently it appeared to me the week before as I wandered by day through the echoing deserted streets, and imagined myself transported to one of those enchanted cities of which my nurse had so often told me. *Then* the whole city was silent as the grave; all was so pale and death-like; the gleam of the sun played on the roofs like gold-leaf on the head of a corpse; here and there from the windows of a mouldering house hung ivy tendrils like dried green tears, everywhere glimmering dreary and dismally petrifying truth. The town seemed but the ghost of a town, a spectre of stone in broad daylight. I sought long and in vain for some trace of a living being. I can only remember that before an old Palazzo lay a beggar sleeping with outstretched open hand. I also remember having seen above at the window of a blackened mouldering little house, a monk, whose red neck and plump shining pate, protruded right far from his brown gown, and near him a full-breasted stark-naked girl was visible, while below in the half-open house-door I saw entering, a little fellow in the black dress of an abbé, and who carried with both hands a mighty, full-bellied wine-flask. At the same instant there rang not far off a delicately ironic little bell, while in my memory tittered the novels of Messer Boccaccio. But these chimes could not entirely drive away the strange shudder which ran through my soul. It held me the more ironly bound since the sun lit up so warmly and brightly the uncanny buildings; and I marked well that ghosts are far more terrible when they cast aside the black mantle of night to show themselves in the clear light of day.

But what was my astonishment at the changed aspect of the city when I, eight days later, revisited Lucca. "What is that?" I cried, as innumerable lights dazzled my eyes and a stream of human beings whirled through the streets. "Has an entire race risen spectre-like from the grave to mock *life* with the maddest mummery?" The previously melancholy houses were bright with lamps, variegated carpets hung from every window, nearly hiding the crumbling grey walls, and above them peered out lovely female

160

faces, so fresh, so blooming, that I well marked that it was Life herself celebrating her bridal feast and Death who had invited the Beauty of Life as a guest. Yes, there marched behind the procession with a full accompaniment of drums and fifes, several companies of troops, besides which there was on each side near the priests in their flowing robes, grenadiers going by two and two. There were almost as many soldiers as clergy, but it requires many bayonets now-a-days to keep up religion and even when the blessing is given cannon must roar significantly in the distance.

1838
James Fenimore Cooper sees Lucca agriculture as gardening

from J.Fenimore Cooper: *Excursions in Italy*

James Fenimore Cooper (1789-1851), the American novelist, is best known for his adventure stories such as The Deerstalker, The Pathfinder *and* Last of the Mohicans. *He lived in Europe from 1826 to 1833 and published his* Excursions in Italy *in Paris in 1838.*

We were up betimes, and went forth to explore Lucca. The town stands on a plain, a mountain basin, and is walled in a semi-modern fashion. If good for nothing in the way of defence, the ramparts make an excellent promenade. We visited the churches and pictures as usual, and then took a fancy to examine the palace, a long, unornamented edifice in the heart of the place. The duke is travelling, and, pretty much as a matter of course, is out of his own dominions, which, though one of the most populous countries of Europe, possessing three hundred and thirty souls to the square mile, has not one hundred and fifty thousand people. When it is remembered that a large portion of even this small territory is mountain and nearly uninhabited gorges, you may form some notion of the manner in which the little plain itself is peopled. The town has only twenty-two thousand souls; but as we walked on the ramparts and overlooked the adjacent country, it seemed alive with peasants of both sexes, labouring in the fields. They resembled pigeons gleaning a stubble, literally forming lines of twenty or thirty, working with hoes. Indeed, the agriculture was gardening.

Lucca was a republic down to the period of the French Revolution, about which time it was given to his sister Eliza, by Napoleon, as a duchy. I believe the palace is owing to her taste, and to the expenditure of an Imperial princess. We found it Parisian in style and arrangement, and in these particulars, I thought, superior even to Windsor. Nature has fitted the French to excel in mantua-making, upholstery, and philosophy.

1839

The Idler finds Lucca *triste* and deserted

from Countess of Blessington: *The Idler in Italy*

The Idler – Marguerite Countess of Blessington (1789-1849) – was a conspicuous beauty, forced to marry a brutish soldier when she was fourteen. Luckily he died by falling from a window in the Kings Bench prison during a drunken orgy. She then married the Earl of Blessington and had a long career as a writer, editor of The Book of Beauty, *and society woman with a famous London salon. In her books she shows a sharp eye for fashion and comportment.*

Lucca is beautifully situated, and is clean; but even more *triste* and deserted than the generality of Italian towns. In the evening, however, it assumes a gayer aspect; for carriages of every form and fashion except that of our own country, are seen traversing it towards the ramparts, which is the promenade resorted to by the aristocracy of Lucca. Thither we proceeded, being assured, by our hostess, that we should be amply repaid for the trouble of our excursion by the view of the *beau monde* of Lucca. The carriages resembled those we see in old pictures, and must have been of very ancient date; the harness laden with ornaments, and the hammer-cloths as antediluvian as the carriages. These last might be heard at a considerable distance, and made more noise than any of our hackney coaches. The liveries of the servants were like those in a comedy of the olden time; but the heterogeneous addition of a chasseur in a rich uniform, stuck up behind, rendered the *tout ensemble* supremely absurd to eyes accustomed to the neat and well-appointed equipages of England. The female occupants of these carriages were dressed in the Paris fashions of three months ago; thanks to the celerity with which *"Le Petit Courrier des Dames"* voyages, conveying to remote regions *les modes nouvelles*, and enabling their inhabitants who cannot visit that emporium of fashion, Paris, to look somewhat like its fair denizens. It was curious to observe even the most elderly women dressed *à-la-mode de Paris*, seated by husbands in the costume of half a century ago; many of the latter comfortably enjoying their *siestas*, while their better-halves fluttered fans of no small dimensions, with an air not unworthy of a Spanish donna. The fan seems an indispensable *accessoire* to a lady's toilette here, and I could have fancied myself in Spain when I saw the female occupant of every carriage waving this favourite weapon, and in vehicles also which accord so well with the descriptions I have read of those to be seen on the Prado at Madrid, Cadiz, or Seville. The young girls too, with their sparkling dark eyes and olive complexions, served to make the resemblance complete; nor were they wanting in those intelligent glances cast at the smart young cavaliers, who passed by on prancing steeds, glances of which report states the ladies of Spain to be so liberal. The *beaux* of Lucca nearly all wear mustachios, and locks that wave in the air as they gallop on horses that show more bone than blood; each covered with more leather accoutrements than would be required to caparison half a dozen chargers in England.

1841

Ruskin, overwhelmed by Lucca's churches, turns to the study of architecture

from John Ruskin: *Praeterita*

John Ruskin (1819-1900) was greatly influenced by his visits to Lucca. Of San Frediano he wrote "the pure and severe arcades of finely proportioned columns at San Frediano, doing stern duty under vertical walls, as opposed to Gothic shafts with no end and buttresses with no bearing, struck me dumb with admiration and amazement." And he loved the walls: "There I have the Pisan mountains, the noble peaks of Carrara, and the Apennines towards Parma, all burning in the sunset, or purple and dark against it, and the olive wood towards Massa, and the wide, rich, viny plain towards Florence – the Apennines still loaded with snow, and purple in green sky, and the clearness of the sky here is something miraculous. No romance can be too high flown for it – it passes fable." His fascination with architecture began in Lucca, as this memory shows.

Another influence, no less forcible, and more instantly effective, was brought to bear on me by my first quiet walk through Lucca.

Hitherto, all architecture, except fairy-finished Milan had depended with me for its delight on being partly in decay. I revered the sentiment of its age, and I was accustomed to look for the signs of age in the mouldering of its traceries, and in the interstices deepening between the stones of its masonry. This looking for cranny and joint was mixed with the love of rough stones themselves and of country churches built like Westmoreland cottages.

Here in Lucca I found myself suddenly in the presence of twelfth century buildings, originally set in such balance of masonry that they could all stand without mortar; and in material so incorruptible, that after six hundred years of sunshine and rain, a lancet could not now be put between their joints.

Absolutely for the first time I now saw what mediaeval builders were, and what they meant. I took the simplest of all façades for

164

analysis, that of Santa Maria Foris-Portam, and thereon literally *began* the study of architecture.

~~~~~

1844

Dickens is appalled by brutality in the Carrara marble quarries

from Charles Dickens: *Pictures from Italy*

Charles Dickens (1812-1870) was an exceptional travel writer as well as novelist, as seen in his American Notes *and* Pictures from Italy. *He is known to have been in Bagni di Lucca and must have visited the city as well. The scree from centuries of marble extraction lies on the mountains of Carrara and can be seen from many miles away, looking like snow. You can visit the quarries, now mechanised, and carry away pieces of marble as pure as those worked by Michelangelo. Dickens wasn't always so squeamish; the next year he queued for seven hours in Rome to see a robber guillotined.*

The Magra safely crossed in the Ferry Boat – the passage is not by any means agreeable, when the current is swollen and strong – we arrived at Carrara, within a few hours. In good time next morning, we got some ponies, and went out to see the marble quarries.

They are four or five great glens, running up into a range of lofty hills, until they can run no longer, and are stopped by being abruptly strangled by Nature. The quarries, or "caves", as they call them there, are so many openings, high up in the hills, on either side of these passes, where they blast and excavate for marble; which may turn out good or bad: may make a man's fortune very quickly, or ruin him by the great expense of working what is worth nothing. Some of these caves were opened by the ancient Romans, and remain as they left them to this hour. Many others are being worked at this moment; others are to be begun to-morrow, next week, next month; others are unbought, unthought of; and marble enough for more ages than have passed since the place was resorted to, lies hidden everywhere: patiently awaiting its time of discovery.

As you toil and clamber up one of these steep gorges (having left your pony soddening his girths in water, a mile or two lower down) you hear, every now and then, echoing among the hills, in a low tone, more silent than the previous silence, a melancholy warning bugle, – a signal to the miners to withdraw. Then, there is a thundering, and echoing from hill to hill, and perhaps a splashing up of great fragments of rock into the air; and on you toil again until some other bugle sounds, in a new direction, and you stop directly, lest you should come within the range of the new explosion.

There were numbers of men, working high up in these hills – on the sides – clearing away, and sending down the broken masses of stone and earth, to make way for the blocks of marble that had been discovered. As these came rolling down from unseen hands into the narrow valley, I could not help thinking of the deep glen (just the same sort of glen) where the Roc left Sinbad the Sailor; and where the merchants from the heights above, flung down great pieces of meat for the diamonds to stick to. There were no eagles here, to darken the sun in their swoop, and pounce upon them; but it was as wild and fierce as if there had been hundreds.

But the road, the road down which the marble comes, however immense the blocks! The genius of the country, and the spirit of its institutions, pave that road: repair it, watch it, keep it going! Conceive a channel of water running over a rocky bed, beset with great heaps of stone of all shapes and sizes, winding down the middle of this valley; and *that* being the road – because it was the road five hundred years ago! Imagine the clumsy carts of five hundred years ago, being used to this hour, and drawn, as they used to be, five hundred years ago, by oxen, whose ancestors were worn to death five hundred years ago, as their unhappy descendants are now, in twelve months, by the suffering and agony of this cruel work! Two pair, four pair, ten pair, twenty pair, to one block, according to its size; down it must come, this way. In their struggling from stone to stone, with their enormous loads behind them, they die frequently upon the spot; and not they alone; for their passionate drivers, sometimes tumbling down in their energy,

166

are crushed to death beneath the wheels. But it was good five hundred years ago, and it must be good now: and a railroad down one of these steeps (the easiest thing in the world) would be flat blasphemy.

When we stood aside, to see one of these cars drawn by only a pair of oxen (for it had but one small block of marble on it), coming down, I hailed, in my heart, the man who sat upon the heavy yoke, to keep it on the neck of the poor beasts – and who faced backwards: not before him – as the very Devil of true despotism. He had a great rod in his hand, with an iron point; and when they could plough and force their way through the loose bed of the torrent no longer, and came to a stop, he poked it into their bodies, beat it on their heads, screwed it round and round in their nostrils, got them on a yard or two, in the madness of intense pain; repeated all these persuasions, with increased intensity of purpose, when they stopped again; got them on, once more; forced and goaded them to an abrupter point of the descent; and when their writhing and smarting, and the weight behind them, bore them plunging down the precipice in a cloud of scattered water, whirled his rod above his head, and gave a great whoop and hallo, as if he had achieved something, and had no idea that they might shake him off, and blindly mash his brains upon the road, in the noontide of his triumph.

1845

The guillotine falls for the last time in Italy

from Rodolfo del Beccaro: *Lucca: History and Legends*

The 29th of July 1845 was a grey day, despite the summer season. A fitting setting for the event that was about to take place. Shortly after 8 a.m. the silence of the town was interrupted by the rhythmic drums of Carlo Ludovico's Bourbon militia and from many churches could immediately be heard "the stroke for the death throes". The door of the San Giorgio prison opened to allow five convicts to emerge. Accompanied by priests and by the Brothers of Charity, they moved towards the field of San Donato, where the platform of the guillotine had been erected, with units of the army drawn up in squares around it. Within ten minutes, five bodies dropped down below the scaffold and five heads rolled into a basket, while at the Porta San Donato "castle" a clerk of the Tribunal recorded in writing that the executions had taken place. There was great commotion, with fainting fits among the crowd, many of whom had come from the countryside, from Pescia and from Pisa.

These were the last capital executions to be carried out by the guillotine in Lucca, and indeed in the whole of Italy. The five executed men belonged to the "band of the seven thieves", and had terrorised the Lucca countryside.

In 1841 and 1842 there had been night-time raids in various parish residences (Vorno, Badia di Cantignano, Castagnori, and so on) with the theft of money and precious objects. These had been violent and impious thefts, accompanied by cruel tortures: under the eyes of a parish priest, bound to a chair, his housekeeper had been forced to sit on the hot stones used for baking chestnut flour.

Perhaps the band was also going to "pay a visit" to the rectory of the old parish church of Santa Maria del Guidice, if, as testified by an old epigraph, the priest, Don Lorenzo Michelotti, died on the 31st of March 1846 "of a bilious fever brought on by frequent iniquitous fear".

The government of Duke Carlo Ludovico unleashed teams of soldiers and policemen, and even operated with spies. For a whole year the investigations produced no result, then the chief of police won. With a promise of impunity one of the members of the band, a certain Filippo Francesoni of Vorno, was lured into revealing the names of his companions, who were staying at various locations. Between August and September 1842 seven members of the band were arrested and taken to Lucca prison. They were Giuseppe Alessandri, 47, nicknamed "caromèo" or "càbala", from Colognora di Valeriano; Giovanni Nardi, son of Luigi, 34, a carpenter of Cocciglia called the "rough abbot"; Demetrio Prosperi di Francesco, 35, of the rich and respected Monti di Villa family living at "Rioli"; Fabiano Bartolomei, 40, called "Faina" (weasel) or the son of "Meo cattivo" or "the American", also from Monte di Villa; Pietro Giuliani, son of Lorenzo, 46, nicknamed "Quere" or "Buèro", a native of Ponte San Pietro but residing in Livorno; Natale Giusti, son of Vincenzo, 43, painter and decorator, living in Lucca; and Francesco Prosperi, 70, father of Demetrio, from Monti di Villa. Tommaso Bartolomeo, 70, born at Monti di Villa, nicknamed "Barbanera" (Blackbeard) and also "Il vecchio della montagna" (The old man of the mountain) escaped arrest.

As from the night before the execution, a large crowd congregated in Lucca. People on foot, in carriages or carts – so many that "the stables and liveries couldn't cope". The cafés, hotels and trattorias were full. The roads were crowded with people, curious and excited. The executioner was called from Parma, because the Lucca executioner, Tommaso Jona, was over 70 years old. (He was displeased by his substitution.) At 7.30 a.m. on the 29th of July the Parma executioner, who had his three sons as assistants, took his place on the scaffold. At five o'clock the condemned men left the prison. With bitter irony Giuseppe Alessandro, known as "càbala", asked: "Are we all ready?", thinking perhaps of the only one pardoned, or the informer, the one who was absent, the old man who had been acquitted. He went straight to the guillotine, followed by Bartolomei, Nardi, Prosperi, and Giuliani.

In 1847 the blade of the guillotine was taken by the populace to Viareggio and thrown into the sea. The scaffold was burned on the glacis of the city walls.

Picnicking on the Torre Guinigi

170

Food and Wine

It hardly seems worth mentioning that the authentic Lucca diet is extremely frugal and traditional. Let's just say that the people of Lucca are consistent, even when they're cooking and eating. Everything they love to have on the table comes from the local countryside – "home made" bread and pasta, *farro* (spelt), chestnut flour, fish, frogs and eels from the Serchio, oil and wine from the hills and mushrooms. These are the things that Puccini ate and drank beside Lake Massaciuccoli or in Celle, that the Romans ate in their houses on the other side of Madam Butterfly's lake or in the forum in Lucca.

Far, in ancient Latin, means "family", and the etymology should be enough to indicate the importance of *farro*, forgotten and all but unknown to most people until about twenty years ago. Before then, it wasn't much grown but it was still to be found in a few little fields in the Garfagnana and, without fuss or fame, it left to travel the world with the emigrants. All the plaster figurine makers, the men who made ice cream, the miners and the fish and chip fryers went to Genoa to board the steamer for the Americas with a bag containing a handful of their native soil and some grains of *farro*. *Farro* was introduced into Lucca by the Romans for whom it was both basic and sacred. Their marriage ceremony, for example, was called the *confarratio*, and consisted of the bridal couple eating a piece of *farro* bread together.

First in France and then in the Garfagnana, the rediscovery of old food (or at least those kinds which had survived) gave new life to *farro*. *Farro* is a hard, "dressed" cereal which means that the outer layer is left on the grain (as it is on barley), and it was possibly introduced into Italy from Palestine or Mesopotamia. It was first of all revived as a gourmet soup to be found only in certain restaurants, and then it went from being quite popular to becoming the theme of food festivals and almost a national dish, though universally acknowledged to be Lucchese. Now we have fashionable *farro* presented in any number of ways, from *hors d'oeuvres* to dessert, cultivated once more on a large scale and so highly selected in the Lucca area that it has a kind of DOC rating.

Many of the plants at the base of the Mediterranean diet were imported and most of them, like *farro*, came from the Middle East.

The chestnut, for example, which was the chief source of food in the Garfagnana, came from Turkey. Up till the end of the Second World War, chestnuts – fresh, roasted, dried in traditional huts, boiled or ground into flour and put to innumerable uses – provided basic food for the people who lived on the mountains all over Italy, and the chestnut tree was therefore called the bread tree. They were eaten as polenta, pancakes, roasted, cooked in milk or wine, boiled with their skins on, made into pasta or turned into *marrons glacé*s. Virgil, Galen the doctor and Columella the great connoisseur wrote about chestnuts.

It was history, trade and man's achievements which created landscape like the countryside of Lucca, where "the vine entwines with the olive", with the chestnut tree and, not so very long ago, the mulberry. In the Maremma there are olive trees which date back more than 2,000 years to the first trees introduced by the Greeks. The trees around Lucca are not so old, but the hills which stretch to Florence and Pisa and almost as far as the coldest parts of the Garfagnana, gleam with silver leaves, a sign of the gold to come.

If Lucca is synonymous with oil, so also is Bertolli, the most important local producer – though nowadays, of course, the raw material comes from all over the world. Bertolli was a good Lucca business man and, as soon as he had made his fortune, opened a bank, as the silk traders did. He is remembered, however, for the richness of his oil which could claim to be the best in the world.

The story of Lucca wine is rather different. There are many people who have a high opinion of it but it also has some detractors. The Romans, for example, who were connoisseurs of wine, mention the *Lunense* from Liguria and some wines from Florence but have nothing to say about our local wine. The DOC wines, however, speak for themselves. Since 1968, these have included the red and white wines from the Lucca hills, produced in the Capannori, Lucca and Porcari areas, and recommended as table wines. The most famous Montecarlo belongs to the following year. (Daniele Vanni)

The medieval peasant diet

The Roman products described by Daniele have been harvested, raised and eaten ever since. An eighth century scribe, Rixolf, described the diet of a Lucca peasant of his day as a loaf of bread, a quarter amphora of wine, a quarter amphora of stew made from beans, flour and oil, and occasionally a little meat. This is not a million miles away from the standard fare you find in Lucca's trattorie. The Lucchesi, like other Tuscans, carry the name "beaneater" (mangiafagioli) and still eat rather sparingly. Pablo Picasso was in Lucca after World War II and might have been expected to comment on its food, even its art and churches, but he is recorded as saying only that he particularly liked the rock candy.

1805
Peter Beckford wishes the Lucca government made better bread

from Peter Beckford: *Familiar letters from Italy*

Peter Beckford (1740-1811) was an eminent sportsman and master of foxhounds, and the first English writer to describe accurately the sport of hunting. A great linguist, he would, according to the Dictionary of National Biography, "bag a fox in Greek, find a hare in Latin, inspect his hounds in Italian and direct the economy of his stables in exquisite French".

Lucca is the capital of a little Republic, containing, at most, one hundred and twenty-five thousand people, who, by extraordinary good fortune, have preserved their liberties in the midst of despotism. Here POMPEY, CAESAR, and CRASSUS met to settle some differences of their own, and formed that plan which afterwards overset the liberties of Rome. Another remarkable circumstance attends this Republic: – not less than two hundred years have elapsed since it saw the face of an enemy. VOLTAIRE, therefore had good reason to say: "Sa Foiblesse la garde; et Lucque est plus tranquille que Dresde, et que Berlin" [Its weakness protects it; and Lucca is more peaceful than Dresden or Berlin].

Surrounded by mountains which, during the winter months are covered with snow, the climate of Lucca is considerably colder than that of Pisa. The soil is good, and well cultivated, but the produce of wheat is not equal to the consumption. As a remedy to this defect, the ovens are all in the hands of Government. Three years provision is kept constantly in store; and bread is sold nearly at the same price all the year round. A monopoly like this is good policy. The gain, if there be any, thus becomes of more general advantage; and the loss, when it happens, is not felt by the public. I wish, by the bye, their Excellencies were better bakers.

... Forty Anziani are chosen; but their turns of service are determined afterwards by lot: nor does any one of them know who is to be his successor till he is chosen. A ridiculous circumstance happened at the last election. An English gentleman, with whom I was in company, newly arrived from India, fell by accident into the procession of the electors, without knowing what they were going about; and seeing those who were before him put their hands into a box, he fancied it was the poor-box, and, had he not been prevented, would have put in a paul. This mistake occasioned some confusion. Luckily it was attributed to its right cause, and laughed at exceedingly.

A Podestà, and four Auditors, try all causes, civil and criminal: they must be foreigners. Forty Sbirri [cops] patrole the streets every night; and two men on the tower of the palace are constantly on the watch, to give an alarm in case of fire; – an excellent regulation, and no where so much wanted as in London. Punishment is more frequent here than in Tuscany. Criminals are sent to the galleys at Venice for eight or ten years, from whence they seldom return.

The revenue of the Republic is small, so are its expences. The former does not exceed one hundred and ten thousand sequins, and yet is more than equal to the expenditure.

We read, that in the year 1314, Lucca alone enjoyed the lucrative monopoly of silk; it was afterwards spread by degrees all over Europe. Silk and oil still form the principal part of her commerce. From the oil alone the Lucchese are said to receive one hundred and fifty thousand sequins annually; a produce that makes ample amends for the twenty thousand sequins they are supposed to lay out in wheat. Silk, linen cloth, wax, and glass, are the chief manufactures. The markets are well supplied, and the veal is famous. The Noblesse are polite and courteous to strangers; Jews only excepted, who are suffered to remain in the town three days only. The Lucchese always wear black, men and women: it gives a gloomy cast to every assembly, and many an ordinary-looking gentleman may be taken for an undertaker. Swords are not allowed to be worn, except by officers. The clocks go *"all' Italiana"*: they also strike every quarter of an hour; a circumstance particularly unpleasant to those who do not understand them.

... The Lucchese are better husbandmen than the Pisans. The very opinion that they are free, renders them industrious. Their hay is excellent: – they spread it as soon as it is cut; and for my own use, I would prefer one load of Lucca hay to all that the Grand Duke has. In this country when their hay is dry, they carry it, though it be on a Sunday. The common people in England would think it the height of impiety were they called from the alehouse on such an occasion.

c. 1820

A Georgian trade card

Peck's Italian Warehouse
No. 175 Strand
LONDON

AMBROSE PECK'S TEA
GROCERY & FOREIGN FRUIT WAREHOUSE
OILS, PICKLES &c.

Lucca Oil – Vegetable Essences – Parmesan Cheese
Mushroom Ketchup – Indian Soy – Cavioe – Covatch

175

Espagnole Sauce – Quin Sauce – Complete Boxes of Rich Fish
Sauces
Sauce Piquant – Sauce Royal – Harvey's Sauce – Cherokee
Sauce
Walnut Ketchup – Essence Anchovies – Lemon Pickle
Wax and Sperm: Soaps, Candles – Starch & Blues – Curry
Powders
Capers – Olives – Vinegar – Pickles – Basket Salt – Salt Petre
Salt Prunella

Isinglass – Vermacelli – Lemon & Peel – Muscatells
French Prunelle – Turkey Figs – Almonds – Morells – Alspice
Ginger – Cinamon – Nutmeg – Mace – Sugars – Pepers
Cocoa Shells – Preserv'd Ginger – Tamarinds – Curious Teas
H[arts] H[orn] Shavings – Arrow Root – Sage & Sage Powder
Macaroni – Tapioca – Truffles – Pistatia Nutts – Prune du Roy
Prune de la Reine – Imperials – Best chocolate – Portugal
Plumbs – Various Honeys – Dry Fruits – Brandy Fruits
Kyan Pepper

1840

A Victorian recipe

from Lady Holland: *Memoir of the Rev. Sydney Smith*

The Rev. Sydney Smith (1791-1845) devised this for Elizabeth, Lady Holland.

SALAD DRESSING

Two boiled potatoes passed through kitchen sieve,
Softness and smoothness to the salad give.
Of mordant mustard add a single spoon,

Distrust the condiment that bites too soon
Yet deem it not, thou man of taste, a fault
To add a double quantity of salt –
Four times the spoon with oil of Lucca crown
And twice, with vinegar procured from Town;
The flavour needs it, and your poet begs
The pounded yellow of two well boiled eggs;
Let onion atoms lurk within the bowl
And, scarce suspected, animate the whole;
And, lastly, in the flavoured compound toss
A magic soupçon of anchovy sauce.
Oh, green and glorious! Oh, herbaceous treat!
'Twould tempt the dying anchorite to eat.
Back to the world he'd turn his fleeting soul,
And plunge his fingers in the salad-bowl.
Serenely full, the epicure would say,
Fate cannot harm me, I have dined today.

1887

Pressing the olives

from Janet Ross: *Italian Sketches*

In the centre was an immense stone basin, in which revolved a solid millstone about five feet in diameter, technically called, I believe, an edge-runner, turned by a splendid white ox, which, to our astonishment, was not blindfolded. Our host told us that it was difficult to get oxen to do this work; it takes time and patience to accustom them to it. The millstone was set up on edge and rolled round in the stone basin, secured to a big column of wood which reached to the ceiling. The whole machine was most old-fashioned and clumsy, and the *padrone* said, laughing, was evidently as old as Noah's ark. Into the stone basin, as clean as a dairymaid's pan, five sacks of olives were emptied, which, in a short time, were

177

reduced to a mass of dark greenish-brown thick pulp. Stones and all were mashed without any noise, save the occasional lowing of the ox when his tasselled and ornamented nose-bag was empty. When Bencino judged that the olives were sufficiently crushed, the pulp was taken out from the mill, with clean new wooden shovels, and put into a circular shallow basket with a large hole through the middle, made of thick cord fabricated from rushes grown in the Pisan marshes, and looking very much like open cocoanut matting. As fast as these *gabbie*, or cages, as they are called, were filled, they were carried by two men, on a handbarrow with long handles at each end, to the press in the corner of the room, and piled with the greatest exactitude one on the top of the other under the press. Then began the hard work. Two huge posts clamped with iron support a colossal beam, through which goes the screw, finishing below in a large square block of wood with two square holes right through it.

Into one of these Carlo stuck a long beam, on the end of which he hooked a rope, which was secured round a turning pillar of wood, about six or eight feet distant, with a handle against which the men threw their whole weight. With many groans and squeaks the big block of wood revolved to the right until the rope was all twisted round the pillar, when it was unhooked, the beam lifted out of its hole in the block, and carried on Carlo's stalwart shoulder to be inserted into the hole further back, the rope untwisted, and again hooked round the end of the beam, and so on until not a drop more could be extracted. The press was then screwed back, and the *gabbie* carried on the handbarrow to the mill, where they were emptied, and their contents again ground for some time; the *gabbie* were then filled anew, and put under the press for the second time, when a great deal more oil came dripping out, but of inferior quality. The refuse that remains, called *sansa di olive*, is almost black, and quite dry and gritty. This is sold for threepence or fourpence a *bigoncia* full, about fifty-five pounds in weight, to some people in the Val di Greve, who buy up the *sansa* from all the country round. They wash it in the running water of the Greve, when the pulp and the skin of the olive floats on the surface, and the crushed stones sink. With large, flat, pierced, wooden ladles the pulp and skins are skimmed off the water and boiled in immense cauldrons previous to being again put under the press.

178

About ten per cent of oil is thus extracted, but of very inferior quality, called *olio lavato*, or washed oil. This is chiefly used in Italy for making soap, but a good deal is exported. It has a nasty, sweet, sickly taste, entirely wanting the aromatic flavour so much prized in the good oil. But to return to the press. At its foot is a large marble underground receptacle, into which the oil ran. This was carefully covered with a hinged, wooden lid to prevent any dust or dirt from falling in. Bencino lifted up the lid and showed us the stream of oil falling into a clean wooden *tinello* or small vat.

Olives contain two-thirds of water and one-third of oil, and for some time it came dripping clear and bright like amber; but when the *gabbie* had been squeezed and squashed down to about half their original size, and the press was screwed back, and the big block of wood raised to admit large heavy rounds of wood, which were screwed down tight again on the pulp, it was more mixed with dirty-yellow water, and had lost its golden tint.

The oil naturally floats on the top of the water, and Carlo Bencino was busily engaged in skimming it delicately off with a big tin scoop. He poured it through a funnel into a clean wooden *barile* (a small barrel with narrow ends, held together by large, flat, wooden hoops, and holding about thirty-six quarts); and when this was full he shouldered it and carried it off to the *chiaritojo*, or oil-clearing room, where the *barile* is emptied into a large *conca*, a terra-cotta vase like an immense flowerpot, well glazed inside. This room was, like everything else, scrupulously clean, and paved with red bricks sloping towards the middle, where there was another underground marble receptacle, in case of an accident, such as the breaking of a *conca*. The temperature is kept as equable as possible, and in cold winter weather a brazier is lighted at night. Nothing spoils the look, though not the flavour, of oil so much as getting frozen; it becomes thick, and seldom quite regains its golden limpidity, even when treated by people who thoroughly understand it.

For fifteen or twenty days it is left to clear in these *conche*, when the thicker or second quality sinks, and the clear, brilliant, yellow oil is carefully put into *barile* and sent down in the ox-cart to the *fattoria*, where it is emptied into tall, well-glazed terra-cotta jars. These are kept in a dark room, with a southern exposure, protected from any violent changes of temperature by a fire during the cold weather.

Ten or twelve *barili* of oil can be pressed in a day, and as all the other *contadini* of the *fattoria* bring their olives and those of the *padrone* up to the press at Bencino's, this process goes on for some time when the crop is abundant. It is hard work, and must be done with cleanliness and nicety. At first our host had some difficulty in getting the *contadini* to see that it was of importance to separate the bruised from the fresh-picked fruit, and to keep the press and implements clean. They thought it was only a whim, which they obeyed, partly from a sense of duty, but chiefly because the *padrone* is extremely beloved by his tenantry.

1902

Picnicking on Torre Guinigi

from Katharine Hooker: *Wayfarers in Italy*

But to return to our entrance into Lucca this particular evening. It was somewhat late to carry out a cherished plan which we had formed long before, so that we lingered not on the way, whatever the temptation, but hastened to the quiet street where the Albergo Croce di Malta stands. We were pleased with its inviting aspect and its quaint rooms. Our own ran along the front of the second story, but differed in level, so that we mounted two or three steps to one and descended as many to another. Besides this there were odd recesses and corners which suggested the remodeling and contriving of an old building, and a curious little boudoir adjoining might have been a chapel now reduced to worldlier uses. After a quick survey we hastened to the carrying out of our plan, which was neither more nor less than to take supper by sunset on the summit of the highest tower in Lucca.

The delectable nature of such a project had occurred to us upon a former visit and had remained with us in the form of a pleasant air-castle thereafter. The tempting peculiarity of this tower was that it bore upon its summit, like a fairy hanging-garden, a tiny grove, provoking curiosity as to how it could sustain life aloft there, exposed to winter storms and the heat that in late summer is said to be intense. Besides, had not Mr. Howells talked of this tower in that book dearest to the heart of Italian travelers, "Tuscan Cities"? Though even he had not enjoyed the bliss we proposed to experience. There was also another precious association. We liked to think that Ilaria had sometimes climbed it, for it was the tower of the Guinigi, of which family her husband was once the head. At first it was somewhat difficult to make our host assimilate the idea that even English-speaking *forestieri* could seriously intend to do anything so unheard of and unreasonable. The head waiter joined our conference – the fattest man in Italy, of a vast bulk that he seemed yet to bear without self-consciousness – but in the end we separated with a promise of cold roast fowls and accompanying viands to be prepared while we meanwhile flew to ascertain whether the powers in authority would yield to our desires. Anyway we drove to the foot of the Palazzo Guinigi, to the very trunk of the tower. The portal was open, the entrance hall empty and silent. We could find no one on that floor.

Across the narrow slit of a street upon which the palace fronted we saw a friendly-looking shoemaker glancing from his tiny shop, a sort of swallow's nest in the wall, and we stepped across to appeal to him. Upon the partition just over his head a notice was fastened which instantly caught the eye: "*Qui non si bestemmia.*" "No swearing allowed here." He was a cobbler of character. We felt protected and reassured at once and explained our difficulty. He displayed a sympathetic interest and nodded his head comprehendingly. The thing might be done. The key, however, was in the hands of the tenants who occupied the highest floor. We sent a long look upward. It was many a flight of stairs to where the tower sprang above the roof. But we began the ascent forthwith. The staircase was massive, well lighted and with broad landings, as befitted the life that once went on there. Up and up we toiled, stopping now and then as the views from successive stories gave us wider and wider prospects, till at last we stood directly under the roof and before the door belonging to the highest apartment. In response to a knock the door opened and a small, bent old woman stood within. To her we submissively imparted our wishes, while she surveyed us as we thought benignantly nor seemed to regard our request with disdainful surprise. She agreed to ask her mistress and courteously invited us to enter while she did so.

If the expedition had been productive of nothing more than the impression the glimpse of this interior gave us, it would have been far from barren in result. We were ushered through an inner passageway into a *salon* with windows looking out from the opposite side of the building. It would be hard to express the peace and aloofness that breathed from this quiet room, with its outlook as from the elevation of a hill-top, all sound of life coming from afar in a subdued murmur, the tranquil valley far beyond the confines of the city wall spread out below. Within, silence, order, a spareness of furnishing and absence of trifling ornament unusual in a place of its class. The principal object in the room was a grand piano drawn in convenient proximity to the light from the open window. Almost an air of asceticism pervaded the place, and yet this instrument with its open keyboard softened all and set one dreaming of long, sweet, leisurely contemplative hours, of tones of Baldassare Galuppi drawn from these yellowed ivories, of strains of Monteverdi and Pergolesi that a listener might catch floating downward in the night air.

Strange to say, for one moment we had a glimpse of a second figure, small, bent and old like the first, which paused an instant in gliding by the doorway to another room. Was it the mistress? If so, did she live here alone? And who, then, touched the keys of this piano, which somehow had the look of use? After a little the old servant returned and brought with her permission to occupy the tower as long as we liked, upon which we hastened away to finish our preparations.

We returned to the hotel for our supper and found the employees of the inn in a group at the door with the hampers, including all necessary dishes, admirably packed, and a servant ready to mount the seat with the coachman and go with us to carry them up. An air of animation and amusement now pervaded the company, for they had evidently arrived at the conclusion that our proceedings were to be regarded humorously. Next in order it was necessary to find a shop where *bucellato*, the specialty of Lucca, was kept, for we wished our feast to have every local element possible. I will admit that we experienced some disappointment in regard to *bucellato*, which is a sweet-cake of unyielding hardness and highly charged with anise. Arrived again at the roof of the Guinigi Palace, the old servant came smilingly forth with a key in her hand and conducting us to a big door, which she unlocked, showed us the beginning of the flights of stairs still to be mounted before reaching our goal. We toiled up and at last through a trap-door came out upon the leafy summit of our tower.

And what shall I say of this realization of our anticipations? It was all and more than we had dreamed it. There we stood as though suspended in the air, far above the roofs of the town, while on every side spread the lovely valley from which rose wooded hills dotted with villas. Beyond all, mountain walls closed in the prospect and away in the direction from which we have come rose Monte San Guiliano, *"perchè i Pisan Lucca veder non ponno."* The hour was perfect; not a breeze rustled the leaves over our heads and the sun, dipping to the horizon, bathed all in the glorifying light that just precedes sunset. Neither was there any disillusionment about our Babylonish garden. The stout little trees were rooted in an abundant amount of soil which had been conveyed to the roof and there disposed in deep beds, between and around which next the parapet was ample room to walk and sit. Two of the trees were ilex, and on measuring we found the trunk of one to be thirty-five inches in circumference. Here, then, we spent an hour or two of such happiness as brings wonder, thankfulness, joy and I know not how many other emotions in a tumult to the heart and fills one with rapture at the heavenly beauty of the earth, while it leaves behind what haunts the memory forever.

Mussolini cries in the tobacco factory

LUCCA AFTER UNIFICATION WITH TUSCANY

c. 1850

A Lear Lucca Limerick

Edward Lear (1812-88)

There was a young lady of Lucca,
Whose lovers completely forsook her;
She ran up a tree
And said Fiddle-dee-dee
Which embarrassed the people of Lucca.

1853

Fra Bartolommeo in his glory

from George Stillman Hillard: *Six Months in Italy*

The situation of Lucca, in the lap of an amphitheatre of hills, is very pleasant; and the walk upon the ramparts is one of the finest promenades in Europe. There is a noble aqueduct, of four hundred and fifty-nine arches, which makes a most picturesque feature in the landscape. The weather was beautiful, the outlines of the neighbouring hills were rounded into the finest curves, and the level plain near at hand, under the most careful cultivation, was revelling in the vivid yellow-green of spring. The whole population seemed to be out of doors. The women wear a graceful head-dress – a sort of handkerchief trimmed with lace, and disposed with much taste. A walk under the arches of the aqueduct was a most agreeable refreshment after all the sight-seeing of the previous hours. I left Lucca at a quarter before five, and reached

Leghorn at half-past six. I noticed that the locomotive on the railway was of Philadelphia manufacture – a small dividend contributed in the shape of the useful arts by the New World towards paying off that great debt of gratitude which all mankind owes to Italy for what it has done in the fine arts.

The brief excursion to Lucca was a most agreeable experience, and, as I have begun to give advice, let me say that this neat and beautifully situated town should at least have a day devoted to it. The view of the glorious company of hills that stand round about it, as seen from the ramparts, is alone worth coming up from Leghorn to look at. The statues and bas-reliefs of Civitali – an artist whose works are hardly to be found anywhere else – have a character and expression of their own, and mark a distinct period in the history of sculpture. And, above all, that great artist Fra Bartolommeo is in his glory at Lucca; and no one who has not been there can have any adequate conception of the power and grandeur of his genius. The impression his works made upon me is, I admit, not quite borne out by the rank assigned to him by writers upon art; but my recollections, which are most distinct, confirm the testimony of records made upon the spot. To me his reputation seems below his merits; and I cannot but think that it would have been higher if the admirable works which adorn a provincial capital like Lucca had found a place of deposit in the Pitti Palace or the Vatican, where every traveller could have seen them, and every writer could have praised them. I know not what heights of art he might not have reached under more favourable circumstances of development, or with a character of firmer tone. Had he been a braver and heartier spirit, and mingled freely in the shocks of life, instead of running and hiding his head in a monastery at the first blast of danger, and thus added variety, invention, and dramatic power to his other gifts, he might have rivalled every name but Raphael's. But it is much better, so far as the interest of travelling in Italy is concerned, that all the good pictures should not be in one place, but that they must be sought in many separate localities. It is agreeable to know that you can judge of certain painters only by going to certain spots. It establishes a relation between an artist and the place where he lived or wrought, which throws over his works a grace like the flavour which wine has, to the mind's taste at least, when drunk on the soil of its growth. Titian, for instance, must be seen at Venice; Correggio, at Parma; Luini, at Milan; Perugino, at Perugia; Fra Bartolommeo, at Lucca; Guido and the Carraccis, at Bologna.

A tourist hears of the death of Lincoln

from Elizabeth Tuckett: Beaten Tracks

Lucca, Hotel de l'Univers: April 27.

We drove to the station at Pisa at three o'clock, noticing, as we left the hotel, a letter from Garibaldi to our host, framed and ornamented, and placed in a conspicuous position on the staircase. It was an acknowledgment of the kindness and attention shown to him when passing through Pisa on his way to Spezzia, after the Aspromonte campaign.

A French paper, bought at the station, contained the sad news of the death of the Czarewitch, and in another column was the fearful and startling telegram announcing the assassination of poor Mr Lincoln. It seems too terrible to be really true, and we are almost hoping there may be some mistake, as there are no particulars, nothing beyond the bare fact that the President is dead, and Mr Seward not likely to recover.

It is only an hour's railway journey from Pisa to this place, where we are comfortably established in a good hotel, and have a pretty sitting-room and an enormous bedroom for E. and me, so large that we shall hardly be able to make ourselves heard across it, with a smaller one beyond for my father. We are, I believe, the only guests, and they have therefore no table d'hôte, though we were shown the *salle à manger*, a curious, low room, round no end of corners and down dim passages and stairs, winding away, I imagine, behind other people's houses, and looking out on a square some distance from the front of the hotel.

We walked at once to the Cathedral, which is full of interest. Amongst the paintings that delighted us the most, were a Virgin and Child with Saints, by Fra Bartolommeo, the same subject by Ghirlandaio, and a beautiful picture by Bronzino, of the Presentation of the Virgin in the Temple, wonderfully rich in colouring, and life-like in the expression of some of the faces. The Altar of Liberty by John of Bologna, is also very beautiful, and interesting as an historical memorial, having been erected by the Lucchesi to celebrate the recovery of their freedom, and consecrated to Christ the Deliverer. It is in white marble, with three figures: those of Our Saviour, St. Peter, and St. Paul. From the Duomo we walked to the Church of San Romano, where a snuffy, fat old *custode* showed us a magnificent painting, by Fra Bartolommeo, called the Madonna della Misericordia, and representing the Virgin interceding for the people of Lucca during the Florentine wars.

After examining the rest of the church, we returned to the hotel for dinner; spending part of the evening in strolling on the ramparts which surround the town, and are planted with trees, making a pleasant shady walk, though not a popular one apparently, as it was quite deserted, whilst the hot dusty square, or Piazza Ducale, in front of the great Ducal palace, was crowded with citizens of all classes, listening to some occasional music from a band stationed below the monument to the Duchess Maria Louisa of Lucca, which was erected in token of the gratitude of the city for the abundant supply of water furnished by the aqueduct, which she caused to be built. The lights and shadows amongst the trees were very pretty, but we are glad to finish our evening quietly in-doors after our busy and interesting day.

... I must leave this letter to E. to finish, so good night!

Lucca: April 28.

I cannot tell you how delighted we are with the churches; the great cathedrals are so wonderfully beautiful; and I can understand now the charm of the black and white marble, which is toned down by the rich gilding and painting, and the coloured glass; and the lines are not staring, as at Genoa, but rather two rich shades of grey, broken up, too, by exquisite tracery, and arch and columns of every size and form; the variety and richness of the wonderful mixture of architecture is quite bewildering. The outside of the buildings at Pisa and Lucca is beautiful; such deep, soft colouring, marked by centuries that have passed over the old marble! The cathedral at Genoa was striped all over, like a bournous; I am sorry if it should be vandalism to say it is unmitigatedly ugly; at all events, in our vague gropings after the beautiful, we have never reached such an ideal.

... It is very interesting to see the different traces of the political feeling of the people, the inscriptions everywhere on the walls, in gilt letters on public buildings, the number of the votes for the king, and over and over again, on houses, in streets and villages, "Vittore Emmanuele nostro Re," and "Abbasso il Papa Re," "Rome for the capital," &c.

We went to San Romano again before breakfast this morning, losing our way completely in the puzzling narrow streets, and wandering away so far that we had to apply to a sweet-faced *contadina*, who guided us back to the great square, parting from us with a stately bend of her gracious head, and a low-voiced "Bon giorno, signorine!"

1874

Henry James sees a small *pays de Cocagne*

from Henry James: *Italian Hours*

The American writer Henry James (1843-1916) himself exemplified a certain type of rich nineteenth century expatriate, many examples of whom appear in his works. He first visited Italy in 1866. Cocagne (Cockaigne) is an imaginary country, a medieval Utopia where life was a continual round of luxurious idleness.

Nothing could be more charming than the country between

Pisa and Lucca – unless possibly the country between Lucca and Pistoia. If Pisa is dead Tuscany, Lucca is Tuscany still living and enjoying, desiring and intending. The town is a charming mixture of antique "character" and modern inconsequence; and not only the town, but the country – the blooming romantic country which you admire from the famous promenade on the city-wall. The wall is of superbly solid and intensely "toned" brickwork and of extraordinary breadth, and its summit, planted with goodly trees and swelling here and there into bastions and outworks and little open gardens, surrounds the city with a circular lounging-place of a splendid dignity. This well-kept, shady, ivy-grown rampart reminded me of certain mossy corners of England; but it looks away to a prospect of more than English loveliness – a broad green plain where the summer yields a double crop of grain, and a circle of bright blue mountains speckled with high-hung convents and profiled castles and nestling villas, and traversed by valleys of a deeper and duskier blue. In one of the deepest and shadiest of these recesses one of the most "sympathetic" of small watering-places is hidden away yet awhile longer from easy invasion – the Baths to which Lucca has lent its name. Lucca is pre-eminently a city of churches; ecclesiastical architecture being indeed the only one of the arts to which it seems to have given attention. There are curious bits of domestic architecture, but no great palaces, and no importunate frequency of pictures. The Cathedral, however, sums up the merits of its companions and is a singularly noble and interesting church. Its peculiar boast is a wonderful inlaid front, on which horses and hounds and hunted beasts are lavishly figured in black marble over a white ground. What I chiefly appreciated in the grey solemnity of the nave and transepts was the superb effect of certain second-story Gothic arches – those which rest on the pavement being Lombard. These arches are delicate and slender, like those of the cloister at Pisa, and they play their part in the dusky upper air with real sublimity.

... To Lucca I was not to return often – I was to return only once; when that compact and admirable little city, the very model of the small *pays de Cocagne*, overflowing with everything that makes for ease, for plenty, for beauty, for interest and good example, renewed for me, in the highest degree, its genial and robust appearance. The perfection of this renewal must indeed have been, at bottom, the ground of my rather hanging back from possible excess of acquaintance – with the instinct that so right and rich and rounded a little impression had better be left than endangered. I remember positively saying to myself the second time that no brown-and-gold Tuscan city, even, could *be* as happy as Lucca looked – save always, exactly, Lucca; so that, on the chance of any shade of human illusion in the case, I wouldn't as a brooding analyst, go within fifty miles of it again.

... Lucca seems fairly to laugh for good-humour, and it's as if one can't say more for her than that, thanks to her putting forward for you a temperament somehow still richer than her heritage, you forgive her at every turn her fortune. She smiles up at you her greeting as you dip into her wide lap, out of which you may select almost any rare morsel whatever. Looking back at my own choice indeed I see it must have suffered a certain embarrassment – that of the sense of too many things; for I scarce remember choosing at all, any more than I recall having had to go hungry. I turned into all the churches – taking care, however, to pause before one of them, though before which I now irrecoverably forget, for verification of Ruskin's so characteristically magnified rapture over the high and rather narrow and obscure hunting-frieze on its front – and in the Cathedral paid my respects at every turn to the greatest of Lucchesi, Matteo Civitale, wisest, sanest, homeliest, kindest of *quattro-cento* sculptors, to whose works the Duomo serves almost as a museum.

1886

Howells recalls the old ducal state

from William D. Howells: *Tuscan Cities*

Another American writer, William Howells, was part of a lively group based in Florence, which included Charles Eliot Norton, the sculptors Thomas Bole, Hiram Powers and Joel Hart, and the

Kentucky painter Frank Duveneck. Howells wrote a number of books about Italy; his illustrator was Joseph Pennell who travelled with him, drawing along the way and sketching in the fields. Pennell also illustrated James' Italian Hours. *The Croce di Malta was a hostelry much used by foreign visitors, located on the via Vittorio Emanuele near the corner of via Burlamacchi. The Hotel Universo still exists.*

Lucca lies as flat as Pisa, but in shape it is as regularly oblong as that is square, and instead of the brick wall, which we had grown fond of there and in Siena, it has a girdle of gray stone, deeply moated without, and broadly levelled on top, where a lovely driveway winds round the ancient town. The wall juts in a score of angles, and the projecting spaces thus formed are planted with groups of forest trees, lofty and old, and giving a charm to the promenade exquisitely wild and rare.

To our approach, the clustering city towers and roofs promised a picturesqueness which she kept in her own fashion when we drove in through her gates, and were set down, after a dramatic rattling and banging through her streets, at the door of the Universo, or the Croce di Malta, – I do not really remember which hotel it was. But I remember very well the whole domestic force of the inn seemed to be concentrated in the distracted servant who gave us our rooms, and was landlord, porter, accountant, waiter, and chambermaid all in one. It was an inn apparently very little tainted by tourist custom, and Lucca is certainly one of the less discovered of the Tuscan cities. At the *table d'hôte* in the evening our commensals were all Italians except an ancient English couple, who had lived so long in that region that they had rubbed off everything English but their speech. I wondered a good deal who they could be; they spoke conservatively – the foreigners are always conservative in Italy – of the good old ducal days of Lucca, when she had her own mild little despot, and they were now going to the Baths of Lucca to place themselves for the summer. They were types of a class which is numerous all over the continent, and which seems thoroughly content with expatriation. The Europeanized American is always apologetic; he says that America is best, and he pretends that he is going back there, but the continentalized Englishman has apparently no intention of repatriating himself. He has said to me

192

frankly in one instance that England was beastly. But I own I should not like to have said it to him.

In their talk of the ducal past of Lucca these English people struck again the note which my first impression of Lucca had sounded. Lucca was a sort of republic for nearly a thousand years, with less interruption from lords, bishops, and foreign dominions than most of her sister commonwealths, and she kept her ancient liberties down to the time of the French revolution – four hundred years longer than Pisa, and two hundred and fifty years longer than Florence and Siena; as long, in fact, as Venice, which she resembled in an arbitrary change effected from a democratic to an aristocratic constitution at the moment when the change was necessary to her existence as an independent state. The duchy of Lucca created by the Congress of Vienna, 1817, and assigned to the Bourbons of Parma, lasted only thirty years, when it was merged by previous agreement in the grand duchy of Tuscany, the Bourbons going back to Parma, in which Napoleon's Austrian widow had meantime enjoyed a life interest. In this brief period, however, the old republican city assumed so completely the character of a little principality, that in spite of the usual Via Garibaldi and Corso Vittorio Emanuele, I could not banish the image of the ducal state from my mind. Yet I should be at a loss how to impart this feeling to every one, or to say why a vast dusty square, planted with pollarded sycamores, and a huge, ugly palace with but a fairish gallery of pictures, fronting upon the dust and sycamores, should have been so expressive of a ducal residence. There was a statue of Maria Louisa, the first ruler of the temporary duchy, in the midst of these sycamores, and I had a persistent whimsey of her reviewing her little ducal army there, as I sat and looked out from the open door of the restaurant where my friend and I were making the acquaintance of a number of strange dishes and trying our best to be friends with the Lucchese conception of a beefsteak.

We did, however, see one Lucchese palace throughout, the Palazzo Mansi, in which there is an admirable gallery of Dutch pictures inherited by the late marquis through a Dutch marriage made by one of his ancestors. The portrait of this lady, a gay, exuberant, eighteenth-century blonde, ornaments the wall of one of the gilded and tapestried rooms which form two sides of the palace court. From a third, standing in an arcaded passage, you look across this court, gray with the stone of which the edifice is built, to a rich brown mass of tiled roofs, and receive a perfect impression of the pride and state in which life was lived in the old days in Lucca. It is a palace in the classic taste; it is excellent in its way, and it expresses as no other sort of edifice can the splendors of an aristocracy, after it has ceased to be feudal and barbaric, and become elegant and municipal. What laced coats and bag-wigs, what hoops and feathers had not alighted from gilt coaches and sedan-chairs in that silent and empty court! I am glad to be plebeian and American, a citizen of this enormous democracy, but if I were strictly cross-examined, would I not like also to be a Lord of the Little Ring in Lucca, a marquis, and a Mansi?

c. 1890

J.P. Morgan under his Lucca Renaissance ceiling

from Stanley Jackson: *J.P. Morgan: the rise and fall of a banker*

John Pierpont Morgan (1837-1913), after amassing one of the great American fortunes, spent much of his later life collecting treasures in Europe, including three copies of the Gutenberg Bible. He was the leading American financier after the Civil War, helping to put together such giants as U.S. Steel. He built a mansion and library in New York to hold his books and paintings, and put a Lucca ceiling in the latter.

Morgan could enter the marble palace by a stone walk that went from his house across a green lawn. Massive bronze doors imported from Italy opened into the lofty, vaulted entrance hall gracefully sectioned by greenish cipollino columns. The vast octagonal skylight was fringed by paintings of the Muses. The library itself was divided between an East and West Room. The former was of "double-cube" design and was elegantly furnished

194

in the Florentine style and adorned with magnificent statuary. Its lofty walls surmounted by medallion portraits were tiered by Circassian walnut shelves glowing with volumes bound in gold, enamel, and ivory. Several of them were gem encrusted. Lapis lazuli columns framed the monumental fireplace.

The West or Red Room was the banker's special retreat; it served as a study and on occasion a salon where he received friends, business associates, and a few privileged art dealers or bibliophiles. Its walls of crimson damask from the Chigi Palace in Rome, embellished by that aristocratic family's crest, set off masterpieces from the hands of Raphael, Perugino, and Botticelli. Among the bookshelves stood a bust by Michelangelo and a rock crystal bowl mounted for Queen Christina. The gilded sixteenth century ceiling from a cardinal's palace in Lucca was complemented by a fireplace of carved marble surmounted by his father's portrait removed from the house next door.

Here he could lounge in a red plush armchair, smoking or playing solitaire at his folding table. Beyond the door was a huge vault with its priceless cache of treasures, including a five-page letter in Washington's hand, four Shakespeare Folios, and a seventy-two page volume of Leonardo's notebooks. At his large square-topped desk he faced a Fra Filippo Lippi altarpiece, with a Pinturicchio Madonna and Child behind him. He could turn to gaze on the bejeweled Ashburnham Bible in its crystal showcase; a bronze statuette of Eros unearthed near Pompeii; and a special favorite of his, a ruby-colored vase of the K'ang Hsi period.

1901

The most fly-in-amber little town in the world

from Hilaire Belloc: *The Path to Rome*

For all my early start, the intolerable heat had again taken the ascendant before I had fairly entered the plain. Then, it being yet but morning, I entered from the north the town of Lucca, which is the neatest, the regularest, the exactest, the most fly-in-amber little town in the world, with its uncrowded streets, its absurd fortifications, and its contented silent houses – all like a family at ease and at rest under its high sun. It is as sharp and trim as its own map, and that map is as clear as a geometrical problem. Everything in Lucca is good.

I went with a short shadow, creeping when I could on the eastern side of the street to save the sunlight; then I came to the main square, and immediately on my left was the Albergo di Something-or-other, a fine great hotel, but most unfortunately right facing the blazing sky. I had to stop outside it to count my money. I counted it wrong and entered. There I saw the master, who talked French.

"Can you in an hour," said I, "give me a meal to my order, then a bed, though it is early day?" This absurd question I made less absurd by explaining to him my purpose. How I was walking to Rome, and how, being northern, I was unaccustomed to such heat; how, therefore, I had missed sleep, and would find it necessary in future to walk mainly by night. For I had now determined to fill the last few marches up in darkness, and to sleep out the strong hours of the sun.

All this he understood; I ordered such a meal as men give to beloved friends returned from wars. I ordered a wine I had known long ago in the valley of the Saone in the old time of peace before ever the Greek came to the land. While they cooked it I went to their cool and splendid cathedral to follow a late Mass. Then I came home and ate their admirable food and drank the wine which the Burgundians had trodden upon the hills of gold so many years before. They showed me a regal kind of a room where a bed with great hangings invited repose.

All my days of marching, the dirty inns, the forests, the nights abroad, the cold, the mists, the sleeplessness, the faintness, the dust, the dazzling sun, the Apennines – all my days came over me, and there fell on me a peaceful weight, as his two hundred years fell upon Charlemagne in the tower of Saragossa when the battle was done, after he had curbed the valley of Ebro and christened Bramimonde.

So I slept deeply all day long; and, outside, the glare made a

196

silence upon the closed shutters, save that little insects darted in the outer air.

1901

Piety, probity, frugality

from Montgomery Carmichael: *In Tuscany*

Lucca is a curiously recondite city. It abounds in treasures and surprises, but few of them are patent. You must live there a long time, and be patient and very courteous, if you would fathom its secrets. Gradually you will become aware that there is matter of interest hidden away in the old town abundant enough to last a lifetime; gradually the full fascination of this unique place grows upon you; with difficulty you tear yourself away from it and go back to the rough, jostling, immoderate and unmeasured life of the world outside, but never do you succeed in rooting out of your heart the sweet ennobling memories of this most favoured spot of God's earth. And perhaps the warmest corner of all in your heart will be reserved for the Lucchesi themselves. What a people! What a nation! Piety, probity, frugality, the quality of honest pride born of long independence under wise, just and free government – perfect skill in manufactures and agriculture, idiosyncratic, unparagoned, the growth of illustrious and sane traditions – all these characteristics of their national individuality still survive in the Lucchesi, and have not yet given way before the automatic uniformity that has too mercilessly been adopted by the modern unity. Heine – the semi-pagan Heinrich Heine – has luminously described the Lucchese territory in a single sentence of two solitary words. *Nirgends Philistergesichter*, he says: nowhere may you see the face of a Philistine.

Lucca at the beginning of the twentieth century

from Evelyn Underhill: *Shrines and Cities of France and Italy*

Evelyn Underhill was 29 in 1904 when she travelled through France and Italy, complementing her diary with sketches of churches and ancient buildings.

Lucca is like her patron-saint, a serving maid in grey and brown. Temperate and discreet she sits enclosed by her tree-ey walls, which hold her from the magic of the hills that guard her and have no part in her, and prevent the dissipation of her gently industrious life.

In Lucca one should always be about forty years old, with a prudent but not cynical outlook. The tone of the city is of an unostentatious activity; of a life in which to do plenty of work. It is not for nothing that her architecture combines the staid and orderly basilica nave with the straight arrowy towers of the Romanesque and crowns them with Ghibelline turrets – the sign of an excellent conservatism.

Without the dreaming magic of Verona and the terrible memories of Ravenna, Lucca is a very trustworthy town. One is not surprised that Dante found her more kindly than many of his resting-places, though it is to be doubted whether she understood him very well. The temperament that converts the awful soil of a Roman amphitheatre into an excellent vegetable market will scarcely bring a sympathetic imagination to the reading of the Divine Comedy. A careful and comely people, however; and a clean small city of white streets and churches of brown and grey. Such pictures as it possesses are exotic and were better away: Fra Bartolomeo and his kind have no place in so calm and reasonable an atmosphere.

Maurel sees a sad relic

from André Maurel: *Little Cities of Italy*

Happy Pisa! Miserable as was her later condition, she at least had won an earlier glory that left her immortal. Life was not given to her entirely unsweetened. Although she perished from the effects of her mad arrogance, boundless avidity, and political aberration, at least she knew how to profit by her early days. Her infancy was fruitful and perpetuates her memory. As faulty as her neighbour, she is forgiven because she was beautiful for an hour.

Pisa is one's first thought upon reaching Lucca and mounting to the top of the ramparts for a view of the entire city.

When the Lombards invaded fruitful Tuscany, they were so charmed by the beauty and wide command of this site that they chose Lucca for their residence. There is no place more pleasing. Between the Apennines and the Pisan Mountains, which spread their fertile sides under her eyes, Lucca, seated on the banks of the Serchio, seems like a proud matron who rests her old age in the sweetness and peace of a fresh and silent country.

But the city herself never smiles, she who formerly was always scolding. She is, however, calm and silent now, and, having stripped off all the military accoutrements that used to bedeck her, she has knotted about her loins a green sash. Her ramparts are crowned with foliage, and from their shade she watches the play of colours across the fertile plain and the pleasant mountain.

... There was a time when she took the lead in Tuscany. Under the Lombards; under the ephemeral kings, Lucca was the capital of this province. She was the haughty and powerful queen until the devout Matilda abandoned her for Mantua.

... For a space of more than three centuries Lucca pursued a fleeting mirage, the reconquering of her royal dominion. She lived in a continual daze of jealous ferocity. Indifferent to aught but herself, ignoring the most sacred principles of life, each day she abjured that which she had done the day before, now allying herself with Florence, now with Siena, now with the Pope, now with the Emperor, now even with Pisa, doing nothing but in the hope of regaining her crown. She lost all conscience and deserved what

Dante said of the city, "there every man is a rogue; for money, they make no of yes." She besmirched herself, became a prostitute with the fury of a noble girl who throws herself into the gutter because she has been violated by a brute.

She was possessed in turn by the most notorious bandits, who after having seated her for some days beside them upon their bloody thrones, cast her back again into the mud. At length, she could not even say to whom she would give herself. Radiant as her poor body had been, she could no longer choose the mud in which she would roll. She was sold like a slave. Three times the tyrants from across the mountains bartered her for money; and, finally, ravaged and withered, she suffered the depths of shame in seeing herself offered to Florence by Mastino della Scala, and hearing Florence answer, "Keep her!"

c. 1914

A friend of Puccini's is ordained

from Dante del Fiorentino: Immortal Bohemian: an intimate
memoir of the life of G. Puccini

Dante del Fiorentino, born 1889, was a young seminarian who saw the accident to Puccini's car in 1903, and became a lifelong friend. He once was the canon in Torre del Lago where Puccini had his principal villa.

The time came for me to be ordained into the priesthood. The long years of preparation and meditation behind the seminary walls came to an end shortly before the outbreak of the war: henceforward I would be granted the power to say Mass and forgive sins in the name of God.

The ordination took place in the cathedral of San Martino in Lucca where for centuries the Puccinis, Giacomo included, had played the majestic organ which hangs over a huge balcony.

200

Trembling I entered the chancel with the other candidates for ordination. I was dressed in a flowing white linen robe. The Bishop pronounced the words, "Are they worthy?" Then we heard the Archdeacon saying we were worthy enough according to his frail knowledge. I lay motionless in the chancel, stretched out on the stones, chanting the litanies. Then I walked to the Bishop who placed the stole over my right shoulder and invested me with the chasuble and anointed my hands. When the ceremonies were over the Bishop demanded a final pledge of obedience, "Will you promise me and my successors reverence and obedience?" Loudly and dramatically we answered, "I do."

We did not know that an age was passing. We saw the old faces of our friends and relatives, men like Don Antonio who had grown feeble with years, for he was past seventy. We must have guessed that the orderly ways of the past would never return. It was Don Antonio who offered to play the organ when I celebrated my first Mass in my parish church of San Michele in Quiesa. I eagerly accepted the offer of the old man whose eyes came blazing to life only when he spoke of music.

That day the church was crowded. As I entered the chancel and approached the altar a quartet was singing an *Ecce Sacerdos*, which had been scribbled on a sheet of ordinary paper by Giacomo Puccini. The organ came to life. Out of that ancient and wheezing instrument there came such a flood of jubilant chords and arpeggios, such diapasons, crescendos and *mancandos* that the statue of San Rocco with a dog at his feet carved by the sculptor Zizzania seemed to smile benignly. Never had the church resounded with such exultant pleading and exultation from the *vox humana*, never had the deep *bourdon* groaned and roared with such heavy accents of warning and pain, and never had the *tuba mirabilis* set up such a sound of trumpeting, so that the old walls began to shake. And then again, when the Mass was over and I had given my blessing to the kneeling throng, what a joyous *tintinnare* resounded from the organ loft. Don Antonio played as though he was young again, with a *saltarella* of skipping notes so gay and summery that the heads of the worshippers were lifted up in broad smiles.

Puccini goes to Brussels (to die)

from Dante del Fiorentino: *Immortal Bohemian: an intimate memoir of the life of G. Puccini*

Puccini suffered from throat cancer after a lifetime of heavy smoking. He went to Brussels to be operated upon and treated with radium needles, but died after the operation.

I remember the last day he spent in Viareggio. It was twilight, and the people were going down to the beach to watch the ceremony of sunset. A breeze stirred the palms along the promenade. The bells of San Paolino, Sant' Andrea, and San Francesco filled the perfumed air: the scent of the flowers, the scent of the pine-groves. The small boats were gliding past the lighthouse far out at sea. The Café Schicchi was bustling with life. Pea, Vianni, Nomellini, Magrini – they were all waiting for the maestro, but Giacomo was in his villa with Toscanini. He was playing *Turandot* on the piano. He looked desperately ill. At the end of the first act he called to Elvira to bring him coffee, then he sipped the black liquid gratefully and went on playing.

"Here Turandot sings," Giacomo said excitedly, and then turned to Tonio, "Put a cigarette between my lips."

Tonio lit a cigarette and put it between his father's lips. Giacomo went on playing. Toscanini was following the score. Giacomo was looking up edgewise to see the expression on the conductor's face. There were tears in Toscanini's eyes. Giacomo winked at me and whispered, "Eh, boy, do you see that? This music must be good if it makes *testa piccina* (tiny head) cry."

One by one the lights in the villa went out. The little group, which had gathered together to hear the first reading of *Turandot*, rode through the night to the railway station, moving in darkness like mourners at a funeral. Only Elvira, at the doctor's orders, remained behind. We were going to put Giacomo on the Rome-

Paris express. Tonio joined his father in the train. Giacomo lowered a window of the *wagon-lit* and leaned out, saying his farewells to the group standing forlornly on the platform. His last words were to Toscanini: "Arturo, if anything happens to me, do not abandon my dear beautiful princess, my *Turandot* – "

Then he withdrew hastily: the excitement had brought on a hemorrhage of the throat.

The train began to move away, the wheels turning with a sobbing rhythm. Someone remarked that Verdi had been inspired by the movement of train-wheels to compose the accompaniment of the *"Miserere"* in *Il Trovatore*.

Miserere di un anima già vicina alla partenza che non ha ritorno.
Pity the soul which is nearing the place whence there is no return.

1924

and senses it

a poem by Puccini

Non ho un amico
mi sento solo,
anche la musica
triste mi fa.
Quando la morte,
verrà a trovarmi
sarò felice di riposarmi

I have no friend,
And I feel alone:
Even my music
Fills me with melancholy.
And when death comes
I shall be happy
To take my rest.

1924

Ringing the bells of San Frediano

from Ada Harrison and R.S. Austin: *Some Tuscan Cities*

When I had walked round all the city on the ramparts, I thought I had seen and admired every shred of the beauty of the environs; but I was woefully wrong. Loitering one afternoon at the back of S. Frediano, I saw an elderly man, accompanied by a sturdy boy and a hopping, chattering crowd of urchins, opening a tiny door in the back of the tower preparatory to climbing up to ring a peal of bells. He was most willing for me to follow him, so up we all went in a file on the steep staircase. At the top was a view indeed! For the single circle of hills seen from the ramparts was a triple and quadruple ring, gloriously sharp in the afternoon sunlight, and backed everywhere against the blue horizon by a snow-mountain of thick white cloud. Instead of the single avenue of chestnuts, were patches and plantations of young autumn trees dotted in all directions on the plain, with the red roofs of outlying villages seeming to crouch in the feathery mist of twigs; and instead of a level view of houses, there was spread below the pattern of the whole red-roofed city, with all her lovely towers picked out against the sky.

Inside the belfry were about eight bells, two very big, and the rest dwindling down to a size manageable by the smallest of the amateur sacristans. In a few moments coats were thrown off, hands spat upon, ropes unloosed, and the two greatest bells slowly set in motion, the old man and the sturdy boy doing the pulling, and the urchins making frantic tugs and dashes at the ropes, and yelling at each other like people who well knew (and what a calamity for an Italian!) that they were soon to be shouted down. Wider and wider swung the slow bells, until at last first one and then the other of the great iron tongues clanged against the side, the belfry was filled with a tumult at once crazy and deep, and the tower rocked. Seldom have I felt such exhilaration as then, standing in the swaying tower almost battered by the iron music, with the huge bells flung backwards and forwards against that bright background of hills, and the man, the boy and all the urchins straining like mad things on the ropes.

When the time came for the deafening peal to end, the boy, like Bessie in our curfew story, jumped and swung for a second on the tongue of his bell, and brought the great bass monster to a standstill. Then he took the rope from the old man, who was practising, but unsuccessfully, a different method, and with a throw lassooed the tongue of his bell into silence. Next we all sat down on the stonework in an exhausted way, and gradually, by gazing at the leashed bells overhead, I drove the aftermath of that terrific clangour from my ears. Two and two, throughout an hour, while the colours changed and darkened the hills, the lesser bells had their say. I stayed up there till all had sung in turn, and even the smallest and most restless of the sacristans was weary; then, when the hills were showing iron hard against the saffron and yellow of the sunset, I came slowly down to Lucca and to earth.

1926

Arnold Bennett tries to cash a cheque

from Arnold Bennett: *Journals*

Arnold Bennett (1867-1931), English writer, visited Lucca in February 1926, finding it "very fine and distinctive ... a rich town, prosperous, clean, self-contained and self-sufficient". This tale of cashing a cheque in an Italian bank is not so far from what visitors experience today.

Italy. – An English bank is inhuman or godlike. Its attitude towards ordinary customers implies that it is conferring a favour upon them by doing business with them at all and that they ought to consider themselves a fortunate lot. It cannot or will not recognize that it is a mere shop for the sale of monetary facilities, and that there are rival shops. That it exists for the convenience of its customers, and not vice versa, is an idea which apparently seldom occurs to them.

Now French and Italian banks are human. They are very human. I have done plenty of business with French and Italian banks. Yesterday I went into a typical large branch of an Italian bank; and everything happened according to precedent. Italian banks close from 12 to 2. Such a system would not work in England, but it works smoothly enough in both Italy and France. At ten minutes past two the numerous staff comes strolling casually in from its lunch, smoking cigarettes. Italian bank-clerks seem to be unable to do business without tobacco. And why should they do business without tobacco? Tobacco is humanizing. Their manners are exquisite; their charm is notable.

At the first guess I went to the right counter, behind which some half-a-dozen clerks were more or less busy in a cubicle. I presented a cheque – not a foreign cheque, but one of the Bank's own cheques. I furnished evidence of identity. I was most urbanely received. The entire half-dozen young males showed a friendly interest in me. Then I said: "I want this money in English sterling."

"*Sterlina!*" exclaimed the youth attending to me, astounded. "Ah! We must go upstairs."

He escorted me upstairs to another and vaster room. He telephoned to the cashier downstairs: "Have we fifty pounds in sterling?" A pause. The clerk smiled. Yes, the Bank had in its coffers fifty pounds in sterling. then began the filling up of forms, with carbon duplicates. A tremendous affair. My full name, the name of my father, my permanent domicile, where I had come from, where I was staying. Then I started to endorse the cheque, which required two separate signatures. With perfect tact, the clerk stopped me.

"Excuse me," said he. "The signature on the front of the cheque ought to have been written before you came into the Bank."

"But I will sign it in your presence," said I.

"Ah, sir! We have our rules." Then followed a long palaver among the staff.

"I must consult the Director," said he.

206

He departed to consult the Director, who presently arrived to see me. The manners of the director were marvellous: a lesson to all Britons. They were comparable to those of the late Lord Chaplin, whose social deportment I have never seen equalled – in England. The Director agreed with me that I might perform the first signature in the Bank itself, and left me with an enchanting bow and smile. Then the second signature. Then more forms which had to be signed. The clerks were in constant consultation as to procedure.

"Now we will go down to the cashier," said my special clerk. "I will accompany you."

We descended to the cashier. A third signature was demanded. In all, I wrote twelve signatures. But I got the sterling. I also got humaneness, charm, and courtesy. Also my affair had engaged the attention of eleven clerks and the supreme Director. At the close everybody appeared to be very pleased and relieved. On everybody's face was an indication that a miracle had been accomplished. I myself felt that a miracle had been accomplished. True, it had taken thirty-three minutes: but a miracle it was. I went forth into the hot blinding sunshine of nearly three o'clock. All this happened in an illustrious city where tourists are as common as flies; and in my view it was quite as interesting as any of the city's storied monuments.

1930

Mussolini cries in the tobacco factory

from Dino Grilli: *I Lucchesi di una Volta*

An exceptional visit in the Fascist period – which caused great confusion in the state tobacco monopoly in via Vittorio – was that of Mussolini, accompanied by the Lucca authorities. Preparations for his visit took many days, until everything was ready on the day of the visit: the "little tobaccists", as they were

207

called, who wore white caps covering their tresses (always obligatory to avoid any hair falling into the tobacco, a damnable thing for smokers) gathered round. The Toscani were praised by the Duce, some caressed... the youngest and prettiest... Then he stopped in front of their new machines which spit out thousands of white Nazionale cigarettes. Il Duce was particularly interested in the preparation of the "toscana" cigar, which had gained a good market, including in Africa; the "leader" wanted to look into all the steps and this curiosity turned into a truly unexpected event, almost... Historic! On the ground floor there were (and I think they are still in existence) the great fermentation pits for the dried tobacco leaves, necessary for a period of "decay". Even though they tried to dissuade him, Mussolini wanted to know how this preparatory stage worked, and went up to one of the pits, which he himself had asked to uncover. All Hell broke loose. A great stench of air impregnated with the maximum possible nicotine overcame Mussolini and those around him.

Throats were irritated, noses ran and – what was worse – eyes began to burn and flood with tears. Coughing, crying and sneezing, the group dashed to the fountain in the courtyard, but it took a long time and a lot of water before Mussolini's eyes stopped disgorging great tears of nicotine.

If you had to design a memorial plaque to commemorate the visit of Mussolini to Lucca, you could write:

When visiting this place, cradle
of exhausting labour of Lucca women
in the years of his reign
il Duce of Fascism wept copious tears
perhaps a presentiment of his tragic end.

A place where life isn't an enemy

from Charles Morgan: *Sparkenbroke*

In the 1936 novel set in Lucca, Lord Sparkenbroke, an English poet, rents a palazzo there; this passage is a dialogue between him and the woman he loves, whom he is about to take to Lucca for the first time.

"And tell me about Lucca. Do you live there alone?"

"Bisset and Italian servants."

"Is there a garden?"

"Between the house and the city ramparts. But it isn't exciting in November. The ramparts themselves will be your garden. I told you of them once, but you have forgotten. A great avenue, raised up, surrounding the whole town, with the roofs and towers inside the circle, and outside, the country and the hills. But they may be dead for you."

"It's odd," she said, "I had imagined Lucca as a hill-town. Is it in a valley after all?"

"In a plain," he answered, and began to tell her how, five years ago, he had gone to Lucca for the first time, driving over from Pisa by chance, for Lucca, having few treasures, was a place little visited except by those who had business there. He had gone again and again.

"But what was it," she asked, "that made you love it?"

If it had been a liking, an admiration or interest, that she had asked him to explain, he might have answered easily, but the word she had chosen was the right one, and to explain a love so personal and intuitive – it was the "feel" of the place, he replied, its ancient smallness, the green enclosure of its trees, its grave, unchanging, cloistered welcome. It was *il riso santo* of Lucca, he exclaimed, like the smile of Dante's Beatrice; an evidence that, within these walls, it was possible to be at once thoughtful and happy.

"But tomorrow," he added, "you will be there. I shall tell you no more about Lucca. You mustn't go there expecting marvels. I have known people – not fools either – say it was disappointing: there was nothing to see – a dull, provincial town without a great school of art of its own, even in the Renaissance. But for me it's a place where life isn't an enemy."

1940s

War Stories

Any Lucchese over sixty will remember the Second World War, and many have fascinating personal experiences to tell. I asked a few friends to tell their remembrances, which are given below.

From Bruno Vanni of Fornaci di Barga

The stories I am about to relate to you refer to the time when my wife Enrica and I were adolescents: episodes of our youth, memories of a far off, unforgettable time, interesting and dramatic, starting from the pre-war Fascist period.

As everyone knows, in the pre-war years, Edda, the Duce's daughter, her husband Count Galeazzo Ciano and their children were accustomed to move from Rome to their country villa at Ponte a Moriano. From there it was their habit to go to the little spa town of Bagni di Lucca for the medicinal baths and to stay in the Albergo Corona. Bagni di Lucca has been famous since the early 1800s and has attracted many Italian and foreign visitors, principally English, who made it their favourite residence. It had a casino and a place for receptions and dances: the renowned Circolo dei Forestieri, a luxurious rendezvous.

Well, the youths now in advanced age who are recounting their adventures remember an evening when they went dancing at that Circolo taking with them for amusement one Pietro, a tiny fellow hardly bigger than a dwarf. When they came into the salon of the Circolo, they saw that among the many people waiting for the dancing to begin was Edda Mussolini Ciano, standing out in her long dress of light blue silk with a rose at her breast. No-one dared to open the ball before her and all waited for the orchestra

210

to strike up. Pietro, egged on by his crafty friends, plucked up the courage to ask the daughter of the Duce to dance, which she accepted with grace. Imagine the miniscule fellow entwined with the tall, noble Edda; it was all the audience could do to keep themselves from laughing. At the end of the dance Pietro returned to his friends, who asked, "But what have you done? Don't you know that she is the daughter of the Duce?" At those words Pietro, taken aback and confused, went up to the lady, begging pardon for his boldness. She replied, "I am very flattered that you opened the dancing with me, and I thank you sincerely".

This is one of many interesting episodes of the Fascist period, but later we in Barga and the Garfagnana unfortunately were caught up in the middle of the war with the Linea Gotica – the massive defensive line in our neighbourhood set up by the Germans under Marshall Kesselring to stop the advancing Allied forces.

I remember that in September 1943 three English airplanes – the famous Spitfires – arrived over us from the chain of Apennine hills near Abetone to strafe targets in our area. Sadly for them, the fighter flown by Major Joe Spencer was hit by German fire; with smoke pouring from the plane's tail the pilot sought for a place to land. Over Ghivizzano he saw a level field of hemp near the Serchio and tried to land. After he touched down, his Spitfire crashed into a tree, losing a wing with the impact and was all but demolished. To the onlookers who rushed up, the condition of the pilot seemed desperate. He constantly called out in English, "Doctor, doctor," but none of the poor bumpkins knew a word of English. He was taken to the medical room of the metal factory in Fornaci di Barga, but even their loving care couldn't save his life.

Another incident on 10 October 1943 showed again the ignorance of airplanes on the part of the people in our valley. On that morning a large formation of American planes came overhead from various directions. They flew at a height of 5,000-6,000 metres, where the air is ice cold; white streams like smoke came out of the planes. The people below were terrified, screaming, "The planes are getting ready to bomb us! Flee, flee!" But nothing fell from the sky. Many years later we learned that those white lines across the sky were nothing but a phenomenon coming from the hot exhaust of the motor when it hit the cold air at great height.

What the advancing Allies would be like, or do to us, we also didn't know. Little more than a year later, on 5 October 1944, Brazilian troops, part of the Allied forces, came into our town at four in the afternoon. My wife, Enrica, then a young girl, saw seven soldiers arriving; since they were all black and none of the kids had ever seen anything but a white face, they all ran away screaming, locking themselves in behind closed doors. But the Brazilians proved themselves to be humane and religious people, who exhibited real friendship to the local people (and were also very greedy for chestnuts, then in season).

Finally the Americans arrived. "Viva la grande America!" For us this was the end of fear, privation and hunger, because the Yankees brought well-being with them. We began to know chewing gum, Camel and Lucky Strike cigarettes, Lux soap, little cans of preserved food, beautiful clothes, hats and shirts, turkey with beans and many other things we had never seen before. Thank you, America!

From Franco Talini, who was a partisan himself in the mountains above Lucca

This story was told to me by an old shepherd many years after the war when the main characters had died and could no longer refute the shepherd's story. The doctor's house was located at the entrance of a mountain village, where the mule track began to climb for five or six kilometres towards the ridge of the mountain. Then it sharply descended towards the village where the Germans still held out in a precarious position. From above, a group of partisans followed their every movement, with their couriers, to maintain control along the side that faced from the white marble Apuan mountains to the pine green seacoast. One dark night in March a young partisan who knew the terrain well was sent to fetch the doctor. One of his comrades had a high fever; his right arm was swollen and black with infection: they had no medicine and his condition was desperate. For the young partisan the foray was dangerous, because the doctor was also the village secretary for the Fascists. He gathered up courage, knocked and told everything to the man, who listened in silence. Then he moved away. The boy was afraid that he would be given up to the Germans and their mission discovered. After a little while, the doctor returned, muffled in a huge cloak with a small bag hidden under its folds. In silence they covered the distance of the narrow mule track. At the camp the doctor carefully examined the patient, gave a few precise instructions to those around and, with what he had available, cut out the deep abscess that had turned septic. All this in silence. Then, leaving some medicine for fever and antiseptics, and without accepting the words of thanks, he departed. The men were relieved about their friend's good treatment but their eyes showed fear of exposure and reprisal. Days passed, the patient improved and nothing adverse happened, as they had feared. They never knew that at dawn's first light, at the last curve before his house, the doctor bumped into Giuseppe the shepherd, who was climbing to graze his little flock. They greeted one another without stopping, but the mind of the shepherd buzzed, speculating about where the doctor had been, coming from a road where there were no houses. Life continued, the doctor still wore the Fascist uniform, but on increasingly less frequent occasions. Giuseppe had his suspicions confirmed when at the much loved doctor's funeral he met the young partisan who during a night long past called him to save a life.

From Diana Laurenzi, whose family villa outside Lucca was commandeered by German officers

I still have in my ears the echo of the cannons' last salute after the Field Marshall's speech in praise and memory of a twenty-year-old angel, who died absurdly in a war in which he was obliged to participate without knowing why. At twenty your reasons for living are the future and love. I was eighteen and I cried behind the closed shuttered windows of our villa, where during the last year of the war successive German commanders stayed, before retreating along the Gothic Line. Their stationing with us was relatively brief, in this case however it was longer, because new recruits were being trained. The soldiers were forbidden to speak to us while training in our courtyard. That is why I never knew the name of this boy. After nearly sixty years I still call him angel. He was handsome as only an innocent blond twenty-year-old can be. I remember that he, together with his comrades, cleaned the courtyard around the villa near the loggia, where I lived in the ground floor. I tried to start a conversation but after my *Guten Morgen* a brief glance silenced me. One morning they all started an exercise in the river: they had to cross the river at its highest point, each carrying his own equipment. It was a beautiful day, the water was quiet, and crossing the river seemed to be a bagatelle. But when they reached the other side, the numbers did not add up. The angel was missing. Later they found him gently lying on the river bed, caressed by the water, a death with no reason. They returned in silence with this fair load. During the night a mortuary was prepared in the chapel of our villa. The day after, we were the first to see him, to tell him he was our brother, our son, even though his uniform was that of our enemy. I remember I begged him to open his eyes once more so I could see again this piece of sky. I cried, refusing to accept this terrible destiny, caused by the cruelty of war, then immediately a miracle happened. Farmers' wives (whose sons were at the front, with the partisans, or dead in arid Africa, or in the Russian snow) entered timidly into the chapel. Each one brought a small bunch of wild flowers and placed it weeping on the lifeless body, which could have been that of their own son. Holding back my tears, I saw in front of me the most beautiful example of love that overcomes hate and revenge, unifying the love of all mothers.

1950

Einstein talks of the man of science

from Albert Einstein: *Ideas and Opinions*

Albert Einstein (1879-1955) was invited to Lucca in 1950 to address the 43rd Conference of the Italian Society for the Advancement of Science. The ageing scientist declined because of poor health, but sent a long letter to the conference about the problems he saw facing the modern scientist in 1950. Written in the aftermath of the development of nuclear power and the bomb, which his own work had done much to underpin, it is a concerned and moving document by one of the greatest scientists of the century.

What, then, is the position of today's man of science as a member of society? He obviously is rather proud of the fact that the work of scientists has helped to change radically the economic life of men by almost completely eliminating muscular work. He is distressed by the fact that the results of his scientific work have created a threat to mankind since they have fallen into the hands of morally blind exponents of political power. He is conscious of the fact that technological methods made possible by his work have led to a concentration of economic and also of political power in the hands of small minorities which have come to dominate completely the lives of the masses of people who appear more and more amorphous. But even worse: the concentration of economic and political power in a few hands has not only made the man of science dependent economically; it also threatens his independence from within; the shrewd methods of intellectual and psychic influences which it brings to bear will prevent the development of really independent personalities.

Thus the man of science, as we can observe with our own eyes, suffers a truly tragic fate. Striving in great sincerity for clarity and inner independence, he himself, through his sheer super-human efforts, has fashioned the tools which are being used to make him a slave and to destroy him also from within. He cannot escape being muzzled by those who have the political power in their hands. As a soldier he is forced to sacrifice his own life and to destroy the lives of others even when he is convinced of the absurdity of such sacrifices. He is fully aware of the fact that universal destruction is unavoidable since the historical development has led to the concentration of all economic, political, and military power in the hands of national states. He also realizes that mankind can be saved only if a supranational system, based on law, would be created to eliminate for good the methods of brute force. However, the man of science has slipped so much that he accepts the slavery inflicted upon him by national states as his inevitable fate. He even degrades himself to such an extent that he helps obediently in the perfection of the means for the general destruction of mankind.

Is there really no escape for the man of science? Must he really tolerate and suffer all these indignities? Is the time gone forever when, aroused by his inner freedom and the independence of his

215

thinking and his work, he had a chance of enlightening and enriching the lives of his fellow human beings? In placing his work too much on an intellectual basis, has he not forgotten about his responsibility and dignity? My answer is: while it is true that an inherently free and scrupulous person may be destroyed, such an individual can never be enslaved or used as a blind tool.

If the man of science of our own days could find the time and the courage to think over honestly and critically his situation and the tasks before him and if he would act accordingly, the possibilities for a sensible and satisfactory solution of the present dangerous international situation would be considerably improved.

1957

The similarity of Lucca and Venice

from Guido Piovene: *Viaggio in Italia*

Lucca is the only Italian city which is completely encircled, like inside a ring, by high walls erected in the sixteenth and seventeenth centuries, which hide it from people arriving from the plains. A superb tree-lined avenue goes along the walls; from various viewpoints one can admire the distant views, or the sweet Lucca plain, or the backdrop of the mountains. Looking inwards, you see the city gathered together as if in a bowl, and can pick out one by one the churches, palaces and towers; up to the Torre Guinigi, which as if recalling the natural world around it, bears a tuft of great wild oaks on its summit. The city centre, seen from the walls, makes one also think of a kind of bank, in which the accumulated wealth of the Lucchesi from the silk industry, financial services and mercantile trade in the centuries of splendour has been deposited, and converted into churches and palaces.

Within this circle of walls the popular imagination has placed the final act of a legend which is both sacred and profane, romantic and operatic. The young Lucida Mansi – from a still existing noble family – and guilty, according to the legend, of having done away with her elderly husband to lead a dissolute life, so in love with her own body that she went to church with a false prayer book lined with mirrors, made a pact with the Devil to have eternal youth. But she was punished in these very walls, when she and her coach fell into the abyss of Hell, which opened up here before her.

Leaving apart Lucida Mansi, it is obvious that Lucca is an exemplary city, with its nearly intact historical shape compressed into a unified outlook. The ring of the fortifications is the last circle of three walls which have enclosed it with comfort and grandeur. You can see in the middle a second circle, which delineated the thirteenth century medieval city, and even further inside there is a trace of the ancient Roman city. So there are three circles, one inside the other. One understands how not only religious festivities but also simple daily life stands out in this restricted, precise and harmonious setting. Lucca is one of the cities with most life on its streets. To be convinced of this, it is enough to enter one of its little streets, which are still the trading streets of the Middle Ages, animated by commerce and still carrying out their traditional function, today as yesterday. Or meet up in a pretty evening in the hot months, when all the citizens, together with visitors from Viareggio and Montecatini, are out walking and taking the fresh air. With its diverse colours, Lucca is like only one other Italian city in the intensity of its street life and maintenance of human scale, for a similar reason – the difficulty of expanding: Venice.

1970

An aura of lightness

from Kate Simon: *Italy: the Places Between*

The aura of lightness may be attributable to the fact that the city was under the control of women at various times, first the

217

Longobard Matilda, early in the twelfth century, and much later, two ladies seriously concerned with the uplift, public works and the cultivation of the arts: the sister of Napoleon, Maria Anna Elisa Baciocchi, and shortly after, Maria Luisa the Bourbon. Add to that the innumerable minute piazze and engaging vicoli, each with its bar or trattoria – three tables on the street and groups of men playing cards, reading newspapers, arguing mildly.

And Lucca offers the people-watching pleasures of an almost interminable *passeggiata* on its shopping streets. The boys stroll together, as do the girls, except for an engaged or extremely enlightened pair. Fluffy baby carriages act as prow for a family cutting its way through the crowd. A girl in a smock, carrying a pile of shoe boxes, a boy with a tray of cakes, still in his white work coat, press purposefully through this leisured world of which they are not yet part. Small gangs of adolescents wander through the crowd like desperate lost sheep and always, enlacing and releasing groups of strollers, little boys who push and pommel each other. The city is for outside, for the mélange of its periods, for the wild joy of decoration on its churches, for the extravagances of ironwork in street lamps and the painted ceilings in shops. A few of the churches are justly famous, and there is an impressive museum that absorbs the treasures of those decayed and abandoned, but with Florence nearby and Pisa round the corner and Siena not too far away, these don't call for studious attention, and that can be a great relief and Lucca's greatest asset.

Wherever one turns there is an invitation: to the vivid piazza that hums around the splendors of Saint Michael's church, to the distinguished museum, to medieval towers and Renaissance palaces. It might be reasonable to start at one of Lucca's earliest monuments and one of the city's prime delights. Carrying the map supplied by the tourist office on via Vittorio Veneto 13, cast a dazzled eye on San Michele (the time for concentration will come later) and go behind it to the via Buia. Pondering the mystery of why this is called the "dark" street in a townful of narrow medieval paths, looking into shopwindows, examining one brilliant display of door handles in a diversity of materials and contortions, you should come to the Piazza dei Mercanti, an outdoor living room filled with tables and umbrellas, flower boxes, potted trees and well-dressed, well-padded people. The toy square opens to the shopping street of Fillungo,

218

which curves and turns easily, almost voluptuously, in its free-of-traffic hours. It shows an impressive number of jewelry shops, one of which is dignified by two sets of triple windows in carved dark wood, like sections of choir stall from a baroque church; perhaps they are. A modern shop of glass and cool order faces a beribboned, ladylike old sweetshop; here and there, glass eaves and biddable iron and suggestions of galleries, in the well-fed, optimistic late-nineteenth-century French style.

1975

Lucca Quartet

from Francis Warner: *Lucca Quartet*

Lucca Quartet *is a collection of four poems about the Lucca area, privately printed in a limited edition of 300 copies, by the English poet and playwright Francis Warner, born in 1937. Warner has been a Fellow at St Peters College in Oxford since 1965, and was Pro Proctor of Oxford in 1989-90 and 1996-97. He received the Italian Constantian Order in 1990.*

Choriambics

We are still wide-eyed awake. Come, shall we tread
   out on the bare-foot paths
With the cool wind on our face? Yes, while no clothes
   bother and night is ours.
We have both whispered to late eagerness sings
   blood is alert. Next door
Two soft brushed children asleep, safe in shared warmth,
   laid like sardines, secure
From all hobgoblins and fears, terrors and ticks,
   giants and walking trees

That bedtime stories have spun, read with a last
   bloodcurdling tender squeeze.
All the still valley's asleep. Cold in neat graves,
   lit by electric coils,
The long past dead of the farms, cemetery snug,
   glimmer their distant light,
While the stream washes, the breeze clouds out of the moon.
   Beauty, star of my sight,
Kiss me once more. Let us stay here
   now, while the first bird calls.
In our flight far from the grey desolate days –
   acres of years misspent –
We've discovered the best. Here let us rest
   living complete content.

1983

Afoot and unhurried in Lucca

from Alfred Alvarez, in Rosenthal and Gelb (eds.): *Beloved Cities*

Alfred Alvarez (b.1929) the widely acclaimed English poet and author is perhaps best known for his close friendship with the American poet Sylvia Plath. His The Savage God *(1971) is an important study of suicide. Here he is in mellower vein.*

In northern Tuscany the tourist trade route runs west along the autostrada from Florence to Pisa, missing Lucca by less than a mile. No doubt this arrangement satisfies Lucca and its citizens perfectly well, since it is a conservative town in a conservative area – one of the few in Tuscany where the Communists have yet to make significant inroads in local politics. The place is elegant, unhurried and spectacularly self-enclosed: it lies behind a dry moat and vast slanting ramparts of mellow brick, their tops thickly wooded and wide enough for a good road and shaded picnic area.

The ramparts, which took a hundred years to build and were finished in 1650, are pierced by arched gateways ornamented with marble figures and coats of arms. Originally the gates were defended by drawbridges, double iron doors and heavy portcullises, all of which have now gone. Yet driving in under the great dark archways still feels like entering a castle – a separate, private world where you have to watch your manners.

Within the walls, of course, the din is like that of any other Italian town. George Orwell pointed out that the Italians can't do anything without making a terrible noise, and the Lucchese are no exceptions. Pedestrians and automobiles and motorbikes jostle each other in the narrow streets and the racket echoes back from the looming buildings. Yet even the noise is intimate, like family chatter. The battalions of booming foreigners who patrol Florence and Pisa, cameras at the ready, are nowhere to be seen.

They ignore Lucca, I suppose, because the place is blessed by having no three-star Grand Tour masterpieces, nor even an art gallery worth mentioning. There is a museum in the Palazzo Guinigi, a fifteenth century brick palace with what looks like a barn for drying hay on its roof and a tall brick tower crowned, incongruously, with trees. But the paintings and historical bric-a-brac on display are mostly second-rate. To the masterpiece addict, the best Lucca can offer is three or four beautiful churches containing three or four beautiful pieces of sculpture – which is not much, in Italy, for a provincial capital with an archbishop and fifty thousand inhabitants. Lucca's real attraction – apart from its olive oil, which is the best and most famous in the world – is its atmosphere, an intricate distillation of that curiously Italian historical richness in which the present and the past are inextricably mingled, and ancient buildings are adapted unselfconsciously to modern uses and modern lives.

At its midpoint is the Antico Café Caselli, now called Di Simo, the unofficial cultural centre of Lucca since the early years of the century. Puccini, Mascagni and the local major poet Giovanni Pascoli were friends of the original owner Caselli, and after Puccini's death he celebrated their memory by awarding annually a Caselli Prize for Literature, the Figurative Arts and Music. The tradition was revived after world War II by the Gruppo Renato Serra, which met weekly from 1947 to 1954. The names of those who attended the meetings are carved on a marble plaque on the rear wall; they include Salvatore Quasimodo, Giuseppe Ungaretti, Mario Praz and the *"poeta Americano"*, Robert Lowell.

The literary gatherings no longer take place, but the atmosphere remains: the turn of the century preserved in lavish mahogany and glass. It is a long room with covered glass counters running half its length, one containing snacks, the other cakes, chocolates and candies. Behind the savoury counter is a bar with an extraordinary display of malt whiskies, behind the other a wallful of imported teas and biscuits and Tiptree jams. There is also the usual extravagant showcase of home-made ice creams. At the back of the main café is a smaller, darker room, opening onto a square, where a handful of silent customers sip coffee and play chess. It is like a London club without the pomp and snobbery: solid, comfortable and somehow out of time, as though its values had a life and harmony beyond fashion. In other words, it is like Lucca itself, the perfect town for those who love Italy and its way of life but dread the occupational hazards of sightseeing – the crowds and what Robert Benchley once called "museum feet."

1995
Prince Charles uses Lucca and Siena as models for Poundbury

Prince Charles' visits to Lucca in the late 1990s caused an understandable stir. The British Crown Prince is well-known for his strong interest in architecture, preferring tradition to Modernism. He has sponsored the development of a model village in Devon – Poundbury – using Italian Renaissance cities as examples.
My wife Veronica met Prince Charles at a reception in Budapest in 1995 and went up to him saying, "You love Lucca" (not "how do you do" or "Delighted to meet you, your Royal Highness"). He didn't understand, of course. She said again, "You love Lucca, because you are building Poundbury after the model of Lucca." He roared with laughter, and said Poundbury actually was mostly based on Siena.

After a long conversation, he parted with the words "Give my love to Lucca", which she has been doing ever since.

In love, in Lucca

from Barbara Cartland: *In Love, in Lucca*

If Mary Shelley's Valperga *seemed sentimental, wait for Barbara Cartland's Lucca love story. The alliteration of Lucca and Love was probably her main interest, although the very brief descriptions of the walls and San Martino are accurate enough. The story deals with a young English girl with Italian relatives in Lucca. She visits the city and gets entangled with a handsome count (who lives in the "Palazzo di Lucca") and a gang of East Indian robbers. She is ultimately rescued from her imprisonment in the walls and marries the count.*

They had left her without undoing the ropes around the ankles, but she now managed with some difficulty to untie them. They had been very tight and hurt her.

The men had left one candle behind. Now she could see more clearly what sort of place it was in which she was imprisoned. The Contessa had told her how thick the walls of the ramparts were. She also said how unusual it was to find intact medieval ramparts like those which encircled Lucca. "There are four kilometres of them," she had said proudly, "and everyone in the City is prepared to subscribe to keep them in good repair."

Paola peeped through the door the men had left open behind them. She could see that this part of the rampart was definitely in need of repair. Bricks had fallen onto the floor. There were holes in the floor itself, and at one place at the end of the passage, she could see the ceiling had fallen in. She guessed that this was why the Big Man and his Indians had been able to find a way into the ramparts. It made a very effective prison.

Shelley lolls about at the Devil's Bridge

BAGNI DI LUCCA

Taking the waters in Bagni

from Jonathan Keates: *Tuscany*

Bagni di Lucca lies fifteen miles north-east of Lucca on the Lima river, a tributary of the Serchio. In the eighteenth and nineteenth centuries it built up an expatriate community, especially English, attracted by its waters, beautiful position, casino and social life. A Protestant church and cemetery were built; the cemetery, which contains the graves and fine tombs of the writers Ouida and Stisted and of President Grover Cleveland's sister, is sadly neglected. It needs urgent restoration, and a group of us under the auspices of the Istituto Storico di Lucca are trying to restore this site to its original state.

Bagni di Lucca, like the other Tuscan curative springs, was well known to early medieval Italy, when Countess Matilda or Frederick II chose to turn aside from war and politics to bathe in its hot springs. Montaigne passed a delightful summer here in 1581, analysing the effects of the waters on his bowels in lurid detail, dancing with the peasantry, climbing the mountains and indulging that insatiable curiosity which provided the foundation for his essays. James Francis Edward Stuart, the Old Pretender, touched for the King's Evil in 1722 (the enraged British government threatened an embargo on Lucca olive oil) and five years later those two quintessentially eighteenth-century spirits Montesquieu and Lord Chesterfield visited the baths together, charming the company by their wit and sententiousness.

Who, indeed, was not at Bagni di Lucca? After the Napoleonic wars, it became a paradise for foreign expatriates, refugees from the sweltering Florentine summers with only a half-hearted interest in the water-cure itself. Here you might have watched Shelley and his friends preparing for that jolly picnic he describes in *The Boat on the Serchio*, Ibrahim Pasha, Viceroy of Egypt, strolling along the chestnut alleys with his exotically-garbed spahis [cavalrymen],

Flaubert arm-in-arm with Victor Hugo, and a crop of those minor novelists, Charles Lever, Francis Marion Crawford and Fanny Trollope, whose works formed the staple fare of English travellers abroad, and can still be enjoyed today by anyone with a good sense of the period.

Under the benign patronage of the harum-scarum Carlo Lodovico, Duke of Lucca, whose chief minister, Thomas Ward, had begun life as a Yorkshire jockey, there were horse-races in the dried-up river-bed and gambling at the casino. The Duke himself was, though charming, a thoroughly bad lot and had no hesitation, when things grew too hot for him financially and politically, in signing away his duchy to Tuscany in 1847 on the "anything-for-a-quiet-life" principle. No wonder Robert Browning, according to his wife Elizabeth, had taken "the strongest prejudice against these Baths of Lucca, taking them for a sort of wasps' nest of scandal and gaming, and expecting to find everything trodden flat by the Continental English", though when the famous pair did arrive, in July 1849, they grew thoroughly enraptured with the beauty of the scene.

Nowadays there is something slightly shabby and depressing about it all. The stucco of the ornamental villas is peeling, the English church, in fantasy Tuscan gothic, is perpetually closed, the pretty neo-classical casino needs a lick of paint, and Prince Demidoff's domed rotunda chapel is fenced off with "Danger" notices. Yet the cures go splendidly onwards, with steam grotto treatment for arthritis and obesity and mud baths for "the pathology of the male reproductive organs". The spa complex, in its attractive little courtyard at the top of the hill, is annually thronged with suffering enthusiasts.

Ghosts and spirits

The people who live in the Lucchesia have preserved their particular culture of traditions and customs to an unusual extent.

Notwithstanding the Roman Catholicism which is omnipresent in Lucca and the Lucchesia, the ritual festivals of May, Christmas, Easter and the Befana (the old woman who comes down the chimney on Twelfth Night with gifts for the children), have a northern pagan flavour. As well as "official" rites, there is also a substratum of beliefs, legends and fables, superstitions and ritual behaviour which still forms an integral part of all that we mean when we speak of the Lucchesia.

There are elves, fairies, befanas, gnomes, wizards, ghost stories, legends, will-of-the-wisps, magic cats, werewolves and hidden treasure here, just as there are in the North. In the mountains there are magic women – sorceresses and fairies, mostly good ones, with appealing names such as Little Star or comical ones, like Longlip – in enchanted grottoes, doing beautiful, delicate work and helping those who come for help. Or who can find them, at any rate.

The best known of the little people in Lucca is the mischief-making *linchetto*. The origin of the word is unknown and the linchetto has never been properly defined, but he's a kind of elf, and according to local legend, elves were born after the battle between the faithful angels and the fallen angels of Lucifer. There were some angels who didn't want to join the rebels but weren't decisive enough to join the other side, so they went and scattered over the world, little baby angels who couldn't make up their minds what to do, but more than willing to play tricks on people. They are invisible, but the country people invented a clever way of tracking them down, long before the invention of finger-printing. What they did was scatter flour in the places where the elves lived, the elves fell into the trap and left their footprints for all to see. The linchetto likes to put things where no-one can find them and hide keys in other people's pockets with wonderful agility. He ties knots in rosaries, puts altogether unsacred pictures in the priest's prayer book, makes lovers count the days wrong ...

This is how Idelfonso Nieri describes the linchetto: "He goes by night, in the dead of night. He gets into bedrooms through the keyhole and takes the blankets off the people there. He makes everything untidy, changes things around and then laughs like a lunatic at all the tricks he's played. He curls the horses' manes and twists the cows' tails into lengths of string and plays other little jokes of a similar nature. But best of all he likes to jump on the chests of people who are sleeping so that they can't breathe properly. It's easy to annoy the linchetto or buffardello, however. What you have to do is go into the room where he usually goes at his usual time, and sit on a chamber pot, eating bread and cows' milk cheese! Another way is to put a plate of millet on your chest which the linchetto is bound to knock over while he's pummelling you, so that all the millet scatters. He'll get so angry picking it all up grain by grain that he'll never come back."

And the devil is here, as he is everywhere. Bridges with bold arches have been built in a single night by devils who have acquired them by exchange and contract. The Ponte del Diavolo looks into the mirror of the River Serchio, like a fine lady damning her soul. Through the arches you can see the bare bleak mountain of the Pratofiorito where women held the witches' Sabbath with the devil himself. Or so they claimed, under torture. The mountain is unique, with two rounded cones, quite bald, like old witches, and these two lobes gave it the name of Montefegatesi. From a distance they look like livers, such as the Etruscans used for telling the future.

Then there are the old traditions which people pass on for fun (but not entirely), about the herbs that witches used, and which are picked before dawn on the 24th of June. These are used to make love potions, of course, or potions to help you fly to the Pratofiorito on Walpurgis Night, and some of them are poisonous or, at any rate, hallucinogenic. You occasionally read in the local newspapers about cases of thorn apple poisoning – witches and sorceresses (not many, in comparison with other places) were burned for using this drug, both in Lucca and in the countryside. For centuries, L'Angiotta and Catarina, both notorious witches, were names to whisper with reverential fear, and not just because their heads, which had flown so often to the Pratofiorito, ended up by dropping into the executioner's basket. Halloween was celebrated here long, long before it became commercialised as a fancy dress party, and it still is today, in one place in particular, and you must surely know by now where that is, without me telling you. (DV)

Montaigne gives a ball

from Michel de Montaigne: *Journal de voyage en Italie*

On the Sunday morning I took another bath, without bathing my head, and after dinner I gave a ball, with presents for the guests, according to the custom of these baths. I was anxious to give the first ball of the season. Five or six days before this date I had caused notice of my entertainment to be given in all the neighbouring villages, and on the day previous I sent special invitations to all the gentle-folk then sojourning at either of the baths. I bade them come to the ball, and to the supper afterwards, and sent to Lucca for the presents, which are usually pretty numerous, so as to avoid the appearance of favouring one lady above all the rest, and to steer clear of jealousy and suspicion. They always give eight or ten to the ladies, and two or three to the gentlemen. Many ventured to jog my memory, one begging me not to forget herself, another her niece, another her daughter.

On the day previous Messer Giovanni da Vincenzo Saminiati, a good friend of mine, brought me from Lucca, according to my written instructions, a leathern belt and a black cloth cap as presents for the men. For the ladies I provided two aprons of taffetas, one green and the other purple (for it must be known that it is always meet to have certain presents better than the bulk, so as to show special favour where favour seems to be due), two aprons of bombazine, four papers of pins, four pairs of shoes – one pair of which I gave to a pretty girl who did not come to the ball, a pair of slippers, which I put with one of the pairs of shoes to form one prize, three head-dresses clear woven, and three netted, which together stood for three prizes, and four small pearl necklaces. Thus I had altogether nineteen gifts for the ladies, the cost of which was six crowns; little enough. I engaged five pipers, giving them their food for the day, and a crown amongst the lot, a good bargain for me, seeing that they will rarely play here at such a rate. The prizes aforesaid were hung up on a hoop, richly ornamented, and visible to all the company.

We began the dance on the piazza with the people of the place, and at first feared we should lack company, but after a little we were joined by a great number of people of all parties, and notably of the gentle-folk of the land, whom I received and entertained to the best of my powers; and I succeeded so far that they all seemed well content. As the day waxed somewhat warm we withdrew to the hall of the Palazzo Buonvisi, which was excellently suited for the purpose. At the decline of day, about the twenty-second hour, I addressed the ladies of the greatest consequence who were present, and said that I had neither wit nor confidence enough to give judgment between these young ladies so richly endowed with beauty and grace and politeness, wherefore I begged them to undertake the duty of deciding, and to award the prizes according to the deserts of the company. We had long discussion over this formal matter, as at first the ladies refused to accept this office, deeming that I had offered it to them merely out of courtesy. At last we agreed to add this proviso, to wit, that they might, if they were so minded, call me into their council to give my opinion. The end was that I went about, glancing now at this damsel and now at that, never failing to allow due credit for beauty and charm, but at the same time determining that graceful dancing meant something else than the mere movement of the feet; that it necessitates also appropriate gestures, a fine carriage of the whole body, a pleasant expression, and a comely charm. The presents, great and small, were distributed on this principle according to desert, one of the ladies aforementioned presenting them to the dancers on my behalf, while I disclaimed all merit thereanent, and referred them to her as the Lady Bountiful. My entertainment passed off in the usual fashion, except that one of the girls would not take her present, but sent to beg me that I would give it with her love to another girl; but this I would not permit to be done, as the damsel in question was not over well favoured. The girls were called one by one from their places to come before the lady and myself, sitting side by side, whereupon I gave to the signora the gift which seemed appropriate, having first kissed the same. Then the signora, taking it in her hand, gave it to the young girl, and said in friendly fashion, "This is the gentleman who is giving you this charming present, thank him for it." I added, "Nay, rather your thanks are due to the gracious signora who has designated you out of so many others as worthy of reward. I much regret that the offering made to you is not more worthy of such merit as yours." I spoke somewhat in these terms to each according to her qualifications. The same order was followed in the case of the men.

The ladies and gentlemen had no part in this distribution though they all joined in the dance. In sooth it was a rare and charming sight to us Frenchmen to look upon these comely peasants dancing so well in the garb of gentle-folk. They did their best to rival the finest of our lady dancers, albeit in a different style. I invited all to supper, as the meals in Italy are like the lightest of our repasts in France, and on this occasion I only provided a few joints of veal and a pair or two of fowls. I had as guests also the colonel of the Lieutenancy, Signor Francesco Gambarini, a gentleman of Bologna, who had become to me as a brother. I also found a place at table for Divizia, a poor peasant woman who lives about two miles from the baths, unmarried, and with no other support than her handiwork. She is ugly, about thirty-seven years of age, with a swollen throat, and unable either to read or write; but it chanced that in her childhood there came to live in her father's house an uncle who was ever reading aloud in her hearing Ariosto and others of the poets, wherefore she seemed to find a natural delight in poetry, and was soon able, not only to make verses with marvellous readiness, but likewise to weave thereinto the ancient stories, the names of the gods of various countries, of sciences and illustrious men, as if she had received a liberal education. She recited divers lines in my honour, which, to speak the truth, were little else than verses and rhymes, but the diction was elegant and spontaneous.

I entertained at my ball more than a hundred strangers, albeit the time was inconvenient for them, seeing that they were then in the midst of the silk harvest, their principal crop of the year. At this season they labour, heedless of all feast days, at plucking, morning and evening, the leaves of the mulberry for their silk-worms, and all my peasant guests were engaged in this work.

231

The Old Pretender touches for the King's Evil

from Olive Hamilton: *The Divine Country:*
the British in Tuscany 1372-1980

James Stuart (1688-1766) was the son of James II, who had been deposed by parliament as King of England and replaced by William and Mary in the "Glorious Revolution". Known as the "Old Pretender", Stuart spent his life abroad, plotting how to regain the British throne with the help of the Jacobites. Thomas Gray says he was "a thin, ill-made man, extremely tall and awkward, of a most unpromising countenance, a good deal resembling King James the Second and has extremely the air and look of an idiot, particularly when he laughs or prays. The first he does not often, the latter continually."

James was so impressed by the hospitality of Lucca that he announced that every Thursday during his visit he would hold at the Palazzo Buonvisi the ceremony of "touching for the King's evil" (scrofula). He had apparently performed the ceremony with some success at the hospitals of Paris in 1715 and 1716, but the proceedings had been nothing to the ceremonial which accompanied it at Bagni di Lucca. The interior of the Palazzo was decorated with rich hangings from the silk looms of Lucca, and a throne draped with crimson silk stood before the niche of the fountain. The ladies of the court were elegantly dressed and wearing high-heeled slippers, the men in powdered periwigs, velvet or satin breeches, silk stockings and buckled shoes. The King was in mulberry-coloured velvet, with a white satin silver-embroidered waistcoat, white satin breeches, silk stockings and diamond-buckled shoes, with fine Mechlin lace at his throat and wrist.

After James was conducted to the throne, and had knelt to pray, the procession of afflicted children approached from the little chapel at Corsena. The King placed his long slender hand on the cheek of each child and hung the "touch-piece" on its white ribbon round his neck. The Comptroller of the Household then held out a silver ewer and basin so that the King could wash his hands, before he slowly retired. The effect produced on those present was profound: as the High Chancellor, Orazio Donati, said afterwards: "The King breathed holiness, so filled was he with its spirit and sweetness as he administered it."

Clementina had intended to take the full course of treatments at the Baths, but before the prescribed number of forty could be taken the weather turned too cold for further immersion. In mid-September it was time for them to depart. James and his wife were entertained in Lucca at the sumptuous Palazzo Mansi (now a museum and art gallery), and at various Lucchese villas. Last of all, they made a solemn religious visit to the most revered shrine in those parts, that of the Volto Santo in the Cathedral of San Martino at Lucca. Then James's envoy, General Forster of Northumberland, took his sovereign's formal thanks to the Republic of Lucca, and in return Senator Spada and Marchese Rafaello Mansi brought to the royal couple the compliments of the government and their wishes for a good journey.

There was an aftermath of the visit, when murmurs of the homage Lucca had paid to the "Pretender" and "Madame the Princess", as they were officially called in England, drifted into Britain, and when a manifesto originating in Lucca appeared in support of James's right to rule over the English nation. The British Government showed its anger and disapproval by threatening to prohibit imports of oil and cloth from Lucca, and to reopen its trade with France instead. But John Molesworth, the British envoy at Turin, was able to calm the situation, and on 9 December 1722 addressed a model letter of diplomacy to his fellow diplomat "Monsieur, l'Ambassadeur de Lucques:

... I receive, Monsieur, with much pleasure the order to signify that though His Majesty [George I] has had much information subject to evil interpretation with regard to the affairs in question, and amongst others that the Declaration of the Pretender scattered in England had been printed at Lucca, His Majesty nevertheless liked to think that the Republic had no share in it, not wishing to attribute to such a wisely governed state the errors of evil-intentioned private people.

Wherefore, Monsieur, you will have the satisfaction of making known to your principals, that the King, my Master, receives their excuses for the past, and believes that as he has never shown anything but esteem for the honoured Republic, those who govern it will in the future prevent those accidents which could give just occasion for complaint."

1817

Metternich in the most charming place in the world

from Clemens Metternich: Memoirs

Prince Clemens Metternich-Winneburg (1773-1859) was one of the most outstanding statesmen and diplomats of the Napoleonic period. After being Austrian Ambassador to France and Saxony, he became Foreign Minister of Austria in 1809, an office he held for nearly 40 years. He played a leading role at the Congress of Vienna in 1815, which restructured Europe after Napoleon's defeat. After the uprisings in 1848, Metternich resigned from his ministry and retired abroad, living in Brighton for a while.

I am here in the most charming spot in the world. The road from Lucca to the waters passes through the most picturesque valley that can be conceived. The mountains which border it are as high as the Styrian Alps (excepting of course the summits covered with perpetual snow). A majestic torrent rushes through it, and this most beautiful road brings us, at a distance of fifteen miles, to the baths and waters. I am living in the part called the Villa de'Bagni, a house which Elisa had built, or rather arranged, for herself; this will tell you that it is comfortable and well situated. I have a bath in the house itself, and the waters for drinking are close by. About a mile from this are the *bagni caldi*; they carry anyone who wishes to go there in a chair. It is a curious sight to see the quantity of open and covered chairs which cross a large wood of chestnuts and a very steep mountain. I can compare the situation to that of Styria; add to that the vegetation of Italy and you embellish the picture amazingly. The air is excellent; it is neither too hot nor too cold; the establishments for the baths are well conducted, and luxuriously carried out. Everything that with us would be of wood is here of the most beautiful Carrara marble.

... Everybody is enchanted with the place; they all declare that there cannot be anything more beautiful, and I am of the same opinion. I think the life of a Prince of Lucca is, without doubt, one of the happiest and most to be envied. This little country has everything and not too much; it contains a town, a country-house, a bath, a seaport, a lake, a river &c.

1818-1820

Shelley lolls about

from Percy Bysshe Shelley: Letters

Percy Bysshe Shelley (1792-1822) spent the last years of his life in Italy with his wife Mary. Their son Percy Florence Shelley was born in Florence in November 1819. Shelley loved Tuscany but was appalled by its cold winters, writing in 1820 "Tuscany is delightful 8 months of the year. But nothing reconciles me to such infernal cold as my nerves have been racked upon for the last ten days." Summers were better, and the Shelleys spent many happy months in Bagni at the Casa Bertini. Shelley often disappeared for the day into the woods with his books, usually beside some stream or waterfall.

In the middle of the day, I bathe in a pool or fountain, formed in the middle of the forests by a torrent. It is surrounded on all sides by precipitous rocks, and the waterfall of the stream which forms it falls into it on one side with perpetual dashing. Close to it, on the top of the rocks, are alders, and above the great chestnut trees, whose long and pointed leaves pierce the deep blue sky in strong relief. The water of this pool ... is as transparent as the air, so that the stones and sand at the bottom seem, as it were, trembling in the light of noonday. It is exceedingly cold also. My custom is to undress and sit on the rocks, reading Herodotus, until the perspiration has subsided, and then to leap from the edge of the rock into this fountain – a practice in the hot weather exceedingly refreshing. This torrent is composed, as it were, of a succession of pools and waterfalls, up which I sometimes amuse myself by climbing when I bathe, and receiving the spray over all my body, whilst I clamber up the moist crags with difficulty.

c. 1820

The Boat on the Serchio

from *Posthumous Poems*

These lines come from a poem which was unfinished at the time of Shelley's death. Mary Shelley published what her husband had written in 1824 and a later version, with additions by Dante Gabriel Rossetti, was published in 1870. Shelley apparently had in mind to describe a day's adventure on the Serchio for two English drop-outs, Melchior and Lionel, who "from the throng of men had stepped aside" and who live on "that hill, whose intervening brow screens Lucca from the Pisan's envious eye".

> The chain is loosed, the sails are spread,
>   The living breath is fresh behind,
> As, with dews and sunrise fed,
>   Comes the laughing morning wind;–
> The sails are full, the boat makes head
> Against the Serchio's torrent fierce,
> Then flags with intermitting force,
>   And hangs upon the wave, and stems
>   The tempest of the ...

236

Which fervid from its mountain source
Shallow, smooth and strong doth come,–
Swift as fire, tempestuously
It sweeps into the affrighted sea
In morning's smile its eddies coil,
Its billows sparkle, toss and boil,
Torturing all its quiet light
Into columns fierce and bright.

    The Serchio, twisting forth
Between the marble barriers which it clove
    At Ripafratta, leads through the dread chasm
The wave that died the death which lovers love,
    Living in what it sought; as if this spasm
Had not yet passed, the toppling mountains cling,
    But the clear stream in full enthusiasm
Pours itself on the plain, then wandering
    Down one clear path of effluence crystalline
Sends its superfluous waves, that they may fling
    At Arno's feet tribute of corn and wine;
Then through the pestilential deserts wild
    Of tangled marsh and woods of stunted pine,
It rushes to the Ocean.

1818

Mary Shelley finds there are too many English

from Mary Wollstonecraft Shelley: *Letters*

Shelley's wife Mary (1791-1851) kept a diary of their days in Italy, and maintained a voluminous correspondence with her friends. She was not as interested in rural pursuits as her husband, but could be persuaded to go out riding with him in the evening, or to the casino. She wouldn't dance there, although Shelley enjoyed it, writing, "The dances, especially the waltz, are so exquisitely beautiful, that it would be a little dangerous to the newly unfrozen urges and imagination of us migrators from the neighbourhood of the pole." She is best known for her novel Frankenstein.

Bagni di Lucca
2 July, 1818

I am sure you would be enchanted with everything but the English that are crowded here to the almost entire exclusion of the Italians ... We see none but the English, we hear nothing but English spoken. The walks are filled with English nurserymaids, a kind of animal I by no means like, & dashing staring Englishwomen, who surprise the Italians who are always carried about in Sedan Chairs, by riding on horseback. – For us we generally walk except last Tuesday, when Shelley and I took a long ride to *il prato fiorito*; a flowery meadow on the top of one of the neighbouring Apennines – We rode among chestnut woods hearing the noisy cicala, and there was nothing disagreeable in it except the steepness of the ascent – The woods about here are in every way delightful especially when they are plain with grassy walks through them – they are filled with sweet singing birds and not long ago we heard a Cuckoo.

1828

Fresh air and security

from L. Simond: *A Tour in Italy and Sicily*

These thermal springs have the high temperature of 60° Réaumur (167° Fahrenheit), and are much frequented. The road to them, by its peculiar smoothness, reminded us of that along the western side of Loch Lomond. We have spent two days in exploring a very fine country. One of our rambles carried us through chestnut woods of luxuriant growth up to the *Prato Fiorito* on the top of a mountain which cannot well be less than six or seven thousand feet high, since we found snow remaining in various places. The extensive pastures well deserved the name they bear, and would have done no discredit to Switzerland; the views from them were varied and magnificent. The inhabitants of these mountains supply the baths with chairmen; six of whom, relieving each other, undertake to carry you in a sedan to Genoa (eighty miles), under the fervent rays of this Italian sun, in the short space of three days, for the sum of eighteen dollars (four pounds sterling). They are deemed very honest; and a shawl having been dropped by our party, one of them went back a mile or two and returned with it, although he might with great plausibility have reported it *not found*. After the dusty roads, the pickpockets, and the cut-throats of Southern Italy, it is really delightful to enjoy the verdure, fresh air, and security of these mountains.

1842

The Lucca Bathites

from Fanny Trollope: *A Visit to Italy*

The Victorian novelist and travel writer Fanny Trollope (1780-1863) was said by the Dictionary of National Biography to "live by the vigour of her portraits of vulgar persons, and her readers cannot help associating her with the characters she makes so entirely her own." Her letters, from which the following is taken, are full of feeling and descriptions of the people she met.

On the following day we returned to the Baths in good time to keep an appointment for going to a ball; by which you may judge a little of the zeal with which we, in common with all the rest of the Lucca Bathites, employ every moment of our time in keeping the foul fiend, *ennui*, from our presence. The three villages are now just about as full as they can be ... every hotel, every house, every cottage is occupied; and as all the good people seem heartily bent upon amusing themselves, there is as little time lost from remissness in that way as possible. I fully expect that, in a few years, this attractive spot will become one of the largest watering-places in Europe, for the increasing demand for dwellings may readily be supplied; the stones which are used for building here may be had for the carrying, for the winter torrents, which tear up the surface of the surrounding Apennines into those deep ravines to which they owe their principal beauty, bring down a supply of stones, which, by the aid of a little mortar, are rapidly piled into walls. It was after this fashion, I believe, that our handsome English church here was built; which church, by the way, must not be forgotten when enumerating the advantages offered by the Baths of Lucca, and the many proofs given by its liberal-minded sovereign of his kind indulgence to the English.

But, notwithstanding all I say of the gaiety of this sweet place, you are not to imagine that it is at all impossible, or even difficult, to live the life of a hermit here, if you like it. You may know everybody, or you may know nobody ... you may be at balls three times in a week, and occupied in riding parties, driving parties, dining parties, and pic-nic parties every day, and all day long ... if you like it; but, if you do not, you may easily turn a deaf ear and a blind eye to all our gaieties, keep company with the sun, moon, and stars, and hold converse with the spirits of the fell instead of gossiping with our beaux and belles.

Elizabeth Browning is also charmed

from Robert and Elizabeth Barrett Browning:
The Brownings' correspondence

Elizabeth Barrett Browning (1806-1861) spent the last years of her life with her husband and son in Italy, particularly at Casa Guidi in Florence, about which she wrote the exquisite Casa Guidi Windows. *The Brownings travelled extensively and several times escaped the Florence heat by going to Bagni. She wasn't always so enraptured of the place; on an earlier occasion she wrote: "We dont go to the Baths of Lucca. We said we would, when I was ill & Robert was frightened, but now in this smooth water we say nothing of the sort – I would'nt go there for the world if I could draw breath anywhere else in Italy. The scenery is beautiful ... but the society ... the ways & means of the place ... nothing can be more detestable! 'divided between Gambling & Church of Englandism', say our informants – meaning no disrespect to the church of England, observe, but simply that the schismatic & controvertial spirit is keen & bitter there. Then there are races, & promenades, & soirees east & west; & people live so close together in the small mountain hive, that one could'nt escape the buzzing & stinging."*

Well, so finding no rest for the soles of our feet, I persuaded Robert to go to the Baths of Lucca, only to see them. We were to proceed afterwards to San Marcello, or some safer wilderness. We had, both of us, but he chiefly, the strongest prejudice against these Baths of Lucca, taking them for a sort of wasps' nest of scandal and gaming, and expecting to find everything trodden flat by the Continental English; yet I wanted to see the place, because it is a place to see after all. So we came, and were so charmed by the exquisite beauty of the scenery, by the coolness of the climate, and the absence of our countrymen, political troubles serving admirably our private requirements, that we made an offer for rooms on the spot, and returned to Florence for baby, and the rest of our establishment without delay. Here we are then ... We have taken a sort of eagle's nest in the highest house in the highest of the three villages which are called the Bagni di Lucca, and which lie at the heart of a hundred mountains, sung to continually by a rushing mountain stream. The sound of the river and of the cicala is all the noise we hear ... the silence is full of joy and consolation. I think my husband's spirits are better already and his appetite improved ... Mountain air without its keenness, sheathed in Italian sunshine, think what *that* must be! And the beauty and the solitude – for with a few paces we get free of the habitations of men – all is delightful to me.

1858

Augustus Hare sees the Grand Ducal family

from Augustus Hare: *The Story of My Life*

Augustus Hare (1834-1903), writer and painter, was born in Rome and lived much of his life in Italy. He is best known for his travel guides, "gathering up [that] which had already been given to the world in less portable form", which several times laid him open to charges of plagiarism. He was in Bagni di Lucca after graduating from Oxford.

About the 10th of June we settled at Lucca baths, in the pleasant little Casa Bertini, a primitive house more like a farm-house than a villa, on the steep hillside above the Grand Duke's palace, possessing a charming little garden of oleanders and apple-trees at the back, with views down into the gorge of the river, and up into the hilly cornfields, which were always open to us. Very delightful were the early mornings, when the mother, with book and camp-stool, wandered up the hill-path, fringed with flowers, to the Bagni Caldi. Charming too the evenings, when, after "*merenda*" at four o'clock in the garden, we used to go forth, with all the little society, in carriages or on horseback, till the heavy dews fell, and drove us in by the light of the fireflies. A most pleasant circle surrounded us. Close by, in a large cool villa with a fountain, was the gentle invalid Mrs. Greville (*née* Locke), singing and composing music, with her pleasant companion Miss Rowland. Just below, in the hotel of the villa, "Auntie" was living with the George Cavendishes, and in the street by the river the pretty widow, Mrs. Francis Colegrave, with her children, Howard and Florence, and her sister Miss Chichester.

An amusing member of the society at the Bagni, living in a cottage full of curiosities, was Mrs. Stisted, the original of Mrs. Ricketts in "The Daltons". She had set her heart upon converting the Duke of Parma to Protestantism, and he often condescended to controversy with her. One day she thought she had really succeeded, but driving into Lucca town next day, to her horror she met him walking bare-headed in a procession with a lighted candle in his hand. Then and there she stopped her carriage and began to upbraid him. When he returned to the Bagni, he went to see her and to reprove her. "There cannot," he said, "be two sovereigns at Lucca, either I must be Duke or you must be Queen," and ever after she was called the Queen of the Bagni. Colonel Stisted had a number of curious autographs, the most interesting being the MS. of the "Lines to an Indian air" – "I rise from dreams of thee" – found in the pocket of Shelley after he was drowned.

Living beneath us all this summer were the Grand Ducal family, and we saw them constantly. They were greatly beloved, but the Grand Duchess-Dowager, who was a Sardinian princess, was more popular than the reigning Grand Duchess, who was a Neapolitan Bourbon, and ultimately brought about the ruin of the family by her influence. The Grand Duchess-Dowager was the step-mother of the Grand Duke, and also his sister-in-law, having been sister-in-law of his first wife. The Hereditary Grand Duke was married to her niece, a lovely Saxon princess, who died soon afterwards: it was said that he treated her very ill, and that his younger brother protected her. We were at a very pretty ball which was given on the festa of S. Anna, her patroness. The Grand Ducal family generally went out at the same hour as ourselves. In the middle of the day nothing stirred except the scorpions, which were a constant terror. One was found in my bath in the morning, and all that day we were in fearful expectation, as the creatures never go about singly; but in the evening we met the companion coming upstairs. There were also quantities of serpents, which in the evening used frequently to be seen crossing the road in a body going down to the river to drink.

Dumas climbs a hill

A poem by Alexandre Dumas père

Alexandre Dumas (1802-1870), the French author, was at Bagni in 1849 at the same time as the Brownings. Immensely fat in his later years, he was noted for having difficulty in getting through the doors of the Hotel Suisse where he was staying. In 1866 he climbed up to the Croce di Ferio and left his signature in the visitors' book. The beautiful view there inspired a poem, sent to his friend in Bagni, Dr. Giorgio Giorgi.

Bains de Lucques, 22 Mai, 1866.

La montagne s'endort dans le ciel obscuri,
Les vallons sont muets et trempés de rosée;
La poussière s'éteint sur la route embrasée,
Le feuille est immobile, et le vent adouci !
Attends encore un peu, tu dormiras aussi.

The mountains are golden amidst the dark sky,
The valleys are mute and drenched in rose;
The dust stretches along the road between them,
The leaves are still, and the wind sweet!
Wait still a while, and you too will sleep.

Puccini at Caffè Caselli

MUSICAL LUCCA

Lucca has had a long and rich musical life, not only in the great churches, but also sponsored by the town's government since very early days. In the Cathedral school there are records of music lessons being given already in 809; music was an important part of the curriculum. Troubadours wrote their love songs: one Rugetto di Lucca was active c.1200-1220. The town records of 1374 show expenses for the organist of San Martino. Three famous composers – Boccherini, Puccini and Catalani – were born in Lucca, the first two from families who produced musicians over many generations.

Music is still flourishing: the Teatro del Giglio has an annual Opera season, and Puccini's operas are presented outdoors in the summer at Torre del Lago. Young opera singers come from all over the world for the summer opera courses and performances. These are held in various beautiful venues – Palazzo Pfanner, Palazzo Mansi, the courtyard of the Palazzo Ducale – as well as in the larger churches.

1399

The Bianchi sing and dance

from Giovanni Sercambi: *Le Croniche*

The Bianchi were named for their white gowns. They were groups of people who were carried away by religious fervour, and sang and danced across Tuscany at the end of the fourteenth century. One of their meeting points was the beautiful church of the Crocifisso in the street of the same name. (It's 20 feet from our mansarda, and I can almost reach out and touch the bells. Luckily for us it is deconsecrated, and they don't deafen us all day and night.)
The Lucca historian Giovanni Sercambi watched them dance and

sing, and wrote it all down in his fascinating Croniche. *He describes how the town authorities wanted to stop Lucca citizens from joining in the frenzy. They prohibited the Lucchesi from leaving, but a large crowd gathered on 19 August 1399 and took a crucifix from San Romano to lead their processions. Word passed quickly from mouth to mouth about the authorities' ban; everyone there quickly put on white and left Lucca, singing this song, transcribed by Sercambi on the spot.*

> Our omnipotent Lord,
> fountain and light of all people,
> Father, don't abandon us.
> We know, Lord, for certain
> that you are holding heaven open,
> having offered us every blessing
> and we don't know how to take them.
> Our Lord, divine King,
> You show us the right path,
> of your heavenly kingdom,
> but we are always doing wicked things.
> We are certain, and more than certain,
> of every blessing you have covered us with,
> always helping our eyes open to
> make us free.

From 1431

The Feast of the Sacks

from Germaine de Rothschild: *Luigi Boccherini: his life and work*

The town council in Lucca was elected by ballots placed in sack-like receptacles (tasche), *and the* Festa delle Tasche *was celebrated in a musical programme which took place over three days. Composers and poets had to be natives of Lucca: the Puccini family composed*

32 tasche works in the eighteenth century. The Boccherini family was also prominent in these festivals.

In accordance with the obligations imposed upon them by the authorities, it was the duty of the artists to provide an accompaniment of music to the morning meal of "Their Excellent Lordships" of the Council; throughout the year they took part also in the services of the Chapel, at Mass on religious feast-days, at the solemn celebrations of the festival of the Holy Cross, and at the Election Feast known by the name of *Tasche* (the sacks). This festival, which is known to have existed as early as 1431, took place every thirty months and was as much a national event as that of the Holy Cross, but with a political character, since it coincided with the election of the magistrates and the Members of the Grand Council of the Republic. It was called the Feast of the Sacks because from one sack were drawn the names of the elected magistrates and from another the order of rotation in which they were to hold the various posts in the government of the Republic. The proceedings were rendered more impressive by an elaborate ceremonial and processions, and in this ritual a specially arranged programme of music, which was expected to be of the highest quality, played a fundamental part.

1467

An English musician is called to the Cathedral school

from George B. Parks: *The English Traveler to Italy*

John Hothby (1410-1487) had an important influence on Italian music during his years in Italy. A Carmelite monk, he helped transmit new musical techniques from Northern Europe to Italy through his teaching and writings. Some of his students were proud to call themselves "Hothbisti". Of his broad range of writings, the Calliopea Legale *was the most influential. Written in Italian, it explores the*

249

problem of the semitone and its varying sizes. Only nine compositions of his survive; one, Diva Panthera *for three voices in C, has a clear reference to Lucca's coat of arms. The title of* magiscolus *allowed him to wear a white mitre, but also obliged him to give instruction in plainsong, not only to clerics, but to any citizen of Lucca, free of charge. Another Carmelite monk, Johannes Ciconia of Belgium (1335-1411) wrote* Una pantera, *definitely related to Lucca, during his many years teaching and composing in Northern Italy.*

John Hothby (or Ottobi) was not actually a professor, but he was a teacher of music and a theorist as well as organist. An English Carmelite, he was lecturing at Oxford in 1435, when William of Worcester heard him; he is called indifferently, in the Italian documents, doctor of music and doctor of theology. We do not know how he came to Italy. It is thought that he was there as early as 1440, at Florence or Ferrara, where some of his manuscripts are known. It is established that in 1467 he was called by the cathedral chapter of Lucca to teach music and singing to the priests and to the musicians in the cathedral school. After a trial term, the chapter induced the Council of the Republic of Lucca to add a monthly stipend to his salary because of his "remarkable learning and high character". Thereafter further benefices were showered upon the *Magister, Cantor, Magischolus, Musicus*, as he was varyingly called. In 1486 he was recalled to England by the king, we do not know why. On his departure the Council of the Republic sent the king a hearty recommendation of their musician's "outstanding honesty, integrity, extraordinary musical knowledge, and high moral character". He had taught them for eighteen years, and we imagine that he had justified the original hope of the chapter that "he would make so many and so excellent disciples in music and in singing (pratica) as to be both useful to the clergy and a great help and joy to all the people".

Goldoni comments on Lucca's musical life

from Carlo Goldoni: *Memoires*

Carlo Goldoni (1709-93) was one of the most important Italian playwrights. He particularly hoped to reform Italian comedy by substituting plays based on everyday life for the more artificial and outmoded scenarios of the Commedia dell'arte, *and wrote some 150 plays. Many are performed today, and the Teatro del Giglio includes Goldoni regularly in its drama season. Browning's sonnet on the erection of a monument to Goldoni in Venice says:*

Goldoni good, gay, sunniest of souls,
Glassing half Venice in that verse of thine,
Though what it just reflects the shade and shine
Of common life nor renders, as it rolls,
Grandeur and gloom? Sufficient for thy shoals
Was Carnival ...

Returning from Florence, another development brought me to Lucca. I was happy to see this republic, which is neither large nor powerful, yet it is rich, peaceful, and governed sagely enough. My wife came with me, and we spent six days there most pleasantly. It was at the beginning of May; the day of the Invention of the Holy Cross and the biggest festival of the city. In the Cathedral there is an image of the Saviour, called the Volto Santo, which they exhibit on this day with great pomp and with a concert so full of singers and instruments that I have not seen the like in Rome or in Venice.

There is a legacy, left by a devout Lucchese, which directs that all musicians who present themselves in the Cathedral will be accepted, and will be paid not only proportionately to their talent, but also to the journey they undertook; the remuneration is based partly on quality and partly on miles.

The concert was more noisy than pleasing, but the opera which was given at the same time in Lucca was better chosen and well devised. The charming Gabrielli was the delight of this harmonious performance. She was in good humour: the celebrated Guadagni, her leading man on stage and in private, submitted the caprices of virtue to the rule of love. She was made to sing every day, and the audience, accustomed to seeing her emaciated, disgusting and loathsome, completely enjoyed her beautiful voice and her great talent.

Having taken care of our business and our curiosity satisfied, we left this respectable city, which under the protection of the Emperor, pro tempore, enjoys a tranquil liberty and concerns itself with even more wholesome and refined good order.

1760

Boccherini asks for a job back home

from a letter in the Archivio di Stato

Luigi Boccherini was born in Lucca on 19 February 1743 and died in Madrid in 1805. Starting out as a gifted cellist, he was engaged by the Court Theatre in Vienna, from which he wrote the following homesick letter. In his own day he was well known in Europe, serving as court composer in Madrid and Prussia. His style was close to that of Haydn, and there was a saying, "Boccherini is the wife of Haydn". Mozart knew and admired his music, such as the string quartets, and may have used Boccherini's Violin Concerto in D as a model for his own violin concerto in the same key. One waspish Stuttgart critic in 1809 said of the two, "Mozart leads his hearers between steep rocks into a thorny forest where flowers grow but thinly, whereas Boccherini leads one into serene country with flowering meadows, clear, rushing brooks and thick groves." (He must have been deaf.) Boccherini's letter was successful: he returned to Lucca in 1761 to play in the theatre orchestra.

To the Grand Council of Lucca:
Luigi Boccherini offers the most profound obeisance, and in all humility represents: that, after having completed his studies in Rome, he was twice summoned to Vienna, and thereafter visited

all the electoral courts of the Empire, where he was gratified with the most indulgent reception of his performances on the violoncello. As there is no one in the town of Lucca who plays the said instrument, so that it is necessary to call in a stranger for every ceremony, and as he desires to settle permanently in his native land and flatters himself that he may be able to employ his modest skill in the service of his most Venerated Prince, he makes so bold as to lay himself at the feet of Their Excellencies, the Magnificent Citizens, and of the most excellent Council, with a prayer that they will graciously render him assistance in obtaining an honourable livelihood by admitting him to the number of the musicians of the chapel of Their Excellencies.

1782

Burney describes Boccherini's music

from Charles Burney: A General History of Music

Dr Charles Burney (1726-1814) was an English composer and music historian, famous throughout Europe in his lifetime. He travelled extensively in Italy to hear the contemporary music (although Lucca is not recorded in his Present State of Music in France and Italy *of 1771). He was a close friend to many musicians, including Haydn, Pacchierotti and C.P.E. Bach. Mrs Thrale met her future husband, the singer Piozzi, in Burney's London home (although she later recalled the meeting as being in Brighton). Samuel Johnson said of him, "My heart goes out to meet him. I much question if there is in the world such another man for mind, intelligence and manners."*

Boccherini, who is still living in Madrid, and whose instrument is the violoncello, though he writes but little at present, has perhaps supplied the performers on bowed-instruments and lovers of music with more excellent compositions than any other master of the present age, except Haydn. His style is at once bold, masterly and elegant. There are movements in his works of every style, and in the true genius of the instruments for which he writes, that place him high in rank among the greatest masters who have ever written for the violin or violoncello. There is perhaps no instrumental music more ingenious, elegant and pleasing than his quintets: in which invention, grace, modulation, and good taste conspire to render them, when well executed, a treat for the most refined hearers and critical judges of musical composition.

1764

Gibbon goes to the opera, but doesn't enjoy it

from a letter dated 9 October 1764

The historian Edward Gibbon (1737-1794) mentions Lucca very briefly in his Memoirs*: "After leaving Florence I compared the solitude of Pisa with the industry of Lucca and Leghorn." In that year he went to the opera in Lucca, which he tells his father about in this letter.*

Dear Sir,
We set out from Florence last Saturday sevenight and are arrived here after a journey of about ten days. We came round by Lucca Pisa Leghorn and Sienna, and I think made a very agreable tour of it. I must acknowledge that I had the least pleasure in what my companion enjoyed I believe the most; the Opera of Lucca. That little republick who could give usefull lessons of gouvernment to many states much more considerable lays out a very large sum of money every autumn in entertaining an exceeding good Opera at the time that public entertainements are very dead in the other towns of Italy, and receives their money again with very good interest from the great affluence of Strangers who resort to Lucca upon that occasion. Of the different tastes which a man may form or indulge in Italy that of musick has hitherto been lost upon me,

and I have always had the honesty never to pretend to any taste which I was in reality devoid of.

Mozart hears abominable Lucca trumpeters

from Emily Anderson (ed.): *The Letters of Mozart and his family*

Wolfgang Amadeus Mozart (1756-1791) travelled three times with his father in Italy, firstly from December 1769 to March 1771, giving recitals and enjoying the rich Italian musical tradition. There is a lovely story of him hearing the Allegri Miserere *in the Sistine Chapel in Saint Peter's in Rome on the same trip – a piece which was not allowed to be performed elsewhere. Mozart (just 14) wrote it out after a single hearing. They spent the summer of 1770 near Bologna, where Mozart was admitted to the ancient Accademia Filarmonica, as was Puccini's great-grandfather in 1771. Mozart went to a concert in Bologna and wrote this letter to his sister Nannerl.*

6 October 1770

I have heard and seen the great festival of St. Petronius in Bologna. It was beautiful but very long. They had to fetch trumpeters from Lucca for the salvo, but they played abominably.

William Beckford wanders about with the castrato Pacchierotti and causes a stir

from William Beckford: *Italy, Spain and Portugal*

William Beckford (1760-1844) was the son of a Lord Mayor of London and cousin to Peter Beckford. A famous art and book collector and writer, his homosexuality drove him from England for many years. Quinto Fabio *is an opera by Bertoni, performed in Lucca several times in this period. Gasparo Pacchierotti (1740-1821) was an Italian soprano castrato, who appeared in many Bertoni operas in Italy and London, at the King's Theatre, where Bertoni was the resident composer. His singing according to Grove "surpassed the expectation of London audiences and he was a favourite of society for his engaging, modest behaviour and cultivated mind."*

Lucca, Sept. 25, 1780

You ask me how I pass my time. Generally upon the hills, in wild spots where the arbutus flourishes; whence I may catch a glimpse of the distant sea; my horse tied to a cypress, and myself cast upon the grass, like Palmerin of Oliva, with a tablet and pencil in my hand, a basket of grapes by my side, and a crooked stick to shake down the chestnuts. I have bidden adieu, several days ago, to the visits, dinners, conversazioni, and glories of the town, and only go thither in an evening, just time enough for the grand march which precedes Pacchierotti in *Quinto Fabio*. Sometimes he accompanies me in my excursions, to the utter discontent of the Lucchese, who swear I shall ruin their Opera, by leading him such extravagant rambles amongst the mountains, and exposing him to the inclemency of winds and showers. One day they made a vehement remonstrance, but in vain; for the next, away we trotted over hill and dale, and stayed so late in the evening, that a cold and hoarseness were the consequence.

The whole republic was thrown into commotion, and some of its prime ministers were deputed to harangue Pacchierotti upon the rides he had committed. Had the safety of their mighty state depended upon this imprudent excursion, they could not have vociferated with greater violence. You know I am rather energetic, and, to say truth, I had very nearly got into a scrape of importance, and drawn down the execrations of the Gonfalonier and all his council upon my head by openly declaring our intention of taking, next morning, another ride over the rocks, and absolutely losing ourselves in the clouds which veil their acclivities. These terrible threats were put into execution, and yesterday we made a tour of about thirty miles upon the highlands, and visited a variety of castles and palaces.

The Conte Nobili, a noble Lucchese, born in Flanders and educated at Paris, was our conductor. He possesses great elegance of imagination, and a degree of sensibility rarely met with. The way did not appear tedious in such company. The sun was tempered by light clouds, and a soft autumnal haze rested upon the hills, covered with shrubs and olives. The distant plains and forests appeared tinted with so deep a blue, that I began to think the azure so prevalent in Velvet Breughel's landscapes is hardly exaggerated.

... Between nine and ten we entered the gates of Lucca. Pacchierotti coughed, and half its inhabitants wished us at the devil.

The Italian première of Rossini's *William Tell*

from Daniele Rubboli: *Le Prime al Teatro del Giglio* (1675-1987)

Gioacchino Rossini (1792-1868) came from Pesaro, and wrote many great operas, including Barber of Seville, La Cenerentola, Il Comte Ory, *and* William Tell. *Gilbert Louis Duprez (1806-1896) was a French tenor and composer, who became famous in Italy as a* tenore di forza *after this performance. Unfortunately Rossini compared his new high C "to the squawk of a capon having its throat cut".*

A single event would be enough to make the Teatro del Giglio historic: the Italian premiere of *William Tell*, a four act tragic melodrama by Gioacchino Rossini, first performed at the Paris Opera on 3 August 1827. It had its Italian debut at Lucca on 17 September 1831 in a translation by Callisto Bassi, a 31-year old poet from Cremona, son of the comedian Nicola Bassi. *William Tell* presented itself in Lucca not only as a new work in the Italian musical theatre, but also as the final melodramatic work of the Pesaro composer which was translated from French. The impetus to do this came from Alessandro Lanari, at this time manager of various theatres from Senigallia to Florence. Wanting to attract public interest in Teatro del Giglio's attractions, Lanari thought of presenting *William Tell*, being curious about Rossini. Wishing, however, to embellish it, he came up with an eccentric idea: to give the tenor role of Arnold (son of the wise shepherd Melchal) to the contralto Rosmunda Pisaroni, already celebrated in Lucca, 38 years old, and full of that artistic splendour which Rossini himself had admired, counting her among his favourite interpreters.

The singer from Piacenza would likely have coined money in Lucca while dressed as a young boy, but she had encountered a negative period: although acclaimed in Paris, in the months before the Tuscan engagement she had come off the rails in London and Milan, and Lanari decided that the speculation was no longer opportune. Fortunately, he stayed true to the opera and gave the role to the tenor Luigi Duprez, 45 years old, who greatly wanted to consolidate his reputation. Looking at the score, and also wanting to show the impresario that he hadn't lost sight of the desire to astonish the public, Duprez began to study ways to enthuse them.

"Everything in the role of Arnoldo," he recalled, "was well within my vocal ability: but in the last part of the great aria, suppressed in Paris but reinstated in the Italian version, there is the warlike, terrible 'Follow me' which culminates in a note which I, a tenor of yesterday, never thought I could reach. My hair stood up in fright. I was struck by the thought that those grave accents, that sublime yell, would say nothing if done with mediocre means. It was necessary, in order not to lose the effect, to place myself at the centre of this evangelic work. I concentrated all my moral and

258

physical forces, and said to myself: 'Perhaps my voice will crack, but I wish to reach that note, and I did ...' It was in this way that I found the *do di petto* (high C from the chest) which electrified the crowd."

⁓

1839

Liszt writes his first song

from Franz Liszt: *Buch der Lieder*

Franz Liszt (1811-1886), although already a prodigy, was refused entrance to the Paris Conservatory by Cherubini on the very dubious grounds that the young Hungarian was a foreigner (Cherubini was from Florence). He travelled extensively in Italy with his lover, the Countess d'Agoult, with whom he had three children. They were in Monte San Quirico, across the Serchio bridge from Lucca, when he wrote a song to these words, presumably a lullaby for his daughter Blandine. Apparently his first Lied, *it is commemorated in a plaque on the old folks' home (where I confidently expected to wind up before this book was completed). Blandine married in Florence Cathedral in 1857 and spent part of her honeymoon in Lucca.*

Angiolin dal biondo crin

Little Angel with blond hair,
Who has seen barely two winters,
May your life be always serene,
Little Angel with blond hair,
Beautiful image of a flower.

May the sun gild you with a ray,
May a benign atmosphere from Heaven
Caress you in its path,

259

Little Angel with blond hair,
Beautiful image of a flower.

When you sleep, your breathing
Is that sigh of love
That can ignore sorrow,
Little Angel with blond hair,
Beautiful image of a flower.

May you ever be happy
For your mother with her sweet laughter,
You tell her of paradise,
Little Angel with blond hair,
Beautiful image of a flower.

You will learn from her as you grow
How much fine arts and nature hold,
You will not learn misfortune,
Little Angel with blond hair,
Beautiful image of a flower.

And if it happens that my name
Stays in your mind when you hear it,
Ah! Repeat it to her often,
Little Angel with blond hair,
Beautiful image of a flower.

1892

Mrs Trollope attends the opera and a mass at San Martino

from Fanny Trollope: *A Visit to Italy*

The moderate-sized and elegant Opera-house of Lucca was well-filled, and the performances much better, as far as the singing went, than at Florence; ... and the whole thing, together with the aspect of the company, had a much more metropolitan air than I expected. I had the honour of being introduced to the learned Marchese Mazzarosa, the well known historian of Lucca, and conversed with him as much as one can converse in an opera box.

The following morning it was necessary (though we were furnished with tickets) to repair at an early hour to the Cathedral, as the crowd was expected to be so great as to render it pretty certain that if we were late we should fail in making our way to the Tribune in which we were to take our places. Nor did we find this statement in any degree incorrect; the majestic old church was filled throughout every part at all within reach of a sight, even a very distant one, of the high altar; and thus filled, and with all the splendid preparations which always attend the ceremony of episcopal inauguration, the venerable-looking and lofty Duomo of St. Martin had a very imposing appearance. The musical part of the ceremony was extremely well performed, and the scene altogether exceedingly impressive. His Royal Highness the Duke was in the Tribune close beside us; and seated next to him was a lady who we were told was his sister. The Duchess was at Marlia, still suffering from constitutional debility.

After this ceremony, which was a very long one, was over, we employed the remainder of the morning in seeing as much of the town and its 320 churches as the time would permit, which was just enough to make us wish that we could see more, for it has an air of unspoiled antiquity about it that is delightful. The first Roman amphitheatre I have ever seen was in this city; and sufficient traces of it remain to be very interesting to one so new to Italy, though not sufficient to lay claim to any of the beauty I have always heard attributed to the form and style of these enclosures. Once more, too, we contrived to get a look from the lovely ramparts at sunset, than which I really have seen nothing more beautiful.

Puccini steals organ pipes from San Paolino to pay for cigarettes

from Howard Greenfield: *Puccini*

Giacomo Puccini (1858-1924) was born in Lucca; his birthplace in via di Poggio near San Michele is now a museum, where one can see manuscripts and portraits, and the piano on which he composed Turandot. *In the adjacent Piazza Cittadella a statue of him reclining in a chair has recently been installed. The church of San Paolino is around the corner in via San Paolino, and is a beautiful, somewhat reserved church. Via San Paolino is full of small shops and stores, little changed since the nineteenth century, and maybe more representative of the traditional Lucca than any other street inside the walls.*

Music – interestingly, in view of Puccini's future, of a rather theatrical nature – was part of Lucca's history; and the Institute, though not on a level with those of Milan, Venice, Bologna, or Naples, was a distinguished one, which numbered among its pupils at one time or another, Boccherini, Luporini, Catalani, as well as Puccini himself.

At the Institute, Puccini found the ideal teacher, Carlo Angeloni. Angeloni had been a pupil of Giacomo's father and was a composer of operas and choral works. He understood Giacomo and seemed to sense, intuitively, the boy's potential. An avid hunter himself, he would ask the boy to join him while he hunted and took the opportunity, while walking through the woods, of instilling in Giacomo a genuine interest in music. He introduced his pupil to the marvels of Verdi's scores – especially *Rigoletto, La Traviata,* and *Il Trovatore* – and Puccini's enthusiasm for opera can be dated from the period when he began to study with Angeloni.

In spite of the enthusiasm engendered by his contact with Angeloni, it was still far from certain that Giacomo would ever apply himself seriously to his studies. There is little information about his early years, but stories, later rather romantically told by his childhood friends, of his adolescent pranks abound. These indicate that he was a cheerful young man, more interested in defying authority, dancing the polka with a pretty girl, hunting birds, or secretly smoking cigarettes than he was in doing his homework. Some of the pranks are significant in that they are most complex and highly theatrical in nature – especially one long story involving the feigned suicide of a friend of his which ended in both the friend and Giacomo being arrested. Nonetheless, Albina apparently made her son understand that, even while young, he had to earn money to contribute to the support of his family. His only way of doing this was through his music. As a result of Angeloni's teaching, by the age of fourteen he was good enough to play the organ at church services in Lucca and in the neighboring villages of Mutigliano, Pescaglia, and Celle. He also occasionally played the organ for the nuns at the cloister of the Servi, for which he was given sweets, which he appreciated almost as much as he did cigarettes. Most of the money earned this way was turned over to his mother, though at times he would take a small amount out of the pay envelope to buy his beloved cigarettes or small cigars. According to reminiscences of some of his friends, another way of getting cigarette money was by ordering his younger brother and friends who acted as organ blowers to steal the organ pipes, which were then sold for the price of the metal to junk dealers. This required considerable ingenuity on Giacomo's part, since he was forced to make appropriate changes in the music, avoiding the notes of the missing pipes so the theft would not soon be discovered.

1884

Verdi muses about the young rival

from Charles Osborne (ed.): *Letters of Giuseppe Verdi*

Giuseppe Verdi (1813-1901) would have met the young Puccini in Milan, although it can't be proved and no biographer of either mentions it. Their approaches to opera were diametrically opposite (compare Verdi's Aida *and Puccini's* Madame Butterfly *as portrayals of exotic foreign women who meet a sad end), but Verdi must have watched Puccini's musical development with interest. Verdi wrote this letter on being asked his opinion of* Le Villi, *which he hadn't seen. Puccini represented the city of Lucca at Verdi's funeral in Milan in 1901.*

10 June, 1884

I have heard the composer, Puccini, well spoken of. I have seen a letter in which he is highly praised. He follows the modern tendencies, which is natural, but he adheres to melody, which is neither modern nor antique. The symphonic element, however, appears to be predominant in him. Nothing wrong with that, but one needs to tread cautiously here. Opera is opera, and the symphony is the symphony and I do not believe it's a good thing to insert a piece of a symphony into an opera, simply for the pleasure of making the orchestra perform.

I say this just for the sake of talking, so don't consider it important. I'm not certain that what I've said is true, though I am certain I've said something that runs contrary to the modern tendencies. Every age has its own imprint.

History will tell us later which epoch was good, and which bad. Heaven knows how many people in the seventeenth century admired that sonnet of Achillini, "Sudate, o fuochi", more than a canto of Dante!

1893

Catalani believes he is the best Tuscan musician

from Mosco Carner: *Puccini: a Critical Biography*

Alfredo Catalani (1854-1893) graduated from the classical Liceo Macchiavelli (still in existence) and the Istituto Musicale Pacini (now the Boccherini) in Lucca. In the latter he studied counterpoint with Fortunato Magi, Puccini's uncle. Specialising in opera, he had a regional and perhaps national fame; although he was eclipsed by Puccini, Toscanini championed his works and named his daughter, Wally, after a Catalani opera. Verdi regarded him with contempt, dismissing him as a "maestrino" (little master); only after Catalani's death did Verdi concede that he was "an excellent musician", having, however, made no effort to hear his works performed.

I know that *Manon* is to be given at Turin on Wednesday, but unfortunately I can't come. I certainly don't wish Puccini what he wished me for the first production of my *Edmea* at La Scala [1886] any more than I wish Ricordi's prophecy should come true, namely, that *Manon* will cast into darkness all the other modern operas; that would be a little too much! The whole Milan press will be there ... and I know that the critics are inspired by benevolence and enthusiasm for P. to compensate him for the excessive attack they had made on his *Edgar*. But the truth I shall find, as usual, in your notice.

I now want to tell you something concerning myself, which Noseda told me and which, in all modesty, pleased me. At the dinner which Franchetti gave in Milan, they talked about Tuscan composers – some extolling Puccini and others Mascagni, trying to make the one or the other into the leader of a school, when Franchetti joined in and said: "Since it seems that a Tuscan school is in the making, it is neither Puccini nor Mascagni who deserves the credit for it but Catalani. At Hamburg, when *Cavalleria* was produced there, they found that it derived from *Le Villi*. But let them give *Loreley* there – *La Wally* is too recent – and you will see what they say."

By God! For twelve long years I have been working and fighting; should I now sit still and watch the ground being taken away from under my feet? Indeed, NO!

The Procession of Santa Croce

Birtwistle writes *Endless Parade*

from a review by Paul Griffiths

Sir Harrison Birtwistle (born 1943) is the greatest living British composer. His virtuoso trumpet concerto Endless Parade *is based on a carnival he saw in Lucca.*

That three English composers should have been writing trumpet concertos at almost the same time is not too surprising; two of these works were commissioned for Hakan Hardenberger to play, and the third, the Davies, was written for another trumpeter, John Wallace. But though all three are very much display pieces – it would perhaps be difficult to write a lugubrious trumpet concerto – the virtuosity is not decoration but substance. These are works about (musically) behaving brilliantly.

Birtwistle's *Endless Parade* (1986-87), the first work he wrote after the première of his opera *The Mask of Orpheus*, has a title that could be applied to almost any of his works, the pulsing and the slow background harmony suggesting a procession while recurrences and the absence of any clear goal make that procession potentially infinite. In this case, though, the composer has acknowledged a concrete event behind the musical parade: a carnival he witnessed in Lucca. "I became interested in the number of ways in which you could observe this event: as a bystander, watching each float pass by ... or you could wander through side alleys, hearing the parade a street away, glimpsing it at a corner, meeting head on what a moment before you saw from behind. Each time the viewpoint was different, yet instantly identified as part of one body."

Puccini gives a rendition of *Suor Angelica* to the nuns in Vicopelago

from Giuseppe Adami (ed.): *Letters of Giacomo Puccini*

A curious episode in the history of *Suor Angelica* was the audition which the composer gave at the convent of Vicopelago near Lucca, where his eldest sister was a nun in an enclosed order. Puccini was greatly moved when he told the story of this performance. The little nuns stood round, absorbed, breathless with attention. His sister turned the pages for him, while Giacomo played and explained the words of the songs to them. Phase by phase, the opening episodes of the novices with their mistress and the monitor, the little scene of the wishes, and then the strange and secret sadness of Sister Angelica, had interested and enthralled them. It may be that each of the listeners found in the music something of her own heart. When he reached the scene of the princess aunt, Puccini stopped in embarrassment. He had to explain the heroine's story, had to tell them of her past and the sin of love which had stained her fair frame, and that of the son who had been taken away from her and whose death was now brutally announced. And there was worse to come. He had to tell them of the despairing suicide and the divine pardon of the miracle. "It was not easy", said Puccini. "Still, with as much tact and skill as I could summon, I explained it all. I saw many eyes that looked at me in tears and when I came to the aria *Madonna, Madonna, salvami per amor di mio figlio,* all the little nuns cried, with voices full of pity but firm in their decision, 'yes, yes, the poor thing'."

BIBLIOGRAPHY

This bibliography has been divided into three sections. The first contains first-hand, eye-witness accounts of Lucca. It is followed by literary works relating to Lucca, and finally by a general bibliography.

A: *First-hand Accounts*

ADDISON, Joseph. *Remarks on several parts of Italy* in *Works* (London: George Bell, 1901).
ALVAREZ, Alfred. *Afoot and unhurried in Lucca* in *Beloved cities* ed. Rosenthal & Gelb (London: Ebury., 1983).
BECKFORD, Peter. *Familiar letters from Italy* (Salisbury: J. Easton, 1805).
BECKFORD, William. *Italy, Spain and Portugal* (London: Richard Bentley, 1840).
BELLOC, Hilaire. *The path to Rome* (London: George Allen, 1902).
BENNETT, Arnold. *Journals* ed. Frank Swinnerton (Harmondsworth: Penguin, 1971).
BLESSINGTON, Countess of. *The Idler in Italy* (London: Henry Colburn, 1839).
BOSWELL, James. *Boswell on the Grand Tour*, ed. F. Brady and F. Pottle (London: Heinemann, 1955).
BROWNING, Robert and Elizabeth Barrett. *The Brownings' correspondence* ed. P. Kelley and S. Lewis (London: Athlone, 1998).
BYRON, George Gordon, Lord. *Letters and Journals* (London: John Murray, 1830).
CARMICHAEL, Montgomery. *In Tuscany* (London: Burns & Oates, 1913).
CAYLUS, Comte de. *Voyage d'Italie 1714-1715* (Paris: Librairie Fischbacher, 1914).
CERONETTI, Guido. *Un Viaggio in Italia* (Milan: Einaudi, 1983).
COOPER, J. Fenimore. *Excursions in Italy* (Paris: A. & W. Galignani, 1838).
DICKENS, Charles. *Pictures from Italy* (London: Bradbury & Evans, 1846).
EVELYN, John. *Diary* (London: Henry Colborn, 1818).
EUSTACE, John Chetwood. *A classical tour through Italy in 1802* (London: J. Marwen, 1815).

Del FIORENTINO, Dante. *Immortal Bohemian: an intimate memoir of the life of G. Puccini* (London: Victor Gollancz, 1952).

GIBBON, Edward. *Gibbon's journey from Geneva to Rome: his journal from 20 April to 2 October 1764* ed. George A. Bonard (London: Nelson, 1961).

—, *Edward Gibbon, Letters*, ed. J.E. Norton (London: Cassell, 1956).

GOETHE, Johann Caspar. *Viaggio in Italia* (Milan: Reale Accademia d'Italia, 1932).

GOLDONI, Carlo. *Memoires* (3 vols., Paris, 1787).

HALLAM, Henry. *Letters from the North of Italy* (London: John Murray, 1819).

HARE, Augustus. *The story of my life* (London: George Allen, 1896).

HARRISON, Ada and AUSTIN, R.S. *Some Tuscan cities* (London: A. & C. Black, 1924).

HAWTHORNE, Nathaniel. *Passages from the French and Italian notebooks* (Boston: Strahan, 1871).

HEINE, Heinrich. *The city of Lucca* trans. Elizabeth Sharp (London: Walter Scott, 1892).

HEWLETT, Maurice. *The road in Tuscany* (London: Macmillan, 1906).

HILLARD, George Stillman. *Six months in Italy* (London: John Murray, 1853).

HOOKER, Katharine. *Wayfarers in Italy* (London: George Newnes, 1902).

HOWELL, James. *Instructions for forreine travell* (London, 1642).

HOWELLS, William D. *Tuscan cities* (Edinburgh: David Douglas, 1886).

JAMES, Henry. *Italian hours* (London: Heinemann, 1909).

JANIN, Jules. *Voyage en Italie* (Brussels: Hauman, 1839).

de la LANDE, M., *Voyage en Italie* (Geneva, 1790).

LASSELS, Richard. *The voyage of Italy* (Paris: du Montier, 1670).

MARCHIÒ, Vincenzio. *Il Forestiere informato delle cose di Lucca* (Lucca: Marescandoli, 1721).

MARTINI, G.C. *Viaggio in Italia 1725-1745* (Lucca: Archivio di Stato, 1969).

MAUREL, André. *Little cities of Italy* trans. Helen Gerard (New York: G. Putnam's Sons., 1911).

METTERNICH, Clemens, Prince of. *Memoirs* trans. Mrs Alexander Napier (London: Richard Bentley, 1881).

MISSON, Maximilian. *Nouvelle voyage d'Italie* (The Hague, 1691).

MONTAIGNE, Michel de. *Journal de voyage en Italie* (Paris: Garnier Freres, 1955).

MONTESQUIEU, Charles Louis, Baron de. *Voyage en Italie* (Bordeaux: Gounouilhon, 1894).

MORGAN, Charles. *The writer and his world* (London: Macmillan, 1960).

MORYSON, Fynes. *An itinerary concerning his 10 years travel* (Glasgow: James Maclehose, 1907, reprinted New York: Da Capo, 1971).

NIKULAS OF MUNKATHVERA. *The pilgrim diary of Nikulas of Munkathvera* trans. F.P. Magoun in *Medieval Studies* 6, pp. 314-354, 1944.

O'FAOLAIN, Sean. *A summer in Italy* (London: Eyre & Spottiswoode, 1949).

PIOVENE, Guido. *Viaggio in Italia* (Milan: Mondadori, 1957).

PIOZZI, Hester Lynch (Mrs Thrale). *Observations and reflections made in the course of a journey through France, Italy and Germany* (London, 1789).

ROGERS, Samuel. *The Italian journal of Samuel Rogers* ed. J.R. Hale (London: Faber & Faber, 1956).

ROSE, William S. *Letters from the North of Italy* (2 vols., London, 1819).

ROSS, Janet. *Italian Sketches* (London: Kegan Paul, 1887).

RUSKIN, John. *Praeterita* (Orpington: George Allen, 1885).

— *Letters to his parents 1845* ed. Harold Shapiro (Oxford: Clarendon, 1956).

SERCAMBI, Giovanni. *Le Croniche* ed. S. Bongi (Rome, 1892).

SHELLEY, Mary Wollstonecraft. *Letters* comp. Frederick L. Jonas (University of Oklahoma, 1944).

SHELLEY, Percy Bysshe. *Letters* ed. Roger Ingpen (London: Bell, 1915).

SIMON, Kate. *Italy: the places between* (London: MacGibbon & Kee, 1971).

SIMOND, L. *A tour in Italy and Sicily* (London: Longman Rees, 1828).

SLADEN, Douglas. *How to see Italy by rail* (London: Kegan Paul, 1912).

SMOLLETT, Tobias. *Travels through France and Italy* (London: R. Baldwin, 1766).

STISTED, Elizabeth. *Letters from the bye-ways of Italy* (London, 1845).

STOKES, Margaret. *Six months in the Apennines* (London: G. Bell, 1892).

TAINE, Hippolyte. *Voyage en Italie* (Paris: Hachette, 1866).

TROLLOPE, Frances. *A Visit to Italy* (London: Richard Bentley, 1842).

TUCKETT, Elizabeth. *Beaten tracks* (London: Longmans Green, 1866).

UNDERHILL, Evelyn. *Shrines and cities of France and Italy* (London: Longmans Green, 1904).

VILLARI, Linda. *On Tuscan hills and Venetian waters* (London: Fisher Unwin, 1885).

Von WERTHEIM, Georg Kranitz. *Paradisus deliciarum Italiae* (Cologne: Conradt Bürgen, 1625).

WHIPPLE, Evangeline. *A famous corner of Tuscany* (London: Jarrolds, 1922).
WILLIBALD, *St. The Hodoeporicon* trans. Rev.Brownlow (London: Palestine Pilgrims' Text Society, 1891).

B. *Literary works relating to Lucca*

BROWNING, Elizabeth Barrett. *The sword of Castruccio Castracani* in *Collected Poems* (London, 1860).
CARTLAND, Barbara. *In Love, in Lucca* (London: Mandarin, 1997).
CERVANTES, Miguel de. *A strange thing happened in Lucca* in *The troubles of Persiles and Sigismunda* (1617, translated by Francesco Ellio, as *Occorse in Lucca un caso dei più strani*, Lucca: Maria Pacini Fazzi, 1997).
Alighieri, DANTE. *Inferno* trans.Robert Pinsky (New York: Farrar Straus & Giroux, 1994).
— *The Divine Comedy* trans. Mark Musa (London: Penguin, 1985).
EICHENDORFF, Joseph von. *Das Marmorbild* in *Werke* (Stuttgart: Cotta, 1957).
LEAR, Edward. *The Nonsense Verse of Edward Lear* illustrated by John Vernon Lord (London: Mandarin, 1992).
LOWELL, Robert. *Day by day* (New York: Farrar Straus and Giroux, 1977).
MORGAN, Charles. *Sparkenbroke* (London: Macmillan, 1936).
SHELLEY, Mary Wollstonecroft. *Valperga, or the life and adventures of Castruccio, Prince of Lucca* (Oxford: Oxford University Press, 1997).
SHELLEY, Percy Bysshe. *Posthumous Poems* (London: John and Henry Hunt, 1824).
TIECK, Ludwig. *Lucca* and *Verso Lucca* in *Werke* (Vienna: Leopold Grune, 1821).
WARNER, Francis. *Lucca Quartet* (Knotting, Beds.: Omphalus Press, 1975).

C. *General bibliography*

ACTON, Harold and CHANCY, Edward. *Florence: a traveller's companion* (London: Constable, 1986).
ANDERSON, Emily, ed. and trans. *The letters of Mozart and his family* (2 vols. London: Macmillan, 1966).

BAKER, Paul R. *The fortunate pilgrims: Americans in Italy 1800-1860* (Cambridge, Mass.: Harvard University Press, 1964).

BARACCHINI, Clara, ed. *Il Secolo di Castruccio* (Lucca: Maria Pacini Fazzi, 1982).

BARTLETT, Vernon. *Tuscan retreat* (London: Chatto & Windus, 1972)

BARONTI, Remo. *Nel cuore della chiesa: le contemplative a Lucca* (Lucca: Maria Pacini Fazzi, 1987).

BARSALI, Isa Belli. *Lucca: guida alla città* (Lucca: Maria Pacini Fazzi, 1988).

BARSOTTI, G. *Lucca sacra* (Lucca: Baroni, 1923).

del BECCARO, Rodolfo. *Lucca: its legends and its history* (Lucca: Baroni, 1999).

BECK, James and AMENDOLA, Aurelio. *Ilaria del Carretto di Jacopo della Quercia* (Milan: Silvana, 1988).

BENTLEY, James. *A guide to Tuscany* (London: Viking, 1987).

BLACK, Christopher F. *Italian confraternities in the sixteenth century* (Cambridge: Cambridge University Press, 1989).

BLACK, Jeremy. *The British and the Grand Tour* (London: Croom Helm, 1985).

BONGI, Salvatore. *Storia di L. Buonvisi lucchese, raccontata sui documenti* (Lucca, 1864).

BORNSTEIN, Daniel E. *The Bianchi of 1399: popular devotion in late medieval Italy* (Ithaca: Cornell University Press, 1993).

BRATCHEL, M.E. *Lucca 1430-1494: The reconstruction of an Italian city republic* (Oxford: Clarendon Press, 1995).

BREWER, Derek S. *Geoffrey Chaucer* (London: G. Bell, 1974).

BRILLI, Attilio. *Viaggiatori Stranieri in terra di Lucca* (Milan: Amilcare Pizzi, 1996).

BROOKS, Van Wyck. *The dream of Arcadia: American writers and artists in Italy 1760-1915* (London: J. Dent, 1959).

BRUCKER, Gene. *Renaissance Florence* (Berkeley: University of California Press, 1969).

BULL, George. *Michelangelo* (London: Viking, 1995).

BURCKHARDT, Jacob. *Die Kultur der Renaissance in Italien* (Leipzig: Phaidon, 1926).

BURNEY, Charles. *A general history of music* (London: T. Beckett, 1782).

del CARLO, Torello. *Storia popolare di Lucca* (Lucca, 1880).

CARNER, Mosco. *Puccini: a critical biography* (London: Duckworth, 1958).

CHELAZZI, Giuliano. *Lucca* (Florence, 1999).

CHURCH, Frederic C. *The Italian reformers 1534-1564* (New York: Columbia University Press, 1932).

CLARKE, Maude Violet. *The medieval city state* (London: Methuen, 1926).

CLOUGH, Shepard B. and SALADINO, Salvatore. *A history of modern Italy* (New York: Columbia University Press, 1968).

DODGE, Thisdore Ayrault. *Hannibal* (Boston: Houghton Mifflin, 1891).

ECHARD, Laurence. *The Roman history* (London: T. Hodgkin, 1699).

EINSTEIN, Albert. *Ideas and Opinions* (New York: Crown, 1957).

FILIERI, Maria Teresa, ed. *Sumptuosa tabula picta: pittori a Lucca tra gotico e rinascimento* (Lucca: Sillabe, 1998).

FONDAZIONE RAGGHIANTI. *Lucca medievale: la decorazione in laterizio* (Lucca: the Fondazione, 1998).

FULVIO, Manlio. *Lucca: le sue corti, le sue strade, le sue piazze* (Empoli: Barbieri Noccioli, 1968).

GIES, Joseph and Frances. *Life in a medieval city* (New York: Crowell, 1973).

GIOVANNINI, Francesco. *Lucca Reiseführer* (Lucca: Baroni, n.d.).

GOETHE, Johann Wolfgang von. *Italian journey* (London: Penguin, 1970).

GREEN, Louis. *Castruccio Castracani: a study on the origins and character of a fourteenth-century Italian despotism* (Oxford: Clarendon Press, 1986).
— *Lucca under many masters* (Florence: Olschki, 1995).

GREENFIELD, Howard. *Puccini* (London: Robert Hale, 1981).

GREGORY, *St. Dialogues* trans. Cuthbert Fursdon (Ilkley: Scolar, 1976).

GRILLI, Dino. *I Lucchesi di una Volta* (Lucca: Maria Pacini Fazzi, 1988).

HALE, J.R. *England and the Italian Renaissance* (London: Faber & Faber, 1954).

HAMILTON, Olive. *Paradise of exiles: Tuscany and the British* (London: Andre Deutsch, 1974).
— *The divine country: the British in Tuscany 1372-1980* (London: Andre Deutsch, 1982).

HAUFE, Eberhard, ed. *Deutsche Briefe aus Italien* (Munich: Beck, 1987).

HAUSER, Ernest O. *Italy: a cultural guide* (New York: Athenaeum, 1981).

HAY, Denys and LAW, John. *Italy in the age of the Renaissance 1380-1530* (London: Longman. 1989).

HEERS, Jacques. *Parties and political life in the medieval West* (Amsterdam: North Holland Publishing, 1977).

HEWITT, Vivien A. *The land of Puccini* (Viareggio: Pezzini, n.d.).

HIBBERT, Christopher. *The Grand Tour* (London: Methuen, 1987).

HOLLAND, Lady Elizabeth. *Memoir of the Rev. Sydney Smith* (London: 1855).

HOLMES, Richard. *Shelley: the Pursuit* (London: Harper Collins, 1994).

HUIZINGA, Johan. *The waning of the Middle Ages* (London: E. Arnholt, 1924).

ISTITUTO STORICO LUCCHESE. *Castruccio Castracani e il suo tempo* in *Actum Luce* XIII-XIV, no. 1-2, 1985.

JACKSON, Stanley. J.P. Morgan: *The rise and fall of a banker* (London: Heinemann, 1984).

JARDINE, Lisa. *Worldly goods: a new history of the Renaissance* (London: Macmillan, 1996).

KAEUPER, R.W. *Bankers to the Crown: the Ricciardi of Lucca and Edward I* (Princeton: Princeton University Press, 1973).

KEATES, Jonathan. *Tuscany* (London: George Philip, 1988).

LAZZARESCHI, Eugenio. *Elisa Buonaparte Baciocchi* (Lucca: Maria Pacini Fazzi, 1983).

— *Lucca* (Bergamo: Istituto Italiano d'Arti Grafiche, 1931).

LAZZARINI, Pietro. *Il Volto Santo di Lucca, 782-1982* (Lucca: Maria Pacini Fazzi, 1982).

LENZI, Eugenio. *Lucca: capitale del Regno Longobardo della Tuscia* (Lucca: Maria Pacini Fazzi, 1997).

LERA, Guglielmo. *Dante e la Città del Volto Santo* (Lucca: Comitato Lucchese della Dante Alighieri, 1983).

— *Lucca: città da scoprire* (Lucca, Maria Pacini Fazzi 1980).

LISZT, Franz. *Buch der Lieder* (Berlin: Schlesinger, 1844).

LIVY (Titus Livius). *History of Rome* trans. George Baker (Philadelphia: M'Carty & Davis, 1840).

LUCAS, Herbert. *Fra Girolamo Savonarola* (London: Sands, 1899).

MACCHIAVELLI, Niccolò. *Opere* (vol. 2, Florence, 1813).

MACRIPO, Alba, ed. *Monete Medaglie Sigilli* (Lucca: Maria Pacini Fazzi, 1992).

MAGRI, Giorgio. *L'uomo Puccini* (Milan: Mursia, 1992).

MANCINI, Augusto. *Storia di Lucca* (Lucca: Maria Pacini Fazzi, 1986).

MARTINELLI, Roberta and PUCINELLI, Giuliana. *Lucca: le mura del Cinquecento* (Lucca: Matteoni, 1983).

— *A Renaissance fortification system: the walls of Lucca* (Lucca: Maria Pacini Fazzi, 1991).

MASSON, David. *The life of John Milton* (Cambridge: Macmillan, 1859).

MAUGHAN, H. Neville. *The book of Italian travel (1580-1900)* (London: Grant Richards, 1903).

MAZZAROSA, Antonio. *Guida di Lucca* (Lucca: Giusti, 1843).

McCARTHY, Mary. *The Stones of Florence* (New York: Harcourt Brace, 1963).

McCRIE, Thomas. *History of the progress and suppression of the Reformation in Italy* (London: William Blackwood, 1827).

MEEK, Christine. *Lucca 1369-1400: politics and society in an early Renaissance city-state* (Oxford: Oxford University Press, 1978).

MENCACCI, Paolo and ZECCHINI, Michelangelo. *Lucca Romana* (Lucca: Maria Pacini Fazzi, 1982).

MONTANELLI, Indro. *Rome: the first thousand years* trans. Arthur Oliver (London: Collins, 1962).

MURRAY, Peter. *The architecture of the Italian Renaissance* (London: B.T. Batsford, 1963).

NETTE, Herbert. *Die Grossen Deutschen in Italien* (Darmstadt: L.C. Wittich, 1938).

OSHEIM, Duane J. *An Italian lordship: the Bishopric of Lucca in the late Middle Ages* (Berkeley: University of California Press, 1977).

OZMENT, Steven. *The age of reform: 1250-1550* (New Haven: Yale University Press, 1980).

— *Magdalena and Balthasar* (New Haven: Yale University Press, 1989).

PARKS, George B. *The English Traveler to Italy* (Rome: Edizione di Stori e Letteratura, 1954).

PASCUCCI, Vittorio. *L'Allusivo iconografico in Santa Maria Corteorlandini* (Lucca: San Marco Litotipo, 1996).

POWER, Eileen. *Medieval people* (London: Methuen, 1924).

PREZZOLINI, Giuseppe. *Come gli Americani scoprirono l'Italia* (Milan, 1933).

PUCCINI, Giacomo: *Letters* ed. Giuseppe Adami, trans. Ena Makin (London: Harrap, 1931).

RAISON, Laura. *Tuscany* (London: Cadogan, 1983).

ROMER, Elizabeth. *The Tuscan year: life and food in an Italian valley* (London: Weidenfeld & Nicolson, 1984).

De ROOVER, Florence Edler. *Le Sete Lucchesi* (Lucca: Istituto Storico Lucchese, 1993).

ROSS, Janet and ERICHSEN, Nelly. *The story of Lucca* (London: J.M. Dent, 1912).

ROSSI, Giuseppina. *Salotti letterari in Toscana* (Florence: Le Lettere, 1992).

De ROTHSCHILD, Germaine. *Boccherini* trans. Andreas Mayor (Oxford: Oxford University Press, 1965).

RUBBOLI, Daniele. *Le prime al Teatro del Giglio (1675-1987)* (Lucca: Maria Pacini Fazzi, 1987).

SALMON, Edward T. *Roman Colonization under the Republic* (London: Thames and Hudson, 1969).

De SANCTIS, Francesco. *History of Italian literature* (New York: Basic Books, 1931).

SARDI, Cesare. *Vita Lucchese nel Settecento* (Lucca: Maria Pacini Fazzi, 1968).

De SISMONDI, J.C.L. *A history of the Italian republics* (London: J.M. Dent, 1910).

SNOWDEN, Frank. *Revolution in Tuscany 1919-1922* (Cambridge: Cambridge University Press, 1989).

SPENDER, Matthew. *Within Tuscany* (London: Penguin, 1992).

STOPANI, Renato. *La Via Francigena* (Florence: Le Lettere, 1992).

TAZARTES, Maurizia. *Una Città allo Specchio* (Lucca: Maria Pacini Fazzi, 1987).

TOUSSAINT, Stephane, ed. *Ilaria del Carretto e il suo monumento* (Lucca: Istituto Storico Lucchese, 1994).

TREVELYAN, Janet Penrose. *A short history of the Italian people* (NewYork: Putnam's Sons, 1920).

TREVES, Giuliann Artom. *The golden ring: the Anglo-Florentines 1847-1882* (London: Longmans Green, 1956).

VASARI, Giorgio. *Lives of the artists* trans. George Bull (London: Penguin, 1965).

VERDI, Giuseppe. *Letters of Giuseppe Verdi* ed. Charles Osborne (London: Victor Gollancz, 1971).

VIGLIONE, Francesco. *L'Italia nel pensiero degli scrittori inglesi* (Milan: Piccolo Biblioteca di Scienze Moderne, 1940).

VILLANI, Giovanni. *Croniche Fiorentine* ed. A. Racheli (2 vols., Trieste, 1857).

WEBB, Diana. *Patrons and defenders: the saints in the Italian city states* (London: Tauris Academic Studies, 1996).

WICKHAM, Chris. *Community and clientele in twelfth-century Tuscany* (Oxford: Clarendon Press, 1998).

— *The mountains and the city: the Tuscan Apennines in the early Middle Ages* (Oxford: Clarendon Press, 1988).

ZECCHINI, Michelangelo. *Lucca Etrusca* (Lucca: San Marco Litotipo, 1999).

ZEYDEL, Edwin. *Ruodlieb: the first courtly novel (after 1050)* (Chapel Hill: University of North Carolina Press, 1986).

INDEX

279

finito di stampare
nel mese di settembre 2002
dalla "litografia varo", pisa
per conto di mp maria pacini fazzi editore